Unchopping a Tree

IN THE SERIES *Politics, History, and Social Change,*
EDITED BY JOHN C. TORPEY

ALSO IN THIS SERIES:

Rebecca Jean Emigh, *The Undevelopment of Capitalism: Sectors and Markets in Fifteenth-Century Tuscany*

Aristide R. Zolberg, *How Many Exceptionalisms? Explorations in Comparative Macroanalysis*

Thomas Brudholm, *Resentment's Virtue: Jean Améry and the Refusal to Forgive*

Patricia Hill Collins, *From Black Power to Hip Hop: Racism, Nationalism, and Feminism*

Daniel Levy and Natan Sznaider, translated by Assenka Oksiloff, *The Holocaust and Memory in the Global Age*

Brian A. Weiner, *Sins of the Parents: The Politics of National Apologies in the United States*

Heribert Adam and Kogila Moodley, *Seeking Mandela: Peacemaking Between Israelis and Palestinians*

Marc Garcelon, *Revolutionary Passage: From Soviet to Post-Soviet Russia, 1985–2000*

Götz Aly and Karl Heinz Roth, translated by Assenka Oksiloff, *The Nazi Census: Identification and Control in the Third Reich*

Immanuel Wallerstein, *The Uncertainties of Knowledge*

Michael R. Marrus, *The Unwanted: European Refugees from the First World War Through the Cold War*

THE UNIVERSITY OF
WINCHESTER

To be returned on or before the day marked above, subject t⁻

Unchopping a Tree

Reconciliation in the Aftermath of Political Violence

Ernesto Verdeja

Temple University Press
Philadelphia

Temple University Press
Philadelphia PA 19122
www.temple.edu/tempress

Copyright © 2009 Temple University
All rights reserved
Published 2009

Printed and bound in Great Britain by
Marston Book Services Limited, Oxfordshire

Library of Congress Cataloging-in-Publication Data

Verdeja, Ernesto.
    Unchopping a tree : reconciliation in the aftermath of
political violence / Ernesto Verdeja.
        p. cm. — (Politics, history, and social change)
    Includes bibliographical references and index.
    ISBN 978-1-4399-0054-3 (cloth : alk. paper)
    1. Political violence. 2. Social conflict. 3. Conflict management.
4. Reconciliation. I. Title.
    JC328.6.V47 2009
    303.6'9—dc22

                                                        2009013156

Contents

Acknowledgments

This is a work about political reconciliation, about the need and challenges of reconciling after severe political violence. I became interested in this subject while living in South America as a child and seeing firsthand the difficulties of engaging with a fraught past. Many years of thinking about these issues led me to graduate school, culminating in a doctoral dissertation on which this book is loosely based. I would like to thank Nancy Fraser and Courtney Jung, who provided valuable suggestions and direction on the dissertation, and Richard A. Wilson and Andrew Arato, who reminded me of the importance of retaining the connection between normative theory and practical politics in my work. Matthew Goldfeder read the text with care and pressed me on a number of points, making the argument more coherent than it otherwise would have been. His patience with my questions was matched only by the wit and clarity of his suggestions.

While at Wesleyan, J. Donald Moon and Nancy Schwartz kindly read the entire manuscript and gave detailed and important feedback on the fundamental arguments. Their intellectual support and friendship helped me enormously in this project. At the University of Notre Dame, the Kroc Institute for International Peace Studies and the Center for the Study of Social Movements and Social Change provided financial support and a wonderful environment in which to write.

I would especially like to thank Daniel Myers for securing this support and making Notre Dame such a welcoming place. A number of persons in Chile and Bosnia and Herzegovina kindly shared their experiences with me, and I am enormously grateful to them. Many thanks also go to Temple University Press and Micah Kleit for taking on this project.

I dedicate this book to my parents, Martha and Ernesto, who have always encouraged me in everything I have done and showed me the beauty of learning, and to my Bettina, whose love and warmth made this long journey possible and worthwhile. Without her support, this would have been a difficult, lonely road.

Unchopping a Tree

1 Theorizing Reconciliation

The past one hundred years witnessed the highest number of political deaths of any century (Rummel 1997). Two major wars, numerous civil conflicts and wars of independence, and systematic state-sponsored atrocities have left behind a battered political landscape. The genocide of Jews, Roma, Armenians, Ibos, Tutsi, Hutu in Burundi, Bengalis, Khmer, the Aché (Paraguay), Guatemalans, Timorese, Bosnian Muslims, southern Sudanese, and Herero and repression, mass terror, and murder in places as disparate as Chile, Argentina, South Africa, Romania, Uganda, China, and Iran illustrate the heterogeneous nature of political violence of the past century but do not by any means exhaust its range and depth. Certainly, a century characterized by massacre and torture is not unique in human history, and there is little reason to believe that the twenty-first will be much different. Although the instruments of violence today may be more sophisticated and the ideologies behind them different from before (and even this is not always the case), horrific violence has long been with us (Kiernan 2007). Nevertheless, what is remarkable are the numerous recent efforts at publicly engaging past atrocities, often through new legal mechanisms but also through a multiplicity of other political and social strategies, with the aim of reconciling former enemies while simultaneously addressing accountability, truth telling, and the concerns of victims. As Martha Minow has eloquently written, these legal and quasi-legal attempts to identify perpetrators and catalogue crimes have "illuminated the hopes and commitments of individuals and societies seeking, above all, some rejoinder to the unspeakable destruction and degradation of human beings" (1998, 1).

Political violence does not end with the last death, however. A common feature of mass murder has been the attempt at destroying any memory of victims, with the aim of eliminating them from history. In the Holocaust, the Aghed (genocide of the Armenians), the Cambodian genocide, the Rape of Nanking, the Rwandan genocide, the Gulag and the Laogai, the tortures and murders of leftists in the Southern Cone, and the rule of apartheid, among many others, perpetrators sought not only to eliminate violently a perceived threat but also to eradicate any possibility of alternate, competing social and national histories.

Surprisingly, in some countries complex and difficult engagements with the past have resulted in remarkable transformations of society. South Africa, Argentina, Chile, and a united Germany are all significantly more democratic and open than before. In other places, such as Cambodia and Rwanda, peace and stability are the most that can be hoped for, at least in the near term. However, all of these societies have had to confront a complicated tangle of questions: How should perpetrators, victims, and bystanders be faced? What is the proper balance between punishment and forgiveness? How much memory is too much, and when is it too little? What does it mean to be reconciled with the past and with each other, and how should this be achieved? What, in other words, are the stakes in reconciling? These and similar concerns occupy a central place in societies emerging from massive violence. This book seeks to contribute to these debates by sketching a normative theory of reconciliation that differs from prevailing approaches.

The difficulty in articulating such a theory finds an echo in Max Weber's essay "Politics as a Vocation" (1958). There, Weber distinguished between two different ethical systems in the political world: the ethic of ultimate ends, which is committed to the attainment of certain ideals regardless of consequences, and the ethic of responsibility, which recognizes that one's conduct must be guided by what is possible in the real world, with all of the limitations that this entails. In the end, Weber was distraught about these alternatives, concluding that the former ran the risk of degenerating into the belief that the ends justify the means—giving us Auschwitz and revolutionary firing squads—and the latter could always be tempted into one more compromise, ultimately condemning action to a series of half steps evacuated of any meaningful content. Something similar haunts any attempt at formulating a model of reconciliation. On one hand, one risks promoting a pure ideal that is unattainable without significantly more violence being done in its wake; take, for example, calls for swift and severe retribution for all human rights violators and their accomplices. Though accountability is desirable as a moral goal—there is, after all, great satisfaction in seeing perpetrators held responsible for gross violations—seeking absolute justice can quickly turn into its own terror. And yet a model that too easily seeks compromise in politically delicate situations can serve as a mere apology for perpetrators, in the process forfeiting any meaningful claim it may make to promoting reconciliation. This book seeks to navigate this Scylla and Charybdis by recognizing that reconciliation is a complex, multileveled process that is best understood as *disjunctured* and *uneven*, with multiple moral claims often in competition with one another. Rather than posit a model, on one hand, equating reconciliation with social harmony between former enemies or, on the other, as a condition of minimal peace with no exploration of past injustices, I outline a conception that emphasizes the importance of shared notions of moral respect and tolerance among erstwhile adversaries as a realistic and morally defensible idea of what we should expect in transitional societies. *Reconciliation, I argue, refers to a condition of mutual respect among former enemies, which requires the reciprocal recognition of the moral worth and dignity of others. It is achieved when previous, conflict-era identities no longer operate as the primary cleavages in politics, and thus citizens acquire new identities that cut across those earlier fault lines.* This model is normative—it stipulates certain moral criteria that are necessary for a society to be reconciled while also recognizing that the dynamics of reconciliation are manifested in different ways depending on what dimension of society one analyzes. That is to say, the dynamics of reconciliation among political elites are different from those among regular individuals in the private sphere, and the requirements of institutional reform contain certain normative imperatives that differ from the demands and expectations that can be placed on civil society.

These different social levels—political society, civil society, institutional, and individual—draw our attention to the myriad ways in which reconciliatory efforts are manifested and develop.

This book is a work of normative political theory. It seeks to make a contribution to current political theory debates about how best to envision reconciliation while remaining realistic about the very significant practical obstacles such efforts face. A number of important recent works have limited their focus to the institutional or administrative policies of transitional justice (such as the use of trials, truth commissions, or reparations) while eschewing broader theoretical explorations of reconciliation (Drumbl 2007; Elster 2004; Freeman 2006; Torpey 2006). Others have focused on comparative analyses of transitions, highlighting the practical challenges faced by incoming elites Barahona de Brito 2001; McAdams 2001). Many of these texts discuss reconciliation to some extent, but only in the context of broader transitional justice policies without elaborating normative understandings of reconciliation as such. Indeed, there has been a remarkably small amount of sustained theoretical work written on reconciliation, and much of this has been a critique of the concept rather than a positive formulation of its normative foundations.[1] I hope to contribute to these normative debates by sketching a viable theory. While I draw heavily from cases, I do not pursue a comparative case studies approach per se nor offer policy prescriptions or recommendations. Instead, I identify the moral claims and counterclaims that arise in transitional settings and explore how they may reinforce (and often work against) one another. Nevertheless, I strongly believe that any normative model must remain sensitive to the particularities and contexts of specific transitions—the type of transition, the outlay of different political and social forces, and the likelihood of the resumption of violence—or it will condemn itself to clever but ultimately useless theorizing. I have attempted, then, to outline a model that shows sensitivity to particularity while also considering the normative claims that seem to emerge across cases. Rather than provide a general, transhistorical model of reconciliation, I restrict my project to cases that share certain features, thus excluding other instances of dealing with past violence that face somewhat different challenges. In subsequent sections, I detail the parameters and normative concepts that are at the core of my model, but before doing so, I outline the scope of the model—what kinds of cases it intends to cover and what kinds it does not—in order to clarify its domain of applicability.

Scope of the Theory

The literature on transitional justice and historical memory is vast, and the types of transitions and political contexts are sufficiently varied that one should be hesitant to offer a nomothetic model of reconciliation that would satisfactorily operate in every instance. Indeed, I believe that this is not possible. My model is intended to be useful in certain kinds of cases: those of extreme domestic political violence where the opposing sides are not territorially separate. In this section I demarcate the bounds of the theory and indicate what falls inside and outside its scope.

Under certain circumstances, partition may be a more just solution than forcing enemies to live together. Biafra, East Timor, Western Sahara, East Pakistan (Bangladesh), and Chechnya are all cases where separation is more desirable than forced integration. This is because of, among other things, the form of political identity involved: Where the opponents can be distinguished principally by territory, rather than by non-territorial religious, linguistic, ethnic, or other affiliation, partition may very well be the optimal solution. Of course, non-territorial categorizations are often interwoven with territorial distinctions as well, but the salience of territoriality plays a crucial role in assessing what options are available (Brilmayer 1991; Lehning 1998). In cases where opponents occupy different territories within a larger political community and one group actively oppresses the other, reconciliation following political violence may not be the most desirable solution, particularly if the oppressed overwhelmingly seek independence and have little chance of achieving satisfactory political and economic protections in the status quo. Thus, the attempt at secession by the Ibo during the Biafran War and the successful separation by the Bangladeshis during their war with Pakistan would both appear legitimate (Harneit-Sievers and Emezue 2000; Ikpeze 2000; Kuper 1981), as would the division of East and West Timor (J. Taylor 1999). This is not, of course, to sanction ethnic cleansing, but only to underscore that in situations where the oppressed group is (1) territorially distinct from the oppressor and has little chance of achieving parity and (2) seeks separation, then reconciliation as discussed in this book would require forcing two (or more) groups to remain together that should be permitted to separate. However, in situations where the opponents are not territorially distinct, separation is not an alternative, and some form of reconciling enemies remains the only option. The violence in Chile in the 1970s and 1980s occurred between groups that cannot be separated by territory; leftists and rightists exist throughout the country, and therefore separation makes no sense. A careful reading of the wars in the former Yugoslavia reveals a great deal of pre-conflict ethnic interpenetration and cohabitation as well, and thus separation was achieved only through massive bloodletting; present-day Iraq is also characterized by significant ethnic and religious overlap (Burg and Shoup 2000; Gagnon 2005).

Wherever the politically salient identities are not territorially based, reconciliation is the only viable solution. What exactly is politically salient depends on the particular case: It could be religious, ethnic, class, or something else (indeed, it is almost always a combination of these), and the relevance of any set of distinctions is always open to change over time, giving credence to the social constructivist's understanding of identity formation (Jung 2000). In any case, the model proposed here is relevant only where *politically salient ascriptions do not neatly square with territorially salient distinctions*; where they do, an alternative solution such as partition may be more desirable (though some form of reconciliation may be necessary in those cases as well). To paraphrase Hirschman (1970), I assume that "exit" is not an option.

Colonialism

In cases where the colonialist and the colonized are territorially separate, the model presented here is inapplicable. Thus, the Japanese use of Korean sex slaves and the Rape of Nanking are not directly relevant to my framework and the specific debate I engage here. These cases require an additional theoretical analysis of the complex relations between the society that perpetrated atrocities and the one that suffered them.

Where the colonized and colonizer do live in the same political territory, the model here may be relevant. The indigenous-colonialist relationships in Canada, the United States, Australia, and New Zealand make interesting candidates for this study, precisely because (the descendants of) the perpetrators and victims must live together. In these situations, there is no "exit." Nevertheless, these are all historical cases, where the primary means of reconciliation occurs through a reassessment of historical memory, and the political order is not in danger of collapse because of renewed attention to historical grievances. I focus, however, on contemporary instances of mass atrocity and reconciliation where actual perpetrators and victims are still alive, the political order is not well entrenched, and renewed violence remains a possibility. So-called "consolidated democracies" normally do not face the same dangers as societies in transition to democracy, though they certainly have a moral obligation to reflect on past atrocities and their consequences. Regardless, the challenges facing those societies are temporally distinct from the focus of this study, requiring an investigation of the historical legacy of violence and its relation to contemporary life (Barkan 2000; Waldron 1992). This project focuses on reconciliation in societies that have undergone recent large-scale political violence where opposing sides drew their identities along non-territorial fault lines.

Why Not Forget?

Before turning to different theoretical models of reconciliation, I should say something about one contending alternative: societal *forgetfulness* as a means of "moving on." The rise in the use of truth commissions gives the impression that engaging the past is necessary after mass violence and that ignoring it is morally wrong. Some scholars cite an "emerging norm of right to the truth" in international law,[2] and international human rights organizations claim there is an obligation on the state to unearth the past, with no exceptions.[3] But these arguments are themselves contentious, and we should first inquire whether forgetfulness may indeed be a legitimate, and possibly better, alternative to the reconciliatory efforts I discuss in this book.

Defenders of forgetting the past argue that to look backward will only re-traumatize a fragile society. Demanding prosecutions and encouraging victims to talk about their experiences will not contribute to reconciliation, but only rekindle the embers of animosity and anger. Reexamining past grievances does little but prolong bitterness and antagonism, preventing a society from moving forward.[4] As such, whatever cathartic benefits for victims may come from truth commissions, trials, or memorials, the likelihood of renewed violence outweighs them. Bruce Ackerman sees these efforts as wasting "moral capital in an ineffectual effort to right past wrongs—creating martyrs and fostering political alienation, rather than contributing to a genuine sense of vindication." "Moral capital" should be used to educate the people on the rule of law, rather than pursuing a "quixotic quest after the mirage of corrective justice" (1992, 72). Though not a supporter of forgetfulness, Michael Ignatieff questions the likelihood that "when the truth is known by all, it has a capacity to heal and reconcile. These are not so much epistemological assumptions as articles of faith about human nature: that the truth is one and, if we know it, it will make us free" (1998, 170). Many contemporary scholars remain skeptical of the benefits of revisiting the past. These arguments assume that fragile societies must privilege the practical needs of the present over morality. Peaceful coexistence requires burying the past.

But if forgetting requires burying awful experiences and behaving as if nothing had happened, what kind of reconciliation is this? Who is reconciled? Without some understanding of what happened, it is difficult to see how people could be reconciled with one another—to know whom to reconcile with means knowing who did what and who suffered what. An agreement to forget the past may bring respite from violence and ease a transition, but it is unlikely to remain for too long (Schwan 1998). In many cases where leaders have called for forgetting the past, public demands for the truth eventually resurface (this brings to mind Uruguay, Brazil, and Spain) and some historical reckoning becomes unavoidable.

Of course, for some, forgetting is a welcome response to the past. Perpetrators and their supporters are likely to encourage historical amnesia for self-interested reasons. Forgetting, however, is hardly apolitical or adopted freely; rather, it masks the power that perpetrators continue to enjoy. To expect victims to surrender their claims to moral acknowledgment constitutes a second moral injury against them, where their suffering is effectively excised from public consciousness and their experiences are disparaged as potentially disruptive to social reconstruction. Public forgetting instrumentalizes victims by signaling that their moral value is less important than stability and peace. It is a form of degradation, and "thus it involves a kind of injury that is not merely tangible and sensible. It is a *moral* injury, and we care about such injuries" (Murphy 1995, 25). The demand that past crimes be forgotten ignores this loss of self-respect. This moral injury results from treating victims as if no wrong had occurred and, consequently, they are not entitled to make claims for moral recognition. Simultaneously, perpetrators feel vindicated, for forgetfulness can in fact serve to confer legitimacy on past policies, at the very least by signaling that past wrongs were not sufficiently awful to demand judgment. The consequences can be devastating. As David Crocker remarks, "Repressed emotions of rage, humiliation, and fear can be expressed in uncontrolled and harmful ways" (1998, 496). A policy of forgetting, of course, is never guaranteed to "succeed," even by crass instrumentalist terms. Silencing the past may only displace it to future generations, who may take up old grievances and return to violence. The state also loses in this calculus, as unaddressed violations may undermine its future legitimacy in the eyes of victims' descendants (Warren 1998).

Nevertheless, advocates argue that certain states have chosen a policy of forgetfulness successfully, effectively burying mutual resentments and resisting calls for accountability and painful confrontations with their recent histories. Mozambique and Cambodia are two countries often identified as successful cases. Today, Cambodia has a United Nations–backed hybrid tribunal to prosecute former high-level Khmer Rouge, and it is no longer accurate to speak of it as a case where social forgetting is the norm. Mozambique, however, still stands out for its seemingly socially sanctioned forgetfulness.

Much has been written about how Mozambique has decided to ignore the legacy of its civil war, creating a new moral and political community founded on the willful ignorance of recent history (Alden 2001; England 2002; Manning 2002). After the 1992 peace agreement that ended sixteen years of vicious fighting, leaders from the two combatant groups Renamo and Frelimo turned to the Catholic church to mediate potential conflicts, and the 1994 elections went ahead without any major contestation occurring along wartime fault lines. Boosters of the transition argued that it was achieved peacefully precisely because Mozambicans chose to renounce the past and move on (Alden 2001).

Nevertheless, though there was no explicit public engagement with the nation's history—certainly not by the political elites who had negotiated the cease-fire and legal amnesty—it was not completely rejected either. Within civil society, villages turned back to a number of autochthonous mechanisms to deal with political conflict. More importantly, these were seen as legitimate by villagers themselves, including the survivors (Bartoli 2001). *Curandeiros*, or traditional healers, served as authority figures who could mediate communal and personal conflict. Specifically, curandeiros played a crucial role in reintegrating former soldiers who had murdered by "rehumanizing" them, casting off the "bad luck" that came from the victim's spirit. The process was complex, but the important point here is that it included an implicit acknowledgment of guilt and sense of responsibility by the soldier, for otherwise the soldier would not require rehumanization. These rituals occurred mostly in rural areas where the majority of the fighting took place. Services conducted by curandeiros served as a method of reconstructing badly broken social relations, allowing for the reintegration of erstwhile enemies into the same moral and social community. Through a complex series of ritualized and meaningful actions, former opponents—on occasion from the same town or even family—were invited to live together as equals (Nordstrom 1997). Writes Rama Mani:

> The traditional belief is that harm is done not just to the individual involved—victim or perpetrator—but to the entire family or community. Consequently, reconciliation and reintegration require that entire communities participate in the ritual to rid themselves of the harm. With the ceremony, the violator is forgiven and the victim is healed, and each can be reconciled and reintegrated into the community as before. (2002, 118)

Though this does not amount to the notion of reconciliation I delineate, it is far removed from the idea of forgetfulness, since the latter term normally precludes any type of moral engagement with the past or acknowledgment of culpability—in this case the very basis of the soldiers' rehumanization. After all, if the goal is to forget completely, why engage in rituals of purification and reintegration? Forgetting usually means letting "bygones be bygones," but here there is at least a recognition that serious wrongs were committed and that there were victims and perpetrators. The fiction that the past does not matter does not hold, since there is such a preoccupation with dealing with it, if only to move away from it. And there is, of course, no guarantee that future calls to revisit the past will not occur, as they have in numerous other countries in similar situations.

The importance of coming to terms with the past may not always be immediately evident, and the force of historical memory may take some time to appear. In spring 2000, Polish historian Jan Gross published *Neighbors: The Destruction of the Jewish Community in Jedwabne, Poland*, an account of how the small town of Jedwabne lost its entire Jewish population in World War II (2001). The Nazis had traditionally been blamed for the murders, though it is now clear that Catholic Poles killed their Jewish neighbors. More disturbingly, it seems that these crimes may have been more common than once believed. The thesis of the book was immensely controversial in Poland, a country that has long thought of itself as *the* victim nation par excellence. Now Poland is engaged in a full-scale reappraisal of its past, investigating its own history of anti-Semitism and the implications for the nation's understanding of itself (Gross 2006; Polonsky and Michlic 2004).

In all of these cases, forgetting has not succeeded. Poland is still confronting crimes committed fifty years ago, and Cambodians have recently begun to demand the truth about their nation's genocide. Even Mozambicans, another people touted as having turned their back on the past, still find it necessary to engage in some form of ritual to reintegrate perpetrators and former combatants into community life. Arguing against social amnesia, Wole Soyinka has written:

> Beyond Truth [*sic*], the very process of its exposition becomes part of the necessity, and, depending on the nature of the past that it addresses, the impact it has made on the lives of the citizens and the toll it has taken on their sense of belonging, it may be regarded as being capable of guaranteeing or founding the future of a nation. Indeed, it may be seen as a therapy against civic alienation. (1999, 12)

Here Soyinka may be overstating the power of truth, and I argue in subsequent chapters that there are other moral claims that require our attention as well. Nevertheless, his point is well-taken; it implies, at the very least, that facing the past is important for societal and communal rebirth and that advocates of social amnesia fail to capture the pull that history can have on a country's historical understanding of itself.

Paradigms of Reconciliation

Facing the past is a crucial element in reconstructing a shattered society. But what it means to reconcile such a society is not self-evident. Reconciliation, like most normatively complex social phenomena, cannot be measured in any exact manner, and it is precisely this elusive yet very real quality that makes any discussion of its nature and sources difficult. Nevertheless, several broad approaches have emerged, ranging from a "minimalist" legal one predicated on coexistence to a "maximalist" approach based on mutual healing, restoration, and forgiveness. These are not hard-and-fast schools of reconciliation, since there are in fact few such fully developed normative theories; rather, they represent general understandings that have informed the way we think of reconciliation. Nor are they purely in opposition to one another; the call for healing and restoration of social relations accepts the importance of minimal coexistence as a starting point but seeks to deepen it substantially through forgiveness and the development of thick ties of solidarity. Nevertheless, I believe that neither approach is satisfactory.

Minimalist approaches formulate reconciliation as simple coexistence between former enemies, a basic agreement by different groups to accept the law rather than violence to resolve disagreements. Rajeev Bhargava discusses this view in the context of "barbaric" societies moving toward "minimal decency":

> A minimally decent society is governed by minimally moral rules. A complete breakdown of such rules characterizes a barbaric society. In this context, what makes these rules moral is their capacity to prevent excess wrongdoing or evil, not their ability to promote a particular conception of the good life, including a substantive conception of justice. Such moral rules include negative injunctions against killing, or maiming or ill-treating others, and also a system of basic procedural due process. (2001, 45)

In this context, procedural justice means accepting basic norms for negotiation, contestation, and decision making while suspending broader issues of redistribution or punishment. Procedural justice is the cornerstone of the minimalist approach. It rejects demands for accountability or transformative policies of material redistribution as unattainable and probably destabilizing while arguing that anything less than basic ground rules for coexistence will result in renewed violence. Reconciliation, therefore, means creating a space where former enemies can become political opponents within the bounds of the rule of law. Writing about Nazism and Stalinism, Stuart Hampshire argues that totalitarianism seeks to create "a bombed and flattened moral landscape" and the destruction of "all notions of fairness and justice from practical politics and, as far as possible, from persons' minds" (1989, 68). In the face of such thorough moral destruction, the only viable alternative is a political order that reinscribes limits for political and state power and imposes a "bare minimum concept of justice," amounting to no more than a method of mediating political contestation absent social solidarity or shared background values (1989, 72). Hampshire considers this "basic level of morality, a bare minimum, which is entirely negative," as the most that can be expected following such extreme political violence. Indeed, procedural justice becomes the only means of achieving a tolerable coexistence between erstwhile enemies "without any substantive reconciliation between them, and without any common ground" (1989, 109).

This argument is certainly compelling, since it reflects a kind of realism and concern about immediately destabilizing conditions, but minimalism leaves a number of normative issues undertheorized, and thus remains problematic as a long-term position on the past. By basing reconciliation on thin proceduralism, minimalists focus on the demands of the present to the near exclusion of engaging the past. We should resist this narrow approach. Victims of atrocity and their descendants have a moral interest in knowing and publicizing the truth about human rights abuses, not in order to pursue a vindictive politics of victimhood, but as a means of achieving legitimate demands for moral recognition. Without some engagement with the past, reconciliation will remain superficial and tenuous at best.

Truth seeking is not only victim oriented, however. Investigating past abuses can undermine apologist histories that perpetrators used to justify their actions. Delegitimizing these histories is crucial for reconciliation, for otherwise abuses remain uncontested and effectively reinforce an equivalence between violators and the violated, with each "side" having its own justifications or interpretation of what happened. Investigating violations can also contribute to addressing the causes of violence, providing a basic groundwork for institutional and political reforms to ensure that the past is not repeated. Minimalism has little to offer in this regard. Because it eschews investigation and disclosure of the past, it contains no mechanism for promoting institutional reform, much less societal transformation. Instead, it risks reifying the power arrangement existing in the transitional period, with the only caveat that enemies not pursue violence to settle disputes. The result is an approach that, unwittingly perhaps, permits apologists to argue for "forgetting and moving on" while maintaining intact the institutions responsible for past crimes.

Similarly, minimalism ignores that often a history of violence may leave a significantly uneven distribution of power and resources benefiting past perpetrators. This is a materialist claim, one that complements the discursive concerns about delegitimizing perpetrator justifications. Minimalists risk underplaying how in negotiated transitions, a thin system of procedural justice may further strengthen existing power relations and ignore a pressing need for distributive justice policies, particularly important where pronounced economic inequalities can further destabilize the country. The political terrain after mass violence is often uneven—particularly after negotiated settlements— with some actors enjoying significant political and economic capital and others living under conditions of impoverishment and destitution nearly identical to the period of violence, albeit perhaps without the overt political oppression of the previous era. A more satisfactory model of reconciliation must attend to these issues of disparate and uneven power relations.

At the other end of the theoretical spectrum lies what I term *maximalist* approaches, which reject the accommodationism and "hasty peace" typical of minimalism.[5] For maximalists, reconciliation occurs when perpetrators acknowledge responsibility, repent, and then are forgiven by their victims. Perhaps the strongest proponent of this approach is Archbishop Desmond Tutu, who served as the South African Truth and Reconciliation Commission's chairman. Tutu famously sought to reground reconciliation on the notion of *ubuntu*, or humane-ness, drawing attention to the importance of generating compassion and forgiveness among former enemies.

In *No Future without Forgiveness* (1999), Tutu discusses this theory of reconciliation at length. While the book is not an academic work, its centrality in debates about reconciliation requires that we give it attention. It is noteworthy for the way it rejects mere cohabitation as normatively problematic, arguing that minimalism simply excuses perpetrators of any responsibility while undercutting moral reflection and placing immediate needs above the more difficult work of moral repair. Of particular concern for Tutu is the fact that minimalism is insufficiently attentive to the needs of victims. For him, reconciliation contains a constitutive element of acknowledgment and forgiveness. Acknowledgment is achieved not only through investigating past actions and publicly disseminating the findings but also more profoundly through the perpetrator's explicit recognition of wrongdoing and the victim's forgiveness:

> If the wrongdoer has come to the point of realizing his wrong, then one hopes there will be remorse, or at least some contrition or sorrow. This should lead him to confess the wrong he has done and ask for forgiveness. It obviously requires a fair measure of humility, especially when the victim is someone in a group that one's community has despised, as was often the case in South Africa when the perpetrators were government agents. The victim, we hope, would be moved to respond to an apology by forgiving the culprit. (1999, 271)

Tutu is careful to qualify his understanding of reconciliation through the use of a soft conditional ("*if* the wrongdoer . . . *then* one hopes" and "the victim, we hope"); however, the result—the overcoming of estrangement—is argued in no uncertain terms. "In the act of forgiveness we are declaring our faith in the future of a relationship. . . . [W]e are saying here is a chance to make a new beginning. It is an act of faith the wrongdoer can change" (1999, 272).

Similarly, political theorist Lyn Graybill (2001) centers reconciliation on mutual forgiveness, which creates the possibility of securing a shared future for everyone affected by the violence. She argues that trials and social amnesia are equally unsatisfactory in this regard, as both ignore the important transformations required to suture old wounds and reintegrate former enemies into a shared community, transformations that can occur only through the power of forgiving. Rodney Petersen espouses a similar definition of reconciliation, characterizing it as a "restoration or even a transformation toward intended wholeness that comes with transcendent or human grace" (2001, 13). Forgiveness is the vehicle of transformation, restoring and transforming practices between former enemies. The transformation must be "grounded in a deep ontological understanding of life" and "rooted in a costly self-immolation in the heart of being itself. It affects my being and the one with whom I exist in a state of alienation insofar as I will allow it" (2001, 11). Achieving this transformation requires a great sacrifice on the part of the perpetrator and the victim; perpetrators must take responsibility for their crimes and repent, in the process critically interrogating their identity and leaving themselves vulnerable to censure and reproach, and victims must move beyond "insincere and grandiloquent language" of facile pity toward seeing their violators "in the present, not as encumbered in the past or as prejudged in the future" (2001, 24).[6]

Arguably, the focus on forgiveness may be burdensome on victims, even if this is not the intention. The state cannot, of course, decree forgiveness, and none of these thinkers argues so. But though forgiving should be a free and unencumbered act, its de facto institutionalization in some truth commissions (such as South Africa's) or in official apologies gives victims little space for opposing it and demanding instead some sort of accountability. In this sense, reconciliation through forgiveness may appear coercive to victims. This is not to say that forgiveness is never appropriate, but only to note that its institutionalization as the prime mechanism for reconciliation is deeply problematic, for it is "morally objectionable as well as impractical . . . to force people to agree about the past, forgive the sins committed against them, or love one another" (Crocker 2000, 108). Forgiveness may be morally praiseworthy, but it should not serve as the lodestar of reconciliation.

These understandings of forgiveness are typically grounded in theological conceptions of moral renewal and solidarity. In an important recent work on South Africa, Claire Moon criticizes Tutu and other maximalist thinkers for constructing a notion of reconciliation that calls "upon the Edenic, or prelapsarian human condition, and hail[s] a return to a condition of harmony and unity that preceded the Fall" (2008, 118). Moon is right to caution against apolitical understandings of reconciliation that problematically naturalize a prior just social order and then trace, as it were, its fragmentation and collapse. Indeed, the term *re*-conciliation itself carries with it an idea of a *return* to a prior desirable state. Such narratives graft onto different societies a general moral story about harmony, rupture, and eventual reunion that risks ignoring important historical and political features.[7]

While Moon may overstate the case that "theological narratives work *against* the possibility of constituting different political configurations and allegiances," she is correct in drawing our attention to the narrative arc of harmony, fall, and return that is common here (2008, 121). The idea of a return to a prelapsarian state is problematic not only for its conceptualization of the past but also for what it requires of the present and future. It risks treating reconciliation as the substantive agreement on moral issues and perspectives as well as a robust harmony between different groups that tends to smooth over real and legitimate differences—differences that are ineradicable elements of any political order. By underplaying political dissension, maximalist approaches face a difficulty in defining the difference between significant political conflict that may degenerate into violence and forceful political dissent, a basic element of democratic politics. In large part, I suspect, this is because they fail to discuss how post-atrocity politics should look. But political life based on forgiveness must still outline the normative criteria to distinguish between extremist political discourse and legitimate political debate; without such criteria, both may be discarded as fundamentally disruptive of the goal of profound reconciliation that forgiveness entails. The demands that forgiveness makes on political discourse risk overdetermining the shape of this discourse, so that it no longer includes contestation but rather is reinscribed with terms such as "love," "fraternity," and "pity."[8] It defines permissible politics according to the likelihood of further antagonism, not according to the actual content of the claims made by actors. Because political contestation may come into opposition with the need to forgive, political contestation risks being delegitimized. But political life includes more than the search for consensus; it also contains something of an *agonistic* dimension, and thus any theory of reconciliation must allow for a distinction between legitimate political contestation and repression. Maximalists struggle to draw this distinction precisely because they focus on forgiveness and the attendant lack of criteria to judge what forms of political contestation are permissible. But there is an even deeper problem with these approaches, one that they share, paradoxically, with minimalist theories discussed earlier.

Both minimalists and maximalists anchor their understandings of reconciliation in specific discourses that do not translate well into other social spheres. In both cases, they draw from a particular type of discourse that functions appropriately within certain bounds but founders in other contexts. In other words, they rapidly reach their limits of applicability outside their specific domains. Consider minimalists: They use an essentially legalistic, proceduralist model that provides a persuasive account of what the minimum basis of post-atrocity politics should be—simple coexistence bound by the rule of law, with a core of human rights protections. But procedural justice tells us little about what reconciliation looks like between individuals. It fails to address that reconciling former enemies interpersonally means more than securing the absence of violence; it also requires thoughtfully engaging issues of responsibility, vengeance, resentment, and even forgiveness, as well as reflection on what the moral contours of new personal relations should be. Minimalists say little about the uses of shame, survivor demands for recognition of their experiences, or complex moral issues surrounding personal apologies and forgiveness. Nor do they tell us much about different types of elite discourse and how political elites can contribute to or undermine societal reconciliation. What should be the role of elites in rebuilding their society, beyond the minimal stipulation that they not use violence to further their own interests? What are the dangers and benefits of having elites promote a revisionist account of the past, and how does this affect personal and broader social historical understandings? Where do official apologies fit in? Related to this is the role of civil society: Certainly, civil society actors can further the process of reconciliation by helping inform public debate on articulating definitions of perpetrators, victims, and bystanders; fostering discussions on the meaning of concepts such as justice, truth, and guilt; and critically examining past legitimizing narratives (they can also, of course, distort or even sabotage efforts at achieving all these things). All of this far exceeds the narrowly tailored proscriptive requirements found in minimalist approaches.

Maximalists suffer from the same limitation. Rather than begin from an overly formalistic legal approach, maximalists tend to rely on the faculty of forgiveness as the wellspring of reconciliation. Here, the problem lies with forgiveness's traditional understanding as a *personal faculty* occurring between individuals qua individuals. It does not travel well into other spheres of social relations, at least not without having to undergo some drastic conceptual changes that result in its substantial redefinition. Consider the use of legal pardons, often seen as the legal twin of forgiveness (Freeman 2002). In the legal sphere, a sovereign grants a pardon in order to eliminate juridical culpability. Pardons do not, however, necessarily require the perpetrator's moral transformation. Indeed, pardons often have little to do with public repentance; rather, they are employed for political reasons, such as ensuring stability or eliminating a potential threat. Furthermore, pardons remain the prerogative of the sovereign, not the victim.[9] Whereas forgiveness can be understood as a faculty that expresses the victim's agency, juridical pardons are firmly rooted in the sovereign, and victims have little influence on their use.

Nor is it clear what it means for forgiveness to play a central role in social discourse. Certainly, elites can apologize for actions committed by members of their group, and other elites may forgive them (Digeser 2001; Tavuchis 1991). But apologies and forgiveness do not necessarily reconcile, nor do they necessarily remove mistrust. Though some civil society groups may encourage forgiveness as a way of reaching closure on the past, how this is to be operationalized remains at best problematic; how do we institutionalize forgiveness in public discourse or public policy while maintaining its transcendental and expiatory character? Another way of putting it is this: If forgiveness requires unpredictability—precisely because it must be the action of a *free* agent, and thus if we know that forgiveness always follows transgressions, the faculty loses its moral force—its institutionalization and routinization will result in predictability and, consequently, its debasement. The deep ontological transformations expected by Tutu and others become muted, or at least significantly attenuated, because there is no mechanism to ensure that the guilty truly repent and the victims forgive them for it. Rather, what is left is a discourse that calls for reintegration through the embrace of the other without providing any insight into how this could operate as a social, rather than merely personal, dynamic. Again, this is *not* to say that forgiveness is inappropriate in post-conflict contexts; it is only to state that we should be wary of placing it at the center of a theory of reconciliation, for it is unclear how forgiveness (as a faculty exercised between individuals) can be used in broader social or institutional contexts. Forgiveness of this sort, as a social mechanism of integration, requires more attention to its operationalization than maximalists have given it.

Both minimalist and maximalist theories are based on too narrow a conception of reconciliation. The former's legalistic understanding fails to capture myriad other elements that need to be addressed at the interpersonal, social, and political levels, and the latter draws on an individualist theory of forgiveness that cannot be satisfactorily projected onto social, legal, or political levels. Because of their restricted origins and applicability, both minimalist and maximalist formulations are *univalent*—that is, they remain anchored to types of discourse that operate at only one societal level. This, in turn, prevents them from identifying how disparate calls for justice, forgiveness, and truth telling—all morally legitimate—interact at different social levels.

Reconciliation as Respect: A Multivalent Approach

This book argues that reconciliation is best understood as a multilevel process, one characterized by specific logics and strategies operating at four levels: the political, institutional, civil society, and interpersonal levels. For example, truth commissions and tribunals address issues of victim recognition, factual accounts of the past, and accountability at an institutional (and in the former case, possibly civil society) level but do not exhaust all the demands for reconciliation. Political leaders may introduce new education policies that discuss the past and may occasionally promote public memory projects (e.g., monuments, museums) to preserve historical memory. Civil society groups, such as nongovernmental organizations (NGOs) and community associations, in many instances have played important roles in bringing attention to crimes and generating public debate about them, as well as fostering discussions about complicity and responsibility. Moreover, sophisticated therapies for treating survivors have emerged to address legacies of

atrocity and trauma at the micro level, further indication that reconciliation is a complex process, operating on multiple levels.

That efforts at reconciliation exist at different levels, from the
political and institutional to the social and interpersonal, is not mere
coincidence. Rather, it points to something more fundamental: Reconciliation develops through the contextually specific actions and
strategies of actors, and thus any theory must maintain sensitivity to
these different contexts. Nevertheless, there is no guarantee that these
different types of responses to the past will work in harmony; they
may, in certain instances, work at cross-purposes, undermining the
larger goal of reconciliation and social regeneration. Trials may end
in acquittals and kindle calls for vengeance, while truth commissions
may bring to light awful crimes but leave perpetrators untouched.
Civil society groups may radicalize public discourse and raise unreal-
izable expectations of justice, or conversely, some actors may actually
serve as apologists for past crimes, arguing that the crimes were legitimate responses to a real or perceived threat. And of course, efforts at
treating trauma will sometimes fail, as survivors fall into further despair. Thus, reconciliation does not unfold harmoniously along different levels. Rather, it is best theorized as *disjunctured* and *uneven*, and
its complex and multivalent character means that institutional responses (tribunals and truth commissions) are by themselves insufficient to guarantee its success.

These four levels are only conceptually distinct; reconciliation
through the smooth and even integration of these levels is rarely, if
ever, achieved empirically. Nevertheless, by theorizing an ideal model,
we can identify how actions and developments at different levels can
affect the larger effort of reconciliation. In this sense, the model serves
as a heuristic and analytical device to interrogate the strengths and
shortcomings of actual reconciliatory efforts, and it identifies the major normative concerns that post-atrocity societies face in a manner
that is more nuanced and sensitive to competing normative claims.
Here, I briefly define the various levels.

By *political society*, I mean the political elite who control the
state, as well as the major actors outside government who represent
defined sectors of the population. Political society also includes formal politics, such as party politics, and serves as a major sphere for
presenting and shaping official accounts of the past. The transitional

context—whether it was negotiated or imposed through military victory—is a major constraining factor in how political elites engage the issue of reconciliation.

The *institutional* level includes formal institutional mechanisms such as tribunals and truth commissions assembled to interrogate the past, address responsibility, and formally recognize victims. The imprimatur of the state sets these types of institutions apart from strictly civil society efforts at investigating the past and examining responsibility.

Civil society is a third crucial level of the reconciliatory process. Civil society actors can contribute to reconciliation by offering more complex and critical interpretations of the past and by opposing statist accounts that simplify or distort the historical record. NGOs and other civil society groups also help inform the categories of bystanders, victims, and perpetrators, as well as concepts such as justice and responsibility. Furthermore, civil society is an important locus for promoting the rule of law and mutual respect, since these values require more than merely legal enforcement.

Finally, there is the *interpersonal* level, where individuals deal with the past by interpreting their personal narratives as part of, or a complement to, the larger public narrative developed at macro levels. Issues of accountability and recognition are transformed into concerns about personal responsibility, revenge, forgiveness, and personal moral transformation. Subsequent chapters show that certain responses have an impact on several levels simultaneously and others remain anchored to only one level (or have only minor repercussions at other levels).

At the center of this multilevel theory is the normative concept of *mutual respect*. Reconciliation, I argue, is based on a normative shift from estrangement and distrust to mutual respect, including (most importantly) among enemies. This means deepening the formal "rule of law" typical of legal minimalism not just to guarantee due process protections and procedural justice in some formal jurisprudential sense but also to recognize the validity of others' claims to participate in the political and social spheres. Respect includes the recognition of others' worth in and of itself and not simply because of political affiliation and limitations on the moral acceptability of certain actions toward them. In the next chapter I elaborate this norm, but I should note here that respect is more substantive than Bhargava's (2001) bare coexistence but not as thick as the conceptions of solidarity animating maximalist accounts of reconciliation. Granted, this idea of respect is a difficult concept to measure empirically. One indication of success is when previous, conflict-era forms of identity no longer represent the dominant modes of carving out political loyalty. Conflict-era identities are constructed on a strongly binary logic: In-groups define themselves through the construction of a dehumanized, disdained, and often-feared out-group requiring suppression, expulsion, or possibly even physical destruction (and often a combination of these). Where these previous identities lose their ability to mobilize loyalty and are instead mitigated by the development of alternative, overlapping political identities, the traditional in-group/out-group boundaries are no longer the most salient. Societies are reconciled to the extent that these new identities signify news ways of organizing political demands and loyalties. Of course, this does not mean that social tranquility and economic development follow, but it is indicative that old forms of enmity have been replaced by new political orientations, and in this sense we can say that reconciliation has been achieved. Nor does it mean the end of contestation and thus the end of politics; rather, it means that former enemies come to respect one another, see each other as moral equals and members of the same polity, and eventually form alliances with one another over new political, social, and economic challenges—the bread and butter, so to speak, of regular politics.

In this sense, I share a general theoretical perspective with Andrew Schaap's *Political Reconciliation* (2005), which argues that society is not a hypostatized entity needing reconstruction after fragmentation, but rather should be understood as a *process*, a fragile undertaking that is never ending and shapes us as much as we shape it. We reconcile, Schaap tells us, through public action and speech, which are inherently perspectival and thus political. His Arendtian approach focuses on "worldliness," a recognition of the necessity of sustaining two fragile but simultaneous moments: one where a shared world is opened to adversaries and another where that world is called into question. The strength of *Political Reconciliation* lies in stressing the centrality of politics and risk and its unwillingness to yield to apolitical conceptions of reconciled society. I agree with much of the argument, though I believe that the idea of moral respect gives greater cohesion to reconciliation while still maintaining sensitivity to the openness and fragility Schaap rightly highlights. This, in turn, necessitates theorizing moral respect across different contexts, as well as examining additional normative concepts that contribute to it, providing a theoretical account that can further elaborate the social relations under consideration in Schaap's work.

In addition to mutual respect, I introduce four other normative concepts that play a role in achieving reconciliation: *truth*, *accountability*, *recognition of victims*, and the *rule of law*, all further defined in the next chapter. These other concepts are crucial not only on their own—they can be justified on their own terms, which is done in the following pages—but also because through their emergence and interaction with one another, they promote respect.

Truth is particularly important, for the most basic requirement for reckoning with past crimes is having an understanding of what actually occurred. Without knowledge of the past, any expectations of developing trust among citizens and between citizens and the state are severely weakened. Accordingly, a society must investigate and publicize past abuses. I elaborate two broad dimensions here: (1) truth in its "objective" or factual sense, requiring the identification and investigation of specific instances of atrocity as well as patterns of violence and (2) a broader theoretical–normative engagement with the justificatory narratives employed by previous elites to legitimize their actions, which is a highly *political* enterprise, all the more so in the unstable context of a political transition.

Holding perpetrators *accountable* is a key element of reconciliation, for it is unlikely that survivors will reconcile themselves with those who continue to enjoy impunity. Accountability can take many shapes, and I argue that it takes different forms depending on the context. This may include the estrangement or public devaluation of violators and the repudiation of past policies, as well as formal prosecutions.

A third norm concerns *victim recognition*, which underscores the importance of inscribing narratives of past atrocity with the manifest recognition of the individuals and communities who suffered. Recognizing victims can serve several functions, including restoring their sense of dignity and self-worth and contributing to and informing broader historical memory by complementing the work of formal historical projects. For these reasons, both instrumentalist and noninstrumentalist, recognizing victims is important to reconciliation.

Finally, the establishment of the *rule of law* is necessary for the achievement of a lasting peace and reconciliation through respect. A commitment to the rule of law means that the successor regime has agreed to reform the relevant state institutions responsible for past crimes and provide the necessary mechanisms of accountability and oversight to ensure that individual rights will be respected. We can say, then, that the rule of law contains an institutional dimension of reform, concerned with revamping problematic state institutions and placing legitimate constraints on state power, as well as a normative dimension centered on accepting that political differences will not be decided through violence or force and political contestation will remain bound within formal and informal spheres of deliberation. Crucially, this means a commitment to transparency and impartiality, the cornerstones of due process. Though the institutional transformations required for successful political transitions are not the focus here, it is important to underscore that both the institutional and normative dimensions of the rule of law are crucial for reconciliation. Clearly, both components are intimately connected.

There is a temporal element that requires some elaboration here. If truth, accountability, and victim recognition often result in further estrangement among different groups (if only because they may destabilize an already politically delicate state of affairs), the rule of law and respect point to a closing of the moral distance between groups, showing that reconciliation requires, in the last instance, a reconstruction of the political order that allows for past enemies to work and live in the same political and moral space. A key difficulty with other approaches that equate reconciliation with forgetting is that they posit a new social order on (morally) insufficiently strong grounds by not grappling with issues of responsibility, impunity, memory, remorse, and frustration, all of which can reemerge following the transition. By underscoring the rule of law and especially mutual respect, I call attention to two important issues: (1) that reconciliation is, in its final calculus, about reintroducing former antagonists back into the same moral sphere and (2) that this requires an honest and sustained engagement with the past and with the moral issues surrounding perpetrators, bystanders, and victims.

It is important to note that these normative concepts all deal with crucial political and ethical problems and therefore should not be treated on a merely instrumental basis for the furtherance of reconciliation; rather, it is precisely because they engage fundamental political and ethical issues that they are important to broad-based reconciliation. To treat them cavalierly and epiphenomenally misses the point entirely.

The following chapter discusses the normative concepts in detail, beginning with the core concept of respect. I provide an account of what each concept means and explain its normative content and limits. Chapters 3 through 6 then tackle the four levels—political, institutional, civil society, and interpersonal, respectively—and discuss why reconciliation at each level is both necessary and, by itself, insufficient for broader societal regeneration. I also discuss how the different levels affect one another, both positively and negatively. These discussions are organized around the five normative concepts. Chapter 7 concludes this book.

One last note: The theory of reconciliation presented here is not directly based on a particular version of contemporary democratic theory. While achieving reconciliation may take a great deal of time, it is largely a phenomenon of the transitional phases between the end of violence and the consolidation of democracy. The discussion I present in this book remains largely agnostic on the question of what type of democracy should follow the transition. Certain theories of democracy may be particularly compatible (or otherwise desirable) with the normative concepts I discuss, but I remain hesitant to expand my argument for reconciliation into a complete theory of democracy. To do so would overburden what I mean by reconciliation and would connect it too tightly to our preferred form of democratic life, without necessarily providing a convincing defense of the logical necessity of such connections. My argument for reconciliation is meant to serve as a groundwork for understanding the normative requirements for future peaceful and just social coexistence, and there are many plausible ways of thinking about this. It is partly decided through public deliberation and debate, as well as through elite negotiation and imposition. As I have argued, and as I argue in subsequent chapters, a peaceful society is not an apolitical society; we should not expect or desire political contestation to disappear. After all, this situation does not hold in established democracies, so there is no reason to believe that it could be achieved in fragile transitions. And, in any case, it would be deeply illiberal and authoritarian. Rather, we should expect reconciled societies to have political contestation, negotiation, argument, bartering, and so on. There are, of course, many ways of understanding these and the necessary normative requirements for democratic justice. At a more theoretical level, one may argue for the virtues of, say, a (late) Habermasian (1996) or Rawlsian (2005) theory of proceduralist democracy above Laclauian (1996) radical democracy, or one may reject both in favor of a radical anarchism, such as Roberto Unger's (1998), or even the more communitarian ideal proposed by Charles Taylor (1989) and Michael Sandel (1998). One could expand this list quite a bit. Each of these theories has strengths and weaknesses that have been debated extensively elsewhere, and I do not pretend that reconciliation must result in any particular democratic theory. While I do draw a number of insights of contemporary democratic theory, especially the recent focus on deliberation and democratic praxis, I do not develop a strong theoretical link between reconciliation and a particular democratic theory model (though I do rely on a number of insights from deliberative theories in my discussion of civil society). At an empirical level, I avoid making a categorical argument in favor of any specific form of democratic power sharing, such as liberal-pluralist above confederal or consociational models. The appropriateness of any one depends on many factors, including the strength and types of demands of territorially based ethnic identities in the given country and their relationships with one another. While these are certainly important issues, they require an analysis of the concrete conditions of particular cases. This book is concerned with establishing and defending the basic normative principles of reconciliation.

2 Key Normative Concepts

A major difficulty for societies emerging from a recent history of mass violence is how to contend with demands for justice, truth, and victim acknowledgment while recognizing the need for stability and peace. Although clearly important, a successful democratic transition requires more than strong leadership. Legacies of violence require that a society engage certain ethical questions in order to arrive at a just peace and meaningful reconciliation.

In the previous chapter I introduced the five normative concepts that underpin my theory of reconciliation as respect. In this chapter, I discuss the concepts at length. I begin by presenting the idea of mutual respect and then introduce the corollary concepts: truth telling, accountability, victim recognition, and rule of law. Although important, each on its own is insufficient for reconciliation. They help promote the development of the norm of mutual respect, which is the heart of reconciliation in badly fractured societies. As will become clear throughout the following discussion and in subsequent chapters, though the concepts themselves are at first framed in general terms, their actualization—that is, how they are manifested in any particular situation—varies significantly, and thus are not part of a universal template. The idea, in other words, is not to create a programmatic model of reconciliation that guarantees a particular outcome when certain steps are followed (which is not, in my opinion, possible). Rather, these normative concepts should be seen as crucial ethical challenges that continuously arise in transitional settings, and demand attention because they point to some of the very basic questions of how a society relates to itself, its past, and its future.

How should a society deal with a legacy of severe human rights abuses? What ethical and practical considerations should frame a response? Societies have turned to international and domestic criminal and civil trials to secure punishment (or amnesties to prevent further violence), truth commissions and other investigative institutions to investigate the past, public apologies and reparations for victims, and museums and monuments meant to preserve history. It is not uncommon to find a combination of measures, even though they may undermine one another. But without an understanding of what a society is trying to accomplish, and without some basic principles to guide its decisions, continued animosity and tensions are likely.

Mutual Respect

Reconciliation requires moving away from estrangement and distrust to a situation of respect and tolerance of others, including, crucially, former enemies. *Reconciliation is the achievement of mutual respect across society.* Such a statement immediately requires some elaboration.

To understand mutual respect, we need to define what it means to be a person, morally speaking. A healthy identity develops from intersubjective recognition among equals, which includes reciprocal recognition of claims to moral worth and dignity. Dignity is a fundamental property of what it means to be a person, as it points to the value of autonomy that is at the core of a healthy sense of self. Kant's second formulation of the categorical imperative, for example, argues that to treat another merely as a means, with no dignity, is a moral wrong (1998). While Kant did not espouse a theory of intersubjective morality, the notion that dignity is a fundamental value is at the basis of both deontological and intersubjective theories of morality. This is particularly important to victims and others who have suffered political abuse and stigmatization and remain mistreated and devalued. A society that seeks to be reconciled must create conditions for the recognition of all citizens as bearers of moral worth and dignity.

We recognize moral worth and dignity by showing respect for others. This is primarily a public relationship—or as Arendt (1989, 243) puts it, of "the domain of human affairs"—and differs from esteem, which refers to holding someone in special regard due to some particular trait of exceptional worthiness that we celebrate in her. Respect is not reserved for exceptional circumstances or for exceptional people;[1] rather, it follows from recognizing others as having inherent rather than instrumental moral worth by virtue of being persons. We show respect by behaving in ways that express that value. We do not, for instance, "respect" another when we measure one's value according to our own desires or goals, for such attitudes and behavior merely relegate the other's value to a measure of utility based on our own calculus. Respect requires that we recognize the other's claim on us to her moral worth and dignity, and we consequently have an obligation to treat her in a way that expresses this recognition. We are responsible for the ways in which we treat others.

Another way of expressing this is to say that as morally autonomous agents, we ought to treat others in such ways that recognize them also as morally autonomous. To the extent that we are autonomous, we can *choose* to act vis-à-vis others in certain ways that are constrained by the moral claims they make on us. Autonomy need not mean monadic individualism, that is, the notion that individuals are theoretically "prior" to socialization or broader cultural influences, but only that personhood includes the possibility of making moral decisions, of choosing. If there were no choice involved and our actions were biologically or socially overdetermined, it would make no sense to speak of moral autonomy or moral responsibility. Without autonomy, there would be no morality. The very idea of respect entails this conception of agency, since without it what appears to be recognition of the value of others is merely coincidental indifference bereft of any normative substance.

Respect is a reciprocal norm: It requires the mutual recognition of moral worth between subjects. Furthermore, it assumes that in engaging with others, we have an obligation to give them reasons for our actions and values that could affect them. We owe them, as moral beings whose dignity we recognize, an account of why we treat them the way we do. In this sense, reason is not private, but intersubjective. It is not morally sufficient for me to be satisfied with my own reasons for values or actions that may affect others; it is not sufficient, in other words, to assume that the values we hold are agent-neutral (in Christine Korsgaard's terms), and thus do not require that we justify them to others (1996). This would be a sign of disrespect, for it disregards the other's ability to judge my reasons and her right to respond to me. Rather, because I acknowledge others as moral, rational beings like me, it is incumbent upon me to give reasons they could recognize as valid. To respect another is to take seriously one's ability to comprehend and judge my reasons and respond to them, and also expect that person to do the same for me. She cannot simply assume that the reasons for treating me in a particular way are normatively satisfactory or show respect for my dignity; she must offer reasons. This by no means requires that we ultimately reach a consensus on ends or policies, nor does it point to deep solidarity or social harmony, but it does mean that we are obligated to engage with one another as moral equals who deserve respect. Nor does it assume that we are strictly rational creatures bereft of emotion. We are also emotional beings who experience pain and joy and develop meaningful commitments and relationships with others, and part of giving reasons is a recognition of the importance of these broader, complex relations for a healthy identity. Giving reasons to others, and expecting the same from them, is an expression of this respect.

Understood in this way, respect refers to something greater than the liminal requirements demanded by political theorists like Chantal Mouffe, who sees political life as fundamentally antagonistic with little room for considering others as moral equals (1997). Respect implies the possibility of discussion and deliberation among former enemies, and reflects the ability to see another as a fellow human being. Nevertheless, it falls short of the deep fraternity that some thinkers place at the core of reconciliation. It certainly falls far short of what theologian and political theorist Miroslav Volf approvingly calls the "will to embrace":

> The will to give ourselves to others and welcome them, to readjust our identities to make space for them, is prior to any judgment about others, except that of identifying them in their humanity. The will to embrace precedes any "truth" about others and any reading of their action with respect to justice. This will is absolutely indiscriminate and strictly immutable; it

transcends the moral mapping of the social world into "good"
and "evil." (2001, 42)

My understanding of respect does not transcend notions of good
and evil, since it takes the problem of accountability quite seriously.
Without just punishment and the rejection of impunity respect is
nearly impossible, and we should not mistake it for absolving perpetrators of responsibility for their actions. Instead, respect underscores the
importance of replacing social relations based on fear and domination
with tolerance toward others in public and semipublic life. Tolerance is
ancillary to respect; to the extent that we see others as deserving recognition as fellow citizens and moral equals, we tolerate their political
claims, ways of life, beliefs, and so on, as long as these do not violate
the fundamental dignity of others or require a return to violence.

The term *tolerance* is not without its ambiguities, and an enormous
amount of literature has been generated to define its conceptual content and boundaries (Mendus 1998, 1999; Nehushtan 2007; Scanlon
2003). Michael Walzer has usefully identified a range of understandings, from "simply resigned acceptance of difference for the sake of
peace" to an "enthusiastic endorsement of difference" (1997, 10–11).
Here, I understand tolerance as more than resigned acceptance to include a basic recognition of others as moral beings. But this does not
mean we should expect an "enthusiastic" endorsement of former enemies. Indeed, tolerance is for those with whom we strongly disagree.
Tolerance includes several core elements: (1) it assumes the existence
of continued, perhaps ineradicable disagreements with persons or
beliefs, which are all more pronounced in the contexts under discussion here and (2) it requires that one's views are not forced on those
with whom one disagrees, or that one not threaten violence or other
sanctions if they do not change their ways (Locke 1983; Newey 1999).
Disagreements and even signs of disapproval toward others are fundamental aspects of social life, even more so following mass political
violence, but their expression must remain within the bounds of mini-
mally acceptable social behavior (i.e., fall short of outright violence or
repression). And yet it implies that we continue to see ourselves as part
of the same community as those with whom we disagree—in other
words, we stay in a relationship with them and recognize that we have
certain obligations toward them, and they toward us. Tolerance, as

part of a larger understanding of reconciliation, is not simply disapproval and complete separation. Rather, tolerance requires that people stay in some nontrivial relationship with one another, and thus points toward a more significant level of reciprocal accommodation and recognition.

Tolerance, then, is the acknowledgment of difference and disagreement combined with a commitment to remain part of the same community. Beneath the disagreements and divisiveness there must be a basic, mutual recognition of moral worth and dignity—of respect—that serves to limit our reactions toward others. It is more than a unilateral act of one toward another, since it is premised on reciprocity. Tolerance and respect develop over time and require that the other normative concepts discussed below be adequately addressed. In this sense, respect develops partially in tandem with the actualization of these other norms, but only after they have been pursued successfully for some period. Over time, mistrust may recede as former antagonists learn to live with one another, although perhaps not embrace each other. It is only then, after erstwhile enemies come to see each other as citizens and moral equals (even if politically at odds), that respect can be said to take root. And it is then that we can talk about reconciliation, for at that point former enemies have made the difficult but important transformation of recognizing and accepting each other as members of the same polity and begin working together. To make sense of this, we now move to the corollary concepts: truth, accountability, recognition, and rule of law.

Truth

Public knowledge of past crimes is an important component of societal reconciliation, for without this perpetrators remain unchallenged, victims are further degraded, and acrimony and resentment between opposing groups remain, undermining future relations and destabilizing political and social life. An accurate rendering of the past can help mitigate these phenomena, first by undermining the self-serving justificatory narratives of perpetrators—and in the process holding them publicly accountable, even if only symbolically—and second, by offering extended recognition to victims and survivors. A generally accurate historical account can also frame future discussions about the past. Depending on the context, truth telling may largely confirm what many already believe happened, rather than uncover unknown crimes. In South Africa, for example, many blacks saw the truth commission's work as a vindication of the struggle against apartheid, as public truth telling provided a broader approval of the widely shared knowledge that the white regime had committed gross and systematic atrocities (though some whites expressed shock at the commission's findings). In other cases, however, truth telling essentially undermines denial. During periods of mass violence, the state may deny responsibility for abuses and employ disappearances and similar strategies that are explicitly designed to obscure the nature of its actions, as occurred in Argentina, Chile, and Guatemala (Garretón 1992). Uncovering the truth in these instances contains both an informative and critical dimension.

The aforementioned are fundamentally consequentialist arguments, for they identify the moral salience of truth telling in its ability to foster profound changes in societies. But public knowledge of the past alone is insufficient to secure reconciliation. New knowledge may only further antagonize opponents and rekindle conflict. But combined with other moral imperatives, truth telling can promote a new political order predicated on mutual respect and tolerance. Truth cannot provide all of this, nor does it serve as a curative elixir capable of magically erasing bitterness and distrust, but the alternative—continued denial, unchallenged dominance of perpetrator justifications, and further victim degradation—is certainly less likely to promote trust, and at any rate is morally unsatisfactory because of the contempt for fellow citizens that it implies. Admittedly, consequentialist arguments remain probabilistic at best, for it is impossible to prove axiomatically that truth telling results in a better society, especially if truth is divorced from other moral imperatives. However, as I argue below, when combined with the other normative concepts, truth telling can work to promote mutual respect and tolerance while remaining practically viable. Without a reasonable understanding of what happened, the other goals of reconciliation are unlikely to be met.

A second set of reasons, essentially non-consequentialist, relies on the moral right to knowledge by victims and society as a whole. Some scholars, such as David Crocker (2000) and Juan Méndez (1997), argue that there exists a deontological aspect to truth telling: Victims have a "right to know" about past abuses, regardless of the broader social consequences of publicizing such knowledge. International human rights law has also endorsed the right to knowledge. UN Special Rapporteur Louis Joinet has written that there exists a non-derogable "fundamental right to truth." This right is understood as both an individual and collective right. "Its corollary is a 'duty to remember,' which the state must assume, in order to guard against the perversions of history that go under the names of revisionism or negationism" (1997, I, II). Theo Van Boven (1993) has also cited the right to truth as a basic right for victims of human rights violations.[2]

The deontological formulation requires further development, however: It should be conceptualized as both a *right* that victims have and a *duty* owed them through which truth telling becomes an expression of respect for their intrinsic moral worth—that is, an important element not captured in more consequentialist arguments. Truth telling acknowledges the dignity and moral value of victims, signaling that past abuses were morally wrong and require repudiation. At its core, a deontological formulation is certainly powerful and intuitively compelling. It justifies itself through the empathy we feel for victims and the claims they make on us to be recognized. By emphasizing a deontological dimension, we place victims at the center of reconciliation while encouraging society to reflect on its responsibility and obligations to those who were harmed.

Truth may be a fundamental aspect of reconciliation, but we are still in need of a satisfactory definition of the term. As I conceive it, reconciliatory truth contains three aspects: (1) an objective, forensic component, (2) a phenomenological, experiential component, and (3) a broadly narrative component that works to combine the first two aspects into an intelligible account that explains the past. I discuss each of these in turn, and then identify some specifically theoretical difficulties that can arise with truth telling.

Factual Truth

Since I accept that there is no socially relevant "fact" prior to its interpretation, I use the term *factual truth* simply to refer to those various types of events and phenomena that are employed in an interpretive process that invariably gives them meaning and places them in a longer chain of comprehension.[3] Primarily, factual truth deals with identifying and investigating specific instances of political atrocity, such as massacres and extrajudicial killings, tortures, rapes, and other empirically identifiable violations of rights. It is concerned with empirically ascertainable events and actions, as well as the concomitant rules and procedures of verification that these require.

But cataloguing discrete violations is insufficient to arrive at a general understanding of political violence. Analysts must also investigate institutionalized patterns of repression, systematized policies of persecution, responsibility of actors and specific units, command structures, and legal codes that facilitated political violence. This is crucial because violence is often part of a broader state policy, and thus to focus solely on specific events and particular perpetrators ignores the larger administrative, legal, and political apparatus that facilitates such violations, as well as those at the top who give the orders for their execution. Mark Osiel has written perceptively on what he terms "administrative massacres," as "the large-scale violation of basic human rights to life and liberty by the central state in a systematic and organized fashion, often against its own citizens, generally in a climate of war—real or imagined" (1997, 9). "Administrative massacres" captures the organized, large-scale and systematized nature of these violations, showing how disparate abuses are in fact often connected through state-centered policies.

For many societies reckoning with past atrocities, the population is often unaware of the extent of the violations. Certainly, there may be a broad understanding that abuses were committed, but their nature is not well-known. How systematic and organized were the abuses? Were they officially sanctioned? Were the targets legitimate political or military foes? How extensive were the violations? These and similar questions determine how justifiable the violations seem in the eyes of the population, whether they were inexcusable crimes or "unfortunate excesses" toward some defensible end. Investigation is crucial. Publicizing hidden violations, however, requires choices of selection and presentation. These choices then make, implicitly and explicitly, claims of moral responsibility, for certain actors are named as perpetrators, others as victims, and still others as morally responsible bystanders. In Althusserian terms, truth telling *interpellates* (Moon 2008). In an important sense, then, searching for the truth is both a historical and political enterprise; it creates winners and losers and reframes historical understanding. Factual truth may be concerned with investigating and classifying empirically identifiable phenomena, but the very process of selection and presentation points to its political nature.

Phenomenological Truth

I term a second form of truth as *phenomenological*. It deals with the physical and psychological legacies of violence on victims and their families, and the ways in which survivors make sense of these experiences. Fear is not easily framed in "objective" language. Nevertheless, personal stories offer insights that are missed in forensic reports. Consider Chanrithy Him's description of the aftermath of a Khmer Rouge (KR) attack on her town in 1975:

> The destruction of something so familiar draws us closer. We dash toward the crumbled buildings, and the stench grows stronger. On the ground along the way, we see a soldier's camouflage hat and burnt pieces of wood from the classrooms. As we move even closer, the smell grows even stronger and buzzing flies swarm. Before our eyes lie piles of dead soldiers in destroyed bomb shelters that had been constructed in rectangular spaces where the flowerbeds used to bloom, between the steps to each classroom. Big flies with greenish heads and eyes swarm the gaping wounds in the soldiers' decaying bodies. One blown-away leg lies beside the step to the first classroom, lonely and morbidly out of place. One soldier's crooked body lies on top of another soldier's, his mouth frozen open in excruciating pain.
>
> I am nine years old.
>
> Never have I seen so much death. For a moment I am hypnotized and spellbound by the ways these soldiers have been killed. [. . .] My stomach begins to move. The breakfast I ate makes its way up my throat, followed by dizziness. Only then do I get hold of myself and feel the repeated tug, the persistent pull of Thavy's brother's hand. (2000, 60)[4]

The power of this account echoes Hans Erich Nossack's claim that "personal truth is the only reality," and to speak it is "revolutionary" insofar as it forces us to confront the immediacy of political terror (2004, xii). But the importance of such stories goes beyond their particularity and immediacy. Victims bring order and meaning to their experiences through narration, simultaneously connecting experience to collective accounts by employing empirical examples. Telling personal stories can "break the silence" imposed through trauma, crucial to the development of a collective understanding of the past (Lira 1997, 5). It establishes a connection between the individual and collective memory, facilitating broader comprehension of what occurred. Thus, phenomenological truth has two dimensions: (1) as a reflection of the individual's personal experiences and (2) as a way of enriching and giving greater substance to social history. But while phenomenological truth plays a role in informing collective understandings of the past, its creation is a dialectical process: Its resonance emerges to the extent that it is both a response to and a further development of broader narratives—that is to say, it is not wholly the product of the speaker but also formed and shaped by other accounts of the past. As Claire Moon (2008) rightly notes, our understandings of violence shape and are shaped by already existing narratives. It is precisely this dialectical process that connects individual experiences to narratives about social conflict, providing a wider and empirically deeper understanding of the past. This is exactly what happens with phenomenological truths of the type presented in Chanrithy Him's account of the Khmer Rouge attack. Her story, and her memoir in general, provides us with a particularized account that both informs and deepens our understanding of the KR era, bringing greater immediacy to our understanding of the Cambodian genocide. And similar to factual truth presented above, phenomenological truth also includes a political aspect, insofar as certain facts and experiences are privileged in presentation; this in turn defines some people as violators, others as victims, and still others as bystanders. This rhetorical element makes these stories both powerful and also potentially problematic, as the combination of fact and empathy can provide a misleading account of events.

The difficulty, then, is how to understand the combination of factual and phenomenological truth as something that is a broadly accurate representation without falling into either a naïve correspondence theory or a radically fractured, deconstructionist notion that replaces the possibility of shared understanding with incommensurability.

Narrative Truth

In transitional settings, any historical inquiry is political charged. Making sense of what constitutes a "fair" appraisal of the past is problematic because of the political and ethical stakes involved and the difficulty of combining factual and phenomenological claims in a coherent, convincing manner. Any such enterprise is also interpretive: It requires making sense of each part, each "fact," in relation to the whole story, which in turn affects the larger narrative picture. The goal of such a hermeneutic combination is to create larger narratives that make sense of events by placing them in culturally intelligible—and persuasive—language. In this book, *narrative truth* refers to these broader social understandings.

Keeping these narrative concerns in mind, it becomes clear that factual truth is not simply the cataloguing of crimes and creation of command-responsibility charts, but more importantly points to the selection (and implicit nonselection) of certain facts and people in an effort to make a larger, coherent story about political responsibility. Not all politically motivated tortures, murders, and rapes receive equal attention in the broader account. Some are used as paradigmatic examples of political atrocity, while others are downplayed because of questions about mens rea (intent), political salience, or other reasons. This is, of course, a political enterprise, insofar as decisions must be made about what events deserve special attention. Accordingly, deciding this is fraught with all sorts of difficulties concerning selection. Phenomenological truths also engage in a kind of hermeneutic of relevance. Individual stories are not totally agent driven, but rather are formed by and inform presiding social narratives, and in the process contribute to our historical understanding. A courtroom may provide a framework for victims to recount their experiences, while simultaneously restricting such presentations through the technical and procedural demands of the trial. Nationalist discourses about historical experiences (e.g., revolutionary struggles, past conflicts, moments of national glory) may be used to justify recent actions—often by all sides—while cultural discourses on responsibility, civility, and threats to the community can serve as the backdrop to debates in the public sphere. Transnational narrative discourses of human rights and popular sovereignty are important, as well as other political-ideological discourses (e.g., Marxism, Fascism, Maoism, anti-imperialism) within which phenomenological and factual truths are framed.

Nevertheless, if narrative truth as I have presented it here aspires to synthesizing truths into a larger overarching story about the past, it is not the case that these truths cohere unproblematically. Personal understandings of an event or series of events emphasize different experiences and downplay others, and can often contradict one another. There is, then, a certain openness that is constitutive of truth claims, insofar as they can never be complete (i.e., totally reflective of all of the events and experiences they represent) nor final. The hermeneutic synthesis required to make larger narratives intelligible is always open to revision, allowing for new interpretations of the past that emphasize some aspects and minimize others. However, this is not the same as wholesale relativism.

Rather, we need a *critical* history that presents the past as accurately as possible, while also ensuring that victims' stories are not erased, nor abuses minimized through ideological manipulation of the past to lessen responsibility. A critical perspective eschews what Nietzsche called "monumental" histories, where the present is justified through the unreflective appeal to the past or any transcendental claim justifying "necessary" actions for its realization (1997 67–70). We need a perspective that interrogates given truths, and thus begins the admittedly difficult and politically delicate process of reconstructing a past that is not based on denials and convenient justifications. This is not an effort at radical deconstruction (if that means a relentless interrogation that risks resulting in incommensurable perspectives with little coherence), but rather a project that remains sensitive to its own assumptions.

Truth is fundamental for reconciliation. Societies need a basic understanding of past events to assign responsibility and resist impunity. The rule of law requires knowing which institutions are most responsible for abuse if they are to be reformed and made transparent and accountable. Punishment, too, requires knowledge of perpetrators, and without some semblance of the truth victims cannot secure the recognition they deserve as human beings; thus the norm of mutual respect stays weak. Certainly, truth alone will not reconcile former enemies. Victims who retell experiences publicly often desire more than merely being heard, even though this is important to them; they may seek reparations, justice for the guilty, and the state's guarantee that it will not violate their rights in the future. Admittedly, new revelations may re-antagonize former enemies and threaten stability, at least in the short term. If we seek to secure a basic condition of mutual respect, the commitment to truth must be matched by a commitment to accountability, recognition, and the rule of law. As such, the truth is necessary but certainly insufficient for securing justice and promoting respect.

Accountability

While truth is undoubtedly important for reconciliation, some form of accountability for wrongdoers is also necessary. Arguably, complete justice would require that all perpetrators be held responsible for past abuses and be appropriately punished—a kind of Kantian commitment to just deserts for all who deserve it. The immense practical obstacles to achieving this in the context of most transitions, as well as the risk of having it degenerate into a new "terror," make it undesirable—however, at the very least, there must be a commitment to seeing that some "justice is done." Before turning to the theoretical and practical limits of accountability, I discuss its normative content.

The Deontological Component of Accountability

Accountability requires publicly holding someone responsible and punishing him or her for an identifiable wrong or violation. While accountability can take many forms, it contains a constitutive element of sanction. This is essentially a form of retributive justice.

As John Borneman (1997) discusses, many (though certainly not all) legal theorists follow Aristotle in dividing justice into two spheres: distributive and corrective—two paradigms that miss the punitive dimension of retribution. Distributive justice, which is concerned with allocating resources according to some principle of fairness or equality, does not explain the element of punishment found in retribution.

Nor does corrective justice. The latter implies returning to the status quo ante, so that the violator and the victim arrive at the relationship existing prior to the harm through the ruling of some impartial third party. For Aristotle, the goal of corrective justice is to compensate the victim for his or her "loss," and in the process remove the perpetrator's "gain," so that "when a measured value is assigned to the suffering, the terms *gain* and *loss* are appropriately used. Thus, the fair is the mean between the greater and the less. . . . That which would be correctively just, then, would be the mean between the loss and the gain" (1984, bk. V, ch. 7, lines 12–20). This assumes that we can return to some prior state, and furthermore that we should focus on the status of the victim, though not necessarily punish the violator. The perpetrator, for example, could be forced to return stolen property or compensate for its destruction, thus addressing the injustice caused, but not be punished for the theft in any meaningful sense. Retribution, however, includes a punitive element.[5] First, it means punishing a perpetrator for his or her actions, and implies that victims are bearers of certain moral rights of dignity and worth (thus certain actions are seen as violations of these rights), and second, it means that perpetrators are also moral actors, to the extent that they are morally responsible for their actions and should thus be held accountable. Retribution means that we understand ourselves as agents with moral rights, and perpetrators as morally responsible actors (Murphy 1998).

Retribution, then, need not be pursued solely for utilitarian ends. While certainly retribution may have an instrumental bent—deterrence, enforcement of rules, expression of intolerance of impunity—this does not exhaust its power. Rather, it is also non-teleological: Violators are punished precisely because they are morally responsible for their actions, and not (solely) because punishing them would benefit the greater good. Kant underscores this when he writes, "Punishment by a court . . . can never be inflicted merely as a means to promote some other good for the criminal himself or for the good of society. It must always be inflicted upon him only because he has committed a crime" (1996, 105).

Retribution can also be understood from the perspective of the victim and her moral claims to respect. A victim expresses self-worth by showing resentment toward the violator and seeking to punish him (or have the violator punished). Unlike Nietzschean envy, resentment here is anchored in the anger that results after experiencing some moral wrong. Indeed, resentment is an expression of self-worth, for it shows the value one places on oneself and subsequent outrage at its violation. Without a sense of human dignity and value, there would be no resentment. It is hard to imagine a person who respects herself, much less others, who does not resent purposeful harms inflicted on her.

Though there can be teleological aims to retribution, and indeed below I indicate what some of these are, retribution is centered on the wrongness of a particular act and the violator's responsibility for the commission of this act. As such, retribution is also communicative, insofar as it communicates our moral condemnation of the violation to its author and to society, a point not lost on Kant (1996) when he argued that any punishment must be expressed publicly, even if the community were to be dissolved immediately afterward. However, *retribution* should not be confused with *revenge*, even though the two terms are often used interchangeably. While revenge also draws its force from the apparent justness of punishment, it risks collapsing into cycles of violence, bereft of any sense of proportionality and with little likelihood of ending. Retributive justice differs from revenge through its inclusion of procedural and substantive protections for the accused, and shifts from the victim's demand for immediate punishment to a measured response based on the rule of law. Unlike vengeance, it requires an evaluation of responsibility and an appropriate penalty.

I use retribution (and accountability) as a measured, legitimate response to harms against people. This formulation serves as an important heuristic device and moral ideal to orient our discussion of post-atrocity justice.

The Teleological Component to Accountability

To the extent that we can normatively separate retribution and vengeance, retribution can serve the broader moral enterprise of reconciliation. I indicated earlier that retribution should not be seen only in instrumentalist terms. Still, under the proper institutional constraints, it can further the project advocated in this book in at least two ways. First, a commitment to accountability sends a clear message that continued impunity will no longer be tolerated. By holding violators accountable for their behavior, the new state condemns past abuses and signals the importance of the rule of law. Second, and more broadly, such a commitment reaffirms (or perhaps affirms for the first time) social values of respect for human rights. These points are closely tied to one another, but I discuss them separately in order to tease out their importance.

Eliminating impunity is possibly the most defensible "forward looking," or instrumentalist, use of retribution in transitional settings. Continued impunity is dangerous for a fragile democracy, weakening the rule of law and frequently jeopardizing the very existence of the new government. Particularly where former elites maintain some political, economic, or even military power, prosecutions may be used as an important way of dissolving this power. Along these lines, a typical defense of retribution rests on its promotion of the common good by sanctioning those who violate society's norms. This utilitarian argument, with roots as far back as Cesare Beccaria (1995) and reformulated by Jeremy Bentham (1995), normally assumes the existence of a relatively stable society with a functioning and impartial judiciary. Transitional societies require that we expand our focus to the role of *the state as violator*. In transitional situations, the emphasis shifts to a hypothetical: What would political and social life be like with the continued existence of significant authoritarian enclaves? Ruti Teitel has perceptively made this point: "Rather than an argument for punishment in the affirmative, the argument [in transitional situations] is generally made in a counterfactual way; What result if there is no punishment?" (2002, 28). The answer is the continued and possibly pervasive undermining of the new order by elites from the previous regime, who would feel unrestrained in their actions.

Accountability also expresses a repudiation of past practices and a commitment to change future relations based on principles of respect for human rights and the law (Kirchheimer 1961; Shklar 1964). Punishment signals the government's interest in establishing a *new* political and social order rooted in the rule of law by underscoring the importance of human dignity and subsuming state interest to human rights. It creates a wall between then and now, and publicly shows that state power must be limited. This is a pedagogical exercise, in many respects. By holding perpetrators accountable, the state signals to society that human rights and respect for individuals should become dominant social norms. Whether this is successful, of course, partly depends on the perceived fairness of the trials themselves—however, accountability reaffirms these norms by highlighting the wrongness of their transgression. In this sense, accountability not only means drawing a line between the past and the future but also signals the importance of endorsing new social values.

Challenges to Accountability

Although accountability is a crucial component for the establishment of a new regime, it nevertheless faces certain pitfalls. I have already mentioned the possibility of punishment degenerating into vengeance, which is a real threat when transitional regimes do not emphasize their commitment to the rule of law and instead replace one illiberal order with another. There are several other recurring problems with retribution.

First, formal retribution can be destabilizing. Trials and demands for punishment undoubtedly antagonize accused elites, who may threaten renewed violence. The threat of destabilization is a serious one, and entering into the delicate calculus of punishment versus stability poses significant dangers for new and fragile regimes. While there is no definitive theoretical solution to this problem, accountability—such as identifying perpetrators, writing new histories that detail complicity and responsibility, and encouraging massive social mobilization against perpetrator elites—should also be pursued in other (nonlegal) social spheres, such as civil society and elite discourse. Here, a commitment to unearthing the truth of violations is particularly important—though legal action may not always be possible, at least the truth can serve to condemn violators in the social imaginary.

Of course, excessive demands for retribution are also problematic. It is not uncommon to see the accused sacrificed for social cohesion, turning them into scapegoats for the sake of "moving forward." Successor regimes are always confronted with the formidable task of establishing a new basis for solidarity, and certain strategies—such as high-profile prosecutions of a handful of prominent or particularly violent perpetrators—can function nicely as symbolic evils with which to suture open wounds. The symbolism of human rights trials, characterized as they are by powerful discourses of villains versus the innocent, or evil versus good, can have a far stronger impact than the bureaucratic reform of the security apparatus and judiciary. At risk, of course, are the due process protections of the accused, shed for the sake of social solidarity. Trials can be made to function as rituals to purge the sins of the past from the present (Walzer 1992). Though vengeance may be a part of this, it need not be; the motive may simply be to select some perpetrators as sacrificial lambs for social solidarity, a more instrumentalist (rather than vindictive) strategy, though a feeling of popular revenge certainly helps. Scapegoating not only affects trials but also broader, category-based forms of punishment such as lustration (purging), where an entire group of people such as party members are systematically denied basic rights, including voting, employment opportunities, government office, or something similar. In the first scenario, a small number of individuals are blamed for widespread violations, even though most mass atrocity involves broad institutional and organizational resources implicating a wide array of people in various ways. In the second scenario, guilt is extended to an entire class of people, who are summarily excluded from certain activities or positions, even though complicity can vary widely among individuals (Wilke 2007). In both situations the desire for social cohesion may undermine justice.

A third problem with accountability concerns the relationship between prosecutorial selectivity and historical representation. The successor regime's desire to show its commitment to accountability, often through a selective number of high-profile cases, can result in a misrepresentation of the past. Certainly, financial and resource constraints are a prime source of selectivity. Given that in most cases the scope of abuse was massive and the complicity widespread, a transitional society with limited resources can only afford to prosecute some violators. The question then becomes "Whom do we prosecute?" The choices rely on a number of factors about potential defendants, including their responsibility for particular abuses, public demands for their punishment, the likelihood of conviction, and what the new government can gain from a successful trial. Regardless of the choices made, greater public scrutiny will be drawn to particular group of individuals while limiting broader historical understandings of the past. Indeed, the past actions of the defendants may become misleadingly representative of all of the regime's actions, thereby risking simplification of what are invariably complex events with many actors.

Closely related is a fourth problem. The repercussions of trials, with their symbolically powerful findings of criminal liability and victimhood, can continue to have an effect on social relations for a long time afterward. Future relations can be shaped for the worse by the public stigma that flows from prosecutions: Those who have even tenuous connections to the prior regime may continue to be disparaged or ignored, regardless of the substance of their political positions, while victims may enjoy continued moral capital well beyond what they should expect, allowing them to exercise political influence over issues that have little to do with their past experiences or victim status. The possibility of creating a shared future where former enemies can see one another as members of the same community can suffer when past culpability continues to delegitimize opposing viewpoints and vigorous public debate. One need only think of the way that under President Paul Kagame, even legitimate political opposition in Rwanda is often accused of treasonous aims.

A strictly liberal legal understanding of culpability requires that individuals be held responsible only for those actions over which they had some control (Fletcher 2001). While understandable, such an approach risks focusing on too small a group of perpetrators, and thereby missing the morally ambiguous category of bystanders. Bystanders, meaning persons who through their inaction and even tacit support facilitated the commission of wrongs though they may have been in a position to oppose or denounce them, carry a particular form of responsibility that lies outside judicial guilt.[6] How are bystanders to be judged, if at all? In some respects, bystanders point to the limits of accountability, and bystander responsibility will be debated in the public sphere among political elites and civil society groups, as well as among individuals in private and semipublic places. However, their responsibility falls outside the purview of courts, and this combined with the troubling fact that substantial public support, or at least acquiescence, is often necessary for political violence means that an understanding of responsibility will likely be highly contentious and politicized. Truth commissions may be able to explore at least some aspects of this, but ultimately bystander accountability will largely be contested in political and civil society, and among individuals.

Although all of these issues point to the limits of accountability, its importance should not be dismissed. Retribution helps promote the rule of law and provides at least some recognition of victims, for it signals the importance of condemning those who harmed them while reinforcing values of human rights and dignity. Accountability is thus a crucial element in the larger project of reconciliation.

Recognition

A common legacy of political violence is the continued contempt and devaluation of victims. Often, victims are seen as having "deserved" their fate, particularly if they belong to groups that have been historically marginalized or disparaged (e.g., indigenous groups in Latin America). Such devaluation makes it difficult for reciprocal respect and tolerance—and hence, reconciliation—to develop, since these require that former enemies come to see one another as moral equals. In response, a society should seek to recognize the moral status of victims as equals, restoring their sense of dignity and establishing their legal rights as citizens. Such an idea of recognition is, certainly, tied to accountability, since both pivot on reinterpreting victims as bearers of moral value and violators as deserving punishment. Nevertheless, while accountability is a crucial element of reconciliation for the reasons discussed above, it does not, in and of itself, focus on victims. Prosecutions and other forms of retribution may provide victims a measure of justice, but these are not aimed primarily toward them. Indeed, following a successful trial, victims may still suffer disparagement and marginalization while continuing to live with the terrible consequences of what happened to them.

Additionally, fellow citizens are less likely to view victims as equals while the state continues to ignore them. Recognizing victims as moral agents may help undermine apologist perpetrator narratives by recasting the consequences of violence in terms of the victims' experiences. This change in emphasis, from violators to those who suffered, can bring attention to the ways in which the endorsement of violent and exclusionary ideologies resulted in crimes with actual victims. This may erode the exclusionary political project of the perpetrators and, perhaps, create the possibility of achieving a more inclusive understanding of plurality and respect. In the following section I discuss the elements of a theory of recognition in transitional settings and then follow with a consideration of some theoretical obstacles and problems peculiar to this context.

Theorizing Victim Recognition

Survivors' reactions to a legacy of violence are complex and varied. Many may call for prosecutions of perpetrators, others may demand programs to help them cope with trauma, and still others simply prefer burying the past (Chakravarti 2008; Verdeja 2000, 2007). The varied responses point to the difficulty of fashioning a general theory of victim recognition that holds across cases. Nevertheless, we can posit one objective: to restore victims' dignity and provide adequate material support so that they may create meaningful lives, and do so in such a manner that neither patronizes them nor undermines their sense of moral agency. The goal should be to provide symbolic and material reparations to victims while simultaneously not degrading them as impotent, lacking in agency, or incapable of achieving self-respect and worth.[7]

The debate surrounding the value of recognition has a long history. Most contemporary theorizations begin from the Hegelian position of identity construction based on a dialogical model of interaction. For theorists in this tradition, recognition is a reciprocal relation whereby subjects see each other as equals entitled to respect. Recognition is thus a principle aspect of subject formation. Beings become full individuals through mutual recognition, underscoring the fundamentally intersubjective (i.e., social) nature of identity formation. This idea that recognition through social praxis is fundamental to stable and healthy identities has been developed by a number of authors (Benjamin 1988, 1995; Taylor 1994). Axel Honneth, for example, argues that a healthy notion of the self is a fundamental element of the good for individuals, and he elaborates the requirements for undistorted identity as consisting of three key components: (1) self-confidence, developed through affective relations between intimates and others who are emotionally proximate, (2) self-respect, accorded through the legal discourse of rights and implying the individual's capacity for autonomous moral action, and (3) self-esteem, developed through participation in communal activities and contributions to a meaningful, ethically substantive social life. These components are all developed through dialogical interactions with other, equal subjects. Moreover, they are crucial for a healthy subject. Without them, the individual risks degenerating into pathologies of self-hatred and denigration (1996).[8]

Some thinkers take these insights significantly further, arguing that the dynamics of individual recognition are mirrored at the macro level. Charles Taylor has discussed how patterns of individual misrecognition parallel those of groups: If the self can suffer mistreatment through devaluation, the same holds for entire groups that are consistently oppressed or suffer discrimination. They are unable to actualize themselves satisfactorily, and natural cultural expression and maturation are truncated or, even worse, fatally arrested. For Taylor, "A person or group of people can suffer real damage, real distortion, if the people or society around them mirror back to them a confining or demeaning or contemptible picture of themselves" (1994, 25). Consequently, certain groups require recognition of their uniqueness in some special, institutionalized manner, a claim that goes beyond the kind of recognition predicated on social equality—in other words, one that is difference-blind.

The criticisms of these approaches are well-known. Seyla Benhabib (2002) has persuasively argued that Taylor and others such as Will Kymlicka fall into traps of cultural essentialism, reifying group identities and privileging authenticity claims above basic justice concerns. Nancy Fraser (2003) has criticized these overly psychologized multicultural approaches for a variety of reasons, including their inability to define satisfactory criteria for distinguishing between just and unjust authenticity claims (and the implicit essentialism this springs from), their reductive assumptions about the primacy of recognition over injustices rooted in political-economic relations, and their inability to theorize from a more objective, sociological position that can distinguish between institutionalized/systematized patterns of subordination requiring justice and culturally salient differences that do not. Benhabib's and Fraser's observations are especially helpful in studying post-atrocity societies. Victim groups often make authenticity claims and special recognition demands in transitional settings. On the face of it, these claims appear quite legitimate, and indeed they often are; the individuals in question suffered devastating violations, offenses that may have been facilitated by historical patterns of categorical subordination and discrimination, but whose overwhelming and immediate barbarity carry a poignant demand that we acknowl-edge their experiences in some nontrivial fashion. The problem is in how we should acknowledge them, and what should be the criteria. Should we recognize victims as a way of enabling their ethical and moral self-realization, as Honneth would argue? While this approach may seem compelling, a theory of victim recognition based wholly on ethical self-realization runs into conceptual challenges because it is incapable of drawing the line between what constitutes satisfactory recognition and what exceeds it. Claims of self-realization, as Fraser points out, are "usually considered to be more restricted" than justice claims precisely because they are based on "historically specific hori-zons of value" (2003, 28). The difficulty here arises with the potential development of so-called "cultures of victimhood," where similar ex-periences become a shared horizon of authenticity that demands cate-gorical respect based not on the content of any particular claim but rather on the status of the speakers. In other words, in some scenarios victim group elites may transform their status as victims into a badge of irreproachable righteousness used to make morally suspect claims (such as a right to oppress internal members), or point to their status as a way to dismiss otherwise valid criticisms or challenges. What if the elites of a particular group that suffered massive human rights viola-tions, say an indigenous group, argue that proper recognition of their identity requires that the state not interfere with the internal subordi-nation of a particular subgroup, such as women (Okin 1999; Warnke 2000)? Should the state accede on the principle that this particular group was victimized and it now requires recognition? It is not uncom-mon for a victim group to claim special recognition rights in the after-math of massive violations, in effect trading on its moral capital to gain further rights, resources, or autonomy.

Of course, victim demands are not always morally dubious. Far from it. In fact they can often be sound, but the principle of ethical self-realization does not give us the conceptual tools necessary to de-cide which claims are legitimate. For Taylor and Honneth, intersubjec-tive recognition is a necessary condition for achieving undistorted, healthy identity. "The conception of ethical life," writes Honneth, can articulate "the entirety of intersubjective conditions that can be shown to serve as necessary preconditions for individual self-realization" (1996, 173). However, to base a theory on claims of ethical self-realization leaves us incapable of discriminating between justice claims and (nonuniversalizable) authenticity claims. A primary concern should be to ensure that any model of victim recognition focus on questions of justice, or "right" (i.e., rather than the "good" entailed by an approach premised on ethical self-realization). Recognition of victims is crucial in transitional societies, but the aim should be for victims to reestablish their dignity and self-worth in such a way that permits them to be full participants in social and political life. This does not mean that all ethical claims are illegitimate. Rather, it means that these claims should be honored to the extent that they promote what Fraser (2003, 29) calls "reciprocal recognition and status equality," a goal that is unachievable if victims continue to find themselves excluded, marginalized, devalued, and forgotten.

Additionally, some theories of recognition tend to reduce all forms of injustice to symbolic misrecognition, while saying little about material inequality, except to consider the latter as a predicate form of injustice. Honneth subsumes the latter under the former when he writes, "the conception of recognition, when properly understood, can accommodate, indeed even entails, a modified version of the Marxian paradigm of economic distribution . . ." (Fraser and Honneth 2003, 3). However, victims often receive symbolic acknowledgment from the state, including an official apology or monument in their in honor, but receive no material support. And yet, they are just as often left impoverished following mass violence, particularly where an entire ethnic group was targeted (e.g., the indigenous in Guatemala, blacks in South Africa). In this context, an apology is insufficient for social reintegration. Consequently, material inequality requires theoretical elaboration in conjunction with symbolic forms, rather than being subsumed into the latter. The goal should be to recognize their experiences as a step toward overturning patterns of discrimination and violence.

Any theory of victim recognition, then, should include both material and symbolic components, while avoiding claims of ethical self-realization to anchor it. As I have argued elsewhere, it does not follow that we must privilege liberal individualist rights and reject all collective claims (Verdeja 2008). That would miss the collective nature of violations, where *groups* were targeted (however defined by the perpetrator) and abuses carried out systematically. It is necessary, however, to distinguish between those policies that protect culturally essentialist claims and those that promote status parity among citizens. A theory that seeks status parity as a goal targets both symbolic misrecognition and material maldistribution. In terms of symbolic recognition, it should emphasize the elimination of cultural views that prevent individuals from recognizing each other as fellow citizens, to achieve what Fraser has termed the "intersubjective condition" of parity of participation (2003, 36). This requires the positive revaluation of "disrespected identities" and, more generally, cultural diversity, as well as the delegitimation of those social values that worked to justify violence and misrecognition (2003, 47). In terms of redistribution, it necessitates addressing economic marginalization that prevents individuals from participating as equal citizens, and secures the "objective condition" of participation parity. This may include a number of initiatives, such as monetary compensation for abuse and increased development programs in places targeted by the violence. The ultimate goal is to restore victims' dignity and self-worth so that they may participate fully in social, economic, and political life, achieving "reciprocal recognition and status equality" with their peers (2003, 36). Without both material and symbolic strategies to correct past injustices, such a goal will remain unrealized. Achieving this goal requires both symbolic and material (i.e., redistributive) claims of justice. I use the terms *victim recognition* and *victim acknowledgment* in this broader sense of status parity (Fraser 2003) that includes both symbolic and material components.[9]

As I understand it, an account of victim recognition consists of four ideal-typical dimensions: "symbolic" and "material" along one axis (a typology of acknowledgment), and "collective" and "individual" along another (a categorization of recipients). These dimensions trace the scope and type of acknowledgment that should be accorded, and though different mechanisms are appropriate within each created space, they contribute to a coherent conceptualization of victim acknowledgment (Verdeja 2006). Below I introduce these four dimensions and follow with a discussion of the normative challenges that each faces.

In most cases of large-scale atrocity, crimes are directed at groups of some type, such as cultural, ethnic, religious, national, ideological, racial, or economic, and often, targeted groups cover different categories. In addition, targeted groups can overlap several different categories, and violations may also be gender-specific (De Vito 2008; Jones 2006a, 2006b). Because of this broadly collective dimension, victim acknowledgment requires theorization of a *collective symbolic* element. Recognizing this means publicly highlighting that violations were part of an organized, coherent strategy against designated collective "enemies," and not merely occasional "excesses" on the part of the perpetrators. Collective symbolic recognition requires recognizing both the way strategies of repression targeted victims as a group, and society and the state's moral obligation to recognize their experiences and treat them as equal citizens. This means fighting discourses that blame victims for what happened to them. Such symbolic recognition can be made in many ways, including through official apologies, public atonement, developing public spaces to honor victims, and establishing museums, monuments, and days of remembrance to promote and preserve collective memory.

Crimes, of course, are not merely collective. *Individual symbolic* acknowledgment consists of the need to recognize victims as individuals and not simply place them in a residual category, thus reducing them to an amorphous group of passive, voiceless survivors. This includes drawing attention to how violence and repression affected individuals qua individuals, and reminds us that "victim experiences" are always more than the aggregate of similar stories, pointing to the importance of recognizing actual persons who suffered in deeply personal ways. Such recognition can in practice be unattainable. Recognizing all victims in a meaningful sense is impossible when confronted with crimes of this magnitude, and not everyone can be given a space to speak publicly. Nevertheless, sensitivity to personal experiences is important because it underscores that victims are actual persons, not simply statistics. As the Argentine writer and torture survivor Jacobo Timerman (2002) reminds us, individual suffering is always more than a symbol of systematic crimes, and part of the process of rehumanizing victims requires attention to this fact.[10] Indeed, such recognition contributes to reaffirming their status as citizens, for it reflects a sensitivity toward fellow humans that is a crucial element of any political order based upon democratic principles of equality and mutual respect. Certainly, symbolic individual recognition is not equivalent to the liberal democratic rights that accompany citizenship, but it is an important prerequisite. Without such recognition of individuals as individuals, and as equals who deserve respect, it is unlikely that victims will maintain their status as citizens.

Symbolic recognition furthers victims' sense of dignity and self-worth, while reaffirming their place as fellow citizens—however, it does not address the material marginalization that is a common legacy of violence. Often, survivors are left impoverished by widespread or systematic violations, and special attention to their economic status is required if reparations are to be more than merely symbolic. Consequently, reparations should include some form of material support that gives victims the capacity to lead meaningful and productive lives. One form this can take is *collective material* reparations. These reparations provide resources to victimized groups as a way of obtaining the material basis and security required for them to participate fully in social, political, and economic life. They may include initiatives such as employment and housing assistance for groups whose economic situation was directly affected by the violence, physical and psychological support for trauma, and infrastructural investment in targeted communities (e.g., better roads, sanitation programs, rural education campaigns, credit allowances for economic development). Although the nature of the programs requires sensitivity to context and the particular needs of the victims, the programs share two characteristics: (1) they are for groups that were targets of violence (and are thus collective) and (2) they are dependent on the redistribution of economic resources, with the aim of enhancing victims' lives so that they may realistically pursue their life plans. In Guatemala, El Salvador, and Peru indigenous groups were the primary victims of political violence, and truth commissions called for significant investments in public education, housing, employment, and economic development to offset the legacy of economic inequality inherited from the civil wars. These measures can help raise the standard of living of the most damaged communities and contribute to reintegrating marginalized groups into society.

Combining reparations programs with broader development programs can be challenging. However, some theorists have argued that combining the two can have positive results.[11] To be sure, society would most likely benefit from increased economic development in poor areas. Nevertheless, combining these two programs can undermine the normative aspect of reparations, since doing so may submerge the specifically moral dimension of reparative justice beneath broader state policies to combat poverty (Wilson 2001). For many victims, reparations are a moral acknowledgment of wrongful suffering, and subsuming them into development strategies obscures this. What the state may consider reparations may very well be part of the duties it has toward its people as citizens. While employing a discourse of reparations may result in greater political and moral capital for state elites, it confuses the normative specificity of reparations with broader obligations. Therefore, any reparations program should be sensitive to this risk, and should be crafted in such a way that maintains its distinctly normative dimension, for example, by explicitly invoking elements of symbolic recognition (e.g., apologies, days of remembrance), even if carried out simultaneously with general economic and infrastructural development plans.

Finally, there is an *individual material* component to theorizing victim recognition. This, too, is a form of distributive justice, insofar as it addresses the importance of redistributing resources to victims, but places greater emphasis on the autonomy of individuals than the collective dimension discussed above. Of course, no compensation can substitute for death or torture, and in this sense money—or any reparatory measure—is always inadequate. But compensation can have an impact for economically destitute victims and show that the state's recognition is not merely symbolic but also material and practical. Individualized reparation schemes normally include familial rehabilitation through access to medical, psychological, and legal services, compensation for losses that can be measured financially, economic redress for harms that are not easily quantifiable, and restitution of lost, stolen, or destroyed property. Individualized payment has the benefit that it maximizes autonomy by allowing victims to use funds as they see fit, and thus minimizes the paternalism inherent in collective material reparations (De Greiff 2006; Goodin 1989; Lomasky 1991).

Victim recognition is a crucial element of reconciliation. Whereas a commitment to truth seeking and to accountability has an impact on victims, a special focus needs to be given to individuals who suffered massive wrongs, not only as a way of reintegrating them into society as fellow citizens but also as a means of recognizing their worth and dignity as fellow humans—that is, as a way of according them moral respect.

Rule of Law

The final normative component of reconciliation as respect is the rule of law. Many commentators have identified the reestablishment of the rule of law—understood as cogent general rules that constrain the actions of the state and establish minimum legal protections for the citizenry—as an important element in democratic transitions (Hampton 1994; Kleinfeld 2005; Nino 1996; Plunkett 1998; Scheuerman 1994). Adopting the rule of law reflects the state's commitment to preventing the recurrence of such violations by reforming relevant state institutions, such as the judiciary and security apparatus. For transitional societies, however, it means more than this. It also means redrawing the boundaries of politics. Of particular importance is tracing some basic normative principles emphasizing that political differences will not be resolved violently—rather, political contestation remains bound within formal and informal spheres of deliberation and negotiation. Consequently, there are two dimensions to the rule of law: one institutional and the other normative. Although I focus on the latter in this book, both elements are necessary for reconciliation, and I briefly discuss the institutional component below before turning to the normative aspect.[12]

Institutional Dimension of the Rule of Law

Institutional reform of the rule of law in post-atrocity societies normally addresses the judiciary, police/state security apparatus, and prison system, though the specifics of this largely depend on the condition of the legal system at the point of the transition.[13] These conditions can vary widely. Rama Mani (2003) has usefully outlined the relative functionality and legitimacy of different systems across numerous transitional cases. Mani notes that in some transitional cases, the legal system still operates, though its legitimacy has largely eroded after years of sanctioning clearly abusive policies by the state. Specifically, the judiciary continues to function and refers to existing law and statutes. Trials, however problematic, are still held for political detainees. Nevertheless, the rule of law is employed as an instrument of repression by the state, and is considered illegitimate by broad sections of the population. The state uses the law as a veil behind which it coerces the judiciary—and often the parliament, if one exists—for its own political ends. Chile, Argentina, and South Africa fall under this rubric. In these situations, legal positivism is insufficient to guarantee popular trust in the state's commitment to the rule of law because the space between written law and popular conceptions of justice remains so wide.

In other instances the rule of law may be significantly weaker. Here, a judiciary and legal order exists throughout the period of violence, but enjoys no autonomy or claims to impartiality. Most persons have no recourse to the legal system; the law becomes an instrument of power for corrupt elites. Public trust in the law disintegrates completely and the rule of law is progressively evacuated of any meaning, ultimately becoming a parody of itself. El Salvador, Guatemala, and Zimbabwe fit this category almost perfectly.

In yet other situations the entire legal system may collapse and no organized system of law, however corrupt and illegitimate, survives. Under situations of chronic war and massive population dislocation, a country can fall into chaos and power is exerted largely through direct violence and explicit coercion. In these conditions, formal legal systems are dismantled or dissolve on their own. Cambodia under the Khmer Rouge and Somalia exhibit this situation most accurately—in neither country were even traces of a legal order left after the violence.

This triptych is not meant to be exhaustive, and cases may show signs of all three stages at different historical periods. Identifying variations in the demise of the rule of law points to the multiplicity of obstacles that reform efforts face, and it follows that different cases exhibit differing needs based on their contexts. Nevertheless, what unites all of these societies is the need for a robust, fair, and transparent legal order as an institutional sine qua non of long-term reconciliation.

In all of these scenarios, building public trust in state institutions is an important aim of reform. As such, the commitment to the rule of law is not only a technical matter of policy implementation and efficiency but also a normative enterprise. The state fosters trust by showing it recognizes the rights of its citizens and places clear, consistent limits over its authority. This includes respecting standard liberal rights such as freedom of speech and association; the right to personal bodily integrity and property; protection against arbitrary detention, arrest, or exile; freedom of movement; and other rights that place restrictions on arbitrary state power. It should also include some basic rights that seek to maximize the individual's ability to participate in the political life of his or her country, such as the right to vote.[14]

Normative Dimension of the Rule of Law

To the extent that the rule of law is a normative concept, it also directly engages with the constitution of the political realm. How do we understand politics in a post-conflict scenario? What are the limits of political contestation, that is, the boundaries between acceptable politics and violent coercion? The reforms discussed above, while fundamental, do not answer these questions. The commitment to the rule of law also highlights the ability of citizens to discuss and debate politically relevant issues without turning to violence or threats of violence. In the aftermath of violence, it is not uncommon for groups to threaten to abandon the realm of debate if they feel that it is unlikely that they will achieve their aims. Even securing this liminal state can be exceedingly difficult, as recent experiences of violence and terror are likely to feed demands for vengeance and sow mistrust.

Admittedly, the idea of a liminal commitment to peace still falls short of the "rule of law" concept as normally understood in liberal democratic theory. This thin conceptualization has more in common with the agonistic notion of contestation found in the works of Schmittians like Chantal Mouffe.[15] For Mouffe, politics is characterized by "the vibrant clash of political positions and an open conflict of political interests" that emerges from the basic friend/foe political category. Because democracy is never fully realizable in any substantive sense (say through the articulation of a Rousseauian "general will"), the best we can expect is a model that accepts the "impossibility of a world without antagonism" while demanding that "the opponent should not be considered an enemy to be destroyed but as an adversary whose existence is legitimate and must be tolerated" (1997, 4). That is, the most we can hope for is a political order that allows for as much contestation as possible without devolving into a violent politics of power. Mouffe's understanding of politics as agonistic is helpful because it draws attention to the incompatibility of essentialist political claims and democratic politics: The attempt to fuse the two, through authoritarian mass mobilizations and plebiscitary politics, is often the harbinger of future

political violence. But her understanding of politics as barely containing conflict is normatively too thin, particularly in transitional situations where political discourse is already badly impoverished and there
is little if any commitment to peaceful debate. Some deliberative demo-
crats have attempted to move beyond this liminal understanding while
still maintaining the complexity and irreducibility that "radical demo-
crats" such as Mouffe emphasize.

David Crocker has been one of the most forceful defenders of deliberation in transitional settings. Drawing from the works of James
Bohman and Amy Gutmann, Crocker argues that society "should aim
to include public debate and deliberation in its goals and strategies for
transitional justice" (2000, 108). Nevertheless, he is careful to note that
the commitment to deliberation is not in itself a solution to pervasive
inequalities or animosity. He acknowledges that it is unlikely that in
"any given society, there will be full agreement about the aims and
means for dealing with past abuses," especially in a nation recently
experiencing massive violence (2000, 109). But the goal of deliberation
committed to the rule of law is to attenuate deep disagreements
through public debate, allowing all affected sides to participate and
seek "morally acceptable" compromises. In transitional situations,
achieving this constitutes a significant political victory. A somewhat
stronger understanding institutionalizes deliberation through proceduralist mechanisms of legitimacy formation. This, in turn, requires a
deliberative process governed by principles of equality and reciprocity
among participants and the right to initiate, debate, and question the
content of discussion. The procedures themselves grant legitimacy to
the outcome of debate. As Seyla Benhabib (1996, 72) notes, "Procedures
can neither dictate outcomes nor define the quality of the reasons ad-
vanced in argumentation nor control the quality of the reasoning or
rules of logic and inference used by participants. Procedural models of
rationality are undetermined."[16] Thus, the substantive good of social
life must remain open; the model remains silent on what constitutes
ethically appropriate social relations. This is one crucial difference in
the construction of the political sphere between a democratic and a
totalitarian regime. In the latter instance, laws and procedures are
subordinated to the creation of an ethically homogeneous society, with
all of the violence and "purification" that this entails. In a democratic
polity, the conflict of values and interests is taken for granted, and

thus the procedural mechanisms in place to process and contain them offer the grounds for legitimacy. The law, understood as a codified series of procedural norms that both limit and permit the possibility of debate (i.e., limits debate insofar as it prohibits the recourse to violence, and permits debate by granting a space for deliberation free from coercion and threat of force), helps move a society from violence toward deliberation. The commitment to the rule of law, then, means agreeing to deliberate within a recognized system of rules rather than turning to violence to solve disagreements. As such, it is more robust than the liminal conception arrived at by Mouffe (1997), but remains wary of the integrative understanding of politics promoted by advocates of "forgiveness in politics," discussed in the first chapter. This understanding of deliberation is essentially proceduralist: It focuses on the procedures developed through open and fair deliberation to give future decisions their legitimacy and binding power.

While this notion of rule of law may seem theoretically overburdened since it includes some of the normative criteria of deliberative democratic theory, I do not believe it is, at least not in the sense I use it here. The commitments to robust debate through meaningful political participation can be satisfied only if basic principles of equality before the law are adopted and violence is rejected. It is in this sense that I use the rule of law to address the importance of peaceful, impassioned debate to replace the politics of violence, and as a fundamental component of reconciliation. I do not mean it in a theoretically more substantive sense requiring a particular set of institutional mechanisms and theoretical links between power, money, and solidarity, as found in, for example, Habermas's *Between Facts and Norms* (1996). While these discussions are important, the theoretical postulates developed from analyzing consolidated, capitalist democracies are of a different order from the cases under study here. Nor do I follow Habermas in positing a strongly rationalist grounding to deliberation. As I discuss in Chapter 5 on civil society, any theory of deliberation for post-atrocity societies cannot assume that competing groups mutually espouse rational rules of discourse, a commitment to forging consensus, or even have shared background norms that allow for a common understanding of the rules of debate.

Alone, the normative dimension of the rule of law may seem silent on issues of social justice and the uneven political standing of different participants. In the aftermath of massive political violence, a model that emphasizes deliberation without reflecting on the material conditions necessary to ensure that participants actually have some equal standing in debate could be accused of naïveté, or worse, deliberately perpetuating modes of domination under the false pretense of liberal (or discursive) equality. But in keeping with the fundamentally integrative approach of my understanding of reconciliation, I emphasize that this goal must be understood in concert with the material component of victim recognition discussed earlier. As indicated there, victims cannot be expected to make meaningful, dignified lives and become full citizens without securing a substratum of material well-being. As such, the model proposed here is not silent on social justice but merely separates it from the theoretically distinct concerns of the rule of law and deliberation (though of course, if debates about distributive justice become salient in the public sphere, the distinction is minimized). Furthermore, a commitment to the rule of law requires a certain measure of accountability, for only if authoritarian enclaves are removed and citizens are bound by principles of open debate without the threat of violence, can the rule of law as normative principle be achieved.[17] It is, thus, constitutively interrelated with other principles.

I have laid out the principle elements of my theory of reconciliation, which centers on moral respect with the corollary norms of truth, accountability, victim recognition, and the rule of law. One may understandably ask whether this conception of political reconciliation is overly Kantian and Western. Does the focus on respect allow it to speak to societies whose cultural values are more communitarian and less focused on the individual? What of those places where morality is understood in collective terms and the individual is not at the center of moral theorizing? These are important concerns, and I should stress that I am not arguing for a full-fledged theory of *liberal* reconciliation, premised on privileging the moral individual as conceptually prior to society. The concept of respect here emphasizes the intersubjectivity of moral identity formation, and while it admittedly has conceptual roots in philosophical language associated with Kantian individualism and rationality, it is not reducible to its origins. Indeed, the basic moral categories of dignity and self-worth emerge in victim narratives in myriad post-conflict settings across the world, even if they are not framed in this specific language (Beah 2008; Hatzfeld 2008; Lifton 1991; Szymusiak 1999). There are many moral vocabularies tied to particular religious, cultural, and philosophical traditions that speak to the importance of the individual's dignity, and Enlightenment thought is only one of these traditions. In any case, my discussion of respect is neither premised on monadic individualism, as should be evident from my emphasis on intersubjective moral recognition as one of its cornerstones, nor based on Kantian rationality devoid of emotional or expressive content, as I showed in discussing the importance of phenomenological truth and recognition. My account of reconciliation as respect, then, should not be taken as an endorsement of liberal individualism or rationality over social theories of ethical life. I believe that reconciliation as respect is sufficiently elastic to operate usefully in the types of cases under consideration here. More importantly, perhaps, is the simple observation that survivors in numerous cultural contexts—from Latin America to Southeast Asia to Africa to North America—often frame human rights violations not only as physical and emotional harms but also as *moral* wrongs. That is, they experience and retell these harms in moral language premised on expectations of moral respect, and their anger and resentment draw on the assumption that the perpetrators should have honored their claims to dignity and to moral personhood. It is this idea of respect as recognition of a person's inherent dignity that I am stressing here and that emerges across settings of mass violence.

Establishing whether such reconciliation has been adequately achieved is obviously quite difficult. Of course, sociological studies, anthropological ethnographies, and surveys can offer much-needed insights into overall patterns (Gibson 2004), but here I want to put forth a rough way to measure progress: When conflict-era forms of political identification are no longer the primary ways of determining political loyalty, some success has been achieved. Political violence and the rhetoric surrounding it depend on a strongly binary logic of identity. In-groups use language that constructs a tightly knit community while simultaneously disparaging and dehumanizing out-groups: This is political identity logic at its most theoretically elegant and empirically venomous. These distinctions can remain relatively stable, reinforcing systematic devaluation and social exclusion (Apter 1998; Levine and Campbell 1972; Staub 1989; Tajfel and Turner 1986; Zimbardo

2004). While it is impossible (and undesirable) to remove all distinctions and forms of differentiation from political life, since a constitutive element of politics is in fact differentiation, we can say that mutual respect and tolerance have been achieved to the extent that previous loyalties (i.e., from the period of violence) are mitigated through the development of alternate, overlapping political identities. Thus, the traditional in-group/out-group distinctions are no longer evident, or at least are no longer primary. This does not mean that political contestation is over, that economic stability is just over the horizon, or that democracy is finally and thankfully here. But it does mean that the most salient forms of political identity that characterized the era of violence can no longer mobilize the passion and viciousness they once did. This is a sign that former enemies are working together, even if only toward their new set of shared interests.

The conception of reconciliation as respect is intimately tied to the other normative concepts presented in this chapter. A culture that values tolerance and espouses deliberation rather than violence to resolve differences cannot emerge where the past is unexamined or where terrible crimes are justified. An honest and truthful understanding of the past is morally necessary, even though this can be painful for victims and unsettling for those who supported the perpetrators. Accountability, too, is necessary, for without some sign that impunity is inexcusable, victims continue to feel marginalized and citizens are not particularly moved to treat one another as equals. Impunity, and the language of superiority and contempt that often accompanies it, reflects a deep disdain for the rights of individuals. Closely tied to this is the importance of recognizing victims as moral equals and fellow citizens. Without meaningful efforts to recognize them, victims are likely to remain mistreated or ignored, receiving none of the respect and dignity they deserve. And the rule of law plays an important role in guaranteeing that personal rights will be respected, the state will remain bound by law, and political differences should be resolved peacefully, even if still contentiously. All of these normative concerns are important if reconciliation is mean more than merely the temporary absence of violence where the powers of the past remain able to intimidate and coerce their opponents.

The key concepts of reconciliation are normatively dependent on one another, and thus the manifestation of one requires the development of the rest. Each normative concept is related to the others—they engage one another and presuppose each other, thus achievement of one is only partial if not accompanied by the others. The multivalent model is integrative, in the sense that it includes all of the concepts as crucial aspects for its sound actualization. They are necessary to promote a conception of reconciliation understood as reciprocal respect, which is the most we can expect from transitional societies. The following chapters are devoted to showing how the concepts interact across social space and how they may reinforce or undermine the project of reconciliation in different settings. We now turn to reconciliation at the level of political society.

3 Political Society

stablishing a new political order after mass violence is a delicate and fraught process. The members of political society, the political elite, must balance a number of competing goals. They may, for example, choose to prosecute those responsible for crimes, therefore risking the dissolution of a fragile peace and the resumption of violence. Others may persecute their adversaries using the full power of the state, and thus weaken the rule of law. Leaders are also confronted with the difficult decision of how to allocate resources, that is, the choice between the particular demands for victim reparations and the general needs for economic development. In addition, elites must work within the set of constraints that were inherited from the transition. In some cases, there may be few limitations on their ability to pass preferred policies, as may happen in the aftermath of a war where one side decisively defeats the other; in other scenarios, they may be severely handicapped by concessions that were given to previous elites who still retain some power.

While the particularities of the transition are important for gauging the range of possible policies open to leaders, there are nevertheless several ways elites can promote reconciliation. First, they can endorse peaceful political contestation over violence as the main means for dealing with conflict. This entails rethinking the domain of politics in such a way that replaces violence and threats with a commitment to respect pluralism and debate within the bounds of law. Combined with respect for the rule of law, such a change in elite political behavior signals the population about the nature of post-atrocity politics.

Additionally, elites can influence interpretations of the past. They may spearhead efforts to recognize injustice and shape society's understanding of its history by focusing on the origins of the conflict and encouraging public debate about violence and responsibility. However, elites should resist ignoring prior violations or promoting social amnesia by encouraging citizens to turn away from the past, and should avoid equating reconciliation with agreement among themselves to avoid the difficult issues of guilt and justice. Because of their special place in the public realm, they have a responsibility to promote thoughtful and honest debate about the past.

Elites can further reconciliation by promoting museums, monuments, and other public art—what Pierre Nora (1996) calls *memory sites*—that make the violent past part of a shared historical narrative. Such sites redefine how society relates to the past, and can engender the kind of passionate (and painful) debate necessary to undermine collective amnesia or triumphalist histories that implicitly legitimate violations. An additional important and increasingly popular step elites may take is to offer a formal apology in the name of the state, or in the name of groups or institutions they represent (e.g., armed forces, former guerrilla movements), thus furthering the process of recognizing the suffering of victims and achieving victim acknowledgment. Apologies give symbolic recognition of the suffering of individuals, and in the process reaffirm their moral worth and dignity in a strong, public manner. Because of their increasing popularity, in this chapter I focus on the normative status of public apologies. Public apologies have become particularly popular in elite discourse over the past twenty years, and a detailed theoretical discussion of their strengths and weaknesses can illuminate a great deal about these attempts at promoting reconciliation and its complex relation toward establishing successor legitimacy and achieving political aims. While this chapter discusses several actions political society can take, the subsequent chapter is devoted to a consideration of certain key state institutions—truth commissions and the judiciary—that also directly engage issues of reconciliation.

Before turning to an analysis of elite actions and apologies more specifically, I provide a discussion of what I mean by political society and the general transitional constraints affecting elite action.

Political Society, Transitional Constraints, and Reconciliation

The literature on political society is large, and includes much disagreement on the precise boundaries between formal political life and informal political mobilization. Nevertheless, most political scientists differ more on their understandings of the relation between civil and political society than on the definition of political society per se. This makes it somewhat easier to arrive at a working definition than one found in civil society debates, where the very definition of civil society is open to some contestation. Scholars normally define political society to include legislators (i.e., the executive and others who occupy decision-making positions in government), as well as the political parties to which these individuals belong. This requires a formal space such as parliaments where these elites compete through legitimate means for the exercise of control over public authority and state institutions. Their "primary goal is to win control of the state or at least some position for themselves within it" (Diamond 1999, 221; Linz and Stepan 1996). Political society is distinct from civil society, which includes those actors who are self-organized and who publicly mobilize to promote their values and interests with the ultimate goal of shaping public policy and discourse, but not the seizure of formal political power. Political society is also distinct from economic society, as the latter is primarily concerned with organizations dealing with production and distribution (J. Cohen and Arato 1992).

Their status means that political elites enjoy significant influence on social and political debates over a nation's treatment of its past. Elites help determine whether ignorance or meaningful reflection becomes the accepted way of looking at the past, though they do not, by themselves, determine whether reconciliation occurs, as this includes a larger set of social actors and institutions. Elites can, however, frame public perceptions of victims and generally set the parameters for realistic and unrealistic expectations of reconciliation. Through public speeches and actions, they establish the terms in which victims and others will be perceived, having a powerful effect on whether the targets of state violence will be considered full members of a new society or fall short of satisfactory moral and legal recognition. Thus, political society remains crucial for reconciliation.

Elite maneuverability to address the past is shaped by the particular nature of the transition. In some circumstances, particularly those following a war or revolution where one side is the clear winner, successor elites enjoy more political space to institute new policies for reconciliation if they so choose, though they may be materially constrained due to war damage or general economic underdevelopment. Nevertheless, they are likely to encounter little if any elite political opposition (e.g., as in the case of Rwanda). Many transitions, however, have not occurred in the aftermath of a complete overthrow but rather were achieved through negotiation among different incoming and outgoing elite factions. Political scientists have called the agreements developing from these negotiations "pacts," or explicit agreements by leaders of opposing sides to shape the rules of governance and power in ways that protect their particular interests (O'Donnell, Schmitter, and Whitehead 1986, 4:37). Pacted transitions occur where outgoing leaders still maintain sufficient power to partially shape future political arrangements and protect themselves from certain threats. The consequences of such transitions are most obvious on the issue of accountability. Often, powerful outgoing elites guilty of crimes demand some form of legal protection, such as an amnesty. This is a function, of course, of the exiting leaders' relative power, and where they are weak their chances of securing protection are reduced (Huntington 1993).

Consequently, successor elites faced with powerful opponents enjoy limited options for securing accountability. The range of these options depends on the specifics of the transition. In Spain, Francoist groups negotiated from a position of power and secured an amnesty and commitment not to delve into the past, a situation that has only begun to change relatively recently; Uruguayan military leaders successfully resisted civilian demands for justice, and an amnesty was reaffirmed through a popular vote driven by fear of a coup. In Argentina the military lost much of its political capital after its defeat in the

Falklands War, and thus negotiated from a somewhat weaker position during the 1983 transition. Nevertheless, subsequent threats to launch a coup proved that the military still maintained significant power, a view reinforced by the amnesty laws that followed (and were not overturned until 2005). Chile represents perhaps the most remarkable case of a pacted transition, with a military securing amnesty and an independent budget. For many Chileans, these were necessary concessions for reinstating civilian rule and keeping a second coup at bay. Only within the last ten years, following Pinochet's arrest in London in 1998, have human rights trials even been considered possible. Government leaders in Sierra Leone offered an amnesty and cabinet position to Revolutionary United Front (RUF) rebels in the Lomé Peace Accords as a way of stabilizing the country, but even this gesture was unable to secure peace, and the country fell back into war until military intervention led by the British largely defeated the insurgents (Barahona de Brito, González-Enríquez, Aguilar 2001; McAdams 2001; Mason and Meernik 2006).

These examples illustrate how particular empirical constraints can shape the options open to transitional societies. Successor elites are often unable—or, given the constraints, unwilling—to seek robust accountability or broad truth telling for fear that peace will collapse. Nevertheless, constraints are not impossibilities; they provide a limited domain of action, but action is still possible. There are options, even moral ones, which elites can use to promote reconciliation in some way, even under difficult conditions. In the following sections, I discuss several of these options, with a focus on the use of public apologies.

Political Elites and the Normative Dimension of the Rule of Law

Political elites play an important role in reframing appropriate forms of political behavior, including emphasizing the importance of debate and deliberation over violence and respect for the rule of law. We should not dismiss the importance of such reframing. Where one side dominates the new state of affairs (e.g., as in Rwanda or Cambodia), rejecting authoritarian rule in favor of inclusive politics is less likely, especially where leaders see political affiliation in absolutist terms and there are few restraints on imposing single-party rule. Successors may consider power a legitimate spoil of victory to be used on enemies, as consistently shown by Cambodian Prime Minister Hun Sen. Conversely, pacted transitions may result in an ossified political culture where continued mistrust and hatred prevent the emergence of the reciprocal norms of respect and openness to political compromise. The violence of the previous era is displaced into politics, and authoritarian apologists continue to equate political success with resisting democratic politics and power sharing. The possibility of securing a sustainable political order in these conditions is low, since significant tensions remain. Of course, even if leaders adopt nonviolent political negotiation, the broader population may remain unmoved. Elite cooperation is important, undoubtedly, but even this may result in a democratic deficit if leaders are perceived to work together for their own benefit and the broader population enjoys little ability to influence them (a common perception, for example, in Nicaragua).

What then, can we expect from political elites? At the very least, leaders should show their commitment to the rule of law and renounce violence. This requires accepting the limits of contestation (i.e., violence is eschewed in favor of deliberation), and stating a commitment to the general "rules of the democratic game." Leaders should accept basic laws that limit state power and acknowledge the right of all sides to compete for power. This requires more than merely stating these commitments; leaders must reaffirm them through practice, for only by *doing* democratic politics are these basic norms and values reinforced over time (Linz 1978).

Elites shape political culture, and through their actions and speech signal to the population what kinds of behavior are proper in democratic society.[1] Establishing the necessary norms of political engagement is possible only when important actors are unwilling to oppose the legitimacy of democratic and constitutional rule. Undoubtedly, there will almost always be spoilers and others who advocate violence; the key is to marginalize them sufficiently so that they do not represent a threat to the fledgling democratic state and the adoption of democratic norms. Crucially, then, major elites from across the political spectrum must act in ways that show respect for the rule of law and the new political order. Adopting a deliberative form of politics shows such a change in behavior. The deliberative approach, as is well-known, is centered on the communicative power of civil society—it both checks and gives legitimacy to political society discourse. Nevertheless, some of its theoretical claims are helpful here to understand how elite discourse should be framed. The core of the approach is its emphasis on public deliberation among a broad scope of actors to develop appropriate state policies. Obviously, deliberation is not endless nor "unfettered," if by this we mean that there are no rules guiding discourse and decision making; elites in parliament operate in what Nancy Fraser (1997, 90) calls "strong publics, whose discourse encompasses both opinion formation and decision making."[2] Thus, in addition to deliberation they are tasked with reaching binding conclusions, or laws. Furthermore, these actors deliberate within a set of rules (e.g., basic procedures for debating, making decisions on legislation). But the point here is more general. A new parliamentary body containing profound cleavages should adopt the basic norms of debate and openness to input from the public.[3] Opponents develop new relations among one another to the extent that they are forced to give reasons for policies and laws and work to secure at least some degree of consensus on common challenges. Such a new relationship can be rather thin and instrumental, and not signal deep agreement or the disappearance of distrust. In fact, a small but important accomplishment is simply accepting terms on *how* to disagree with one another. Nevertheless, spirited debate can signal to the population what constitutes proper political behavior. In a parliamentary setting, elites are forced to interact with one another in the search for mutually acceptable ends, and over time and through rounds of negotiation and argument they may come to see that political success need not always be measured in zero-sum terms. Rather, the legitimacy of particular policy outcomes should be seen as a product of the durability and legitimacy of the rules or practices of debate, so that disagreement and contention occupy a prominent but not necessarily destructive role in political life. In this regard, the turn toward deliberative politics represents a major shift from a politics based on violence and coercion, that is, where rightness is equated with power.

Elites must also endeavor to reestablish, or establish for the first time, public trust in the state. At the very least, the state should have clear limitations on its power and show respect for the rights of its citizens, as well as ensure citizen access to politics through voting and holding office. Rebuilding public trust takes a great deal of time, and its success is not amenable to easy measurement. Furthermore, trust can be damaged by other events that are not directly related to human rights, such as severe corruption (Philip 2008; Reno 2008). Some of this probably is unavoidable and should be expected. Western consolidated democracies rarely enjoy deep and sustained public trust in state institutions, and it is naïve to expect more from fragile, transitional societies. Rather, what we should aim for is the generation of basic social trust in the main state institutions associated with past violence, such as the police, armed forces, and the judiciary. The judiciary must be autonomous and function transparently according to basic rules of due process and security forces must remain under the control and authority of civilian leadership. Political society more generally also must show itself responsive to public will. Indeed, the rule of law aims to "lessen the risk of conferring trust, by lending assurances to expectations about how others will behave. Creating trust is thus a long-standing purpose of legal rule and institutions" (Osiel 1997, 38), which can be promoted only if elites are committed to enforcing the rule of law.

Securing the rule of law and showing a commitment to debate and democratic practice are undoubtedly important—achieving these goals constitutes a significant step away from the threat of violence. A society emerging from war or severe authoritarian rule can take some measure of confidence that these are important accomplishments, particularly when considering the alternatives. But elites can do more and should be expected to do so. More substantively, leaders should be tasked with bringing to public attention past wrongs that have remained hidden and retelling national history to incorporate these experiences. By bringing these experiences to the public, leaders can start a larger discussion about the consequences of abuses. They can also confront and resist consistent denials about the past to help the public overcome the painful and damaging silence that often follows violent histories. Without elite recognition, abuse remains a topic relegated to private discussion and solitary suffering, given little attention in schools or in the media.

Mere recognition, of course, is not enough. It is not uncommon for leaders to acknowledge violations but then treat them superficially;

more is required if the justifications of perpetrators are to be interrogated, resisted, and overturned. Michael Ignatieff (1996, 113) has called the past an "argument," that is, a narrative that is interpreted and fought over in many ways. Political leaders can contribute to these arguments by encouraging critical investigations of the past, highlighting the experiences of victims, and calling for public reflection on complicity and responsibility. This is more than simply the recognition of past wrongs in some passive sense; it highlights the need to condemn wrongs and those who committed them, and requires deeper and broader reflection on issues of responsibility and obligation toward fellow citizens. It entails a shift in how society sees itself and the obligation that citizens reflect on who is part of their moral community.

Public memory projects can begin this process of reinterpretation and reflection. These can include monuments, memorial parks, and museums that serve as signposts to give shape and contour to broader historical memory. Some authors note their importance by claiming that "people are forgetful and need their social memory bolstered by powerful mnemonic devices," and "monuments are needed to transmit it across generations" (Savage 1994, 129). These projects are not, of course, final statements on the past, and should not be seen or used as such, though the temptations can be strong; as both moral and political devices, they are part of a larger struggle over collective memory and identity. Rather, they should be understood as encouraging citizens to reflect critically on the past, fomenting public discussion and deep moral reflection. Public memory sites not only honor victims and acknowledge their suffering but also demand a reassessment of society's obligations to its members. In this respect, then, they are *critical* devices, for they question what kinds of historical interpretations are normatively appropriate. But they are also symbolically laden, for they serve a ritualistic role in reconceiving society's sense of itself. This is clear in the tendency of victim memorial sites to draw our attention to how the abuses were wrongs not only against specific individuals but also against society as such. Placing victims at the center of such narratives challenges society to rethink the moral consequences of past violence, and its own responsibility for the abuse. Nevertheless, no public memory site can give a definitive, authoritative history; individuals approach the past from different perspectives and consequently draw different interpretations about its significance. Memory sites cannot determine these interpretations, as tempting as this may be, but they can situate them by providing a framework for making sense of history. In Chile, a public park and memorial was created on the site of one the military's most infamous torture centers, Villa Grimaldi, and today it serves as a physical marker of a reconceived social imaginary, offering a stark and powerful counter-memory to the triumphalist discourse of the Pinochet regime and its apologists. In Argentina, the state-backed *Museo de la Memoria* has functioned as a place where survivors' myriad individual stories are connected to the larger events of the Dirty War, and the exhibit allows such personal stories to resonate with the larger public in the creation of a new history. In Sierra Leone and Liberia, incoming governments have sought to reposition victims at the center of understanding their civil wars to draw attention to the consequences of violence.

While civil society actors undoubtedly play a role in creating and shaping historical memory, elites enjoy a special status—and thus responsibility—for promoting public memory projects. In their capacity as leaders, they can mobilize state resources to create monuments and museums, thereby conferring official legitimacy to critical reflection. To be sure, remembering is neither static nor passive, and certainly cannot be commanded; individuals do not simply place pre-existing memories in ready-made frameworks. Remembering is a dialectical process whereby memories influence broader understandings of the past while simultaneously shaping those broader understandings, and in this sense individuals as well as communities have complex relationships with their histories. Memory sites can play a role in these dynamics by helping question ossified historical understandings. Through these sites and public speeches, leaders help engender a morally sensitive reflection on events that still remain raw and traumatic.

Of course, memory sites do not guarantee such reflection. When used by leaders for explicitly political ends or building social solidarity with little attention to actual historical events, they can be amount to little more than an alternate, equally simplistic and problematic "monumental history," to draw on Nietzsche's felicitous phrase (1997 66). Replacement only reifies a new "correct" interpretation, preempting reflection (Mosse 1991; Winter 1995). Memorials can introduce a new narrative that seeks interpretive closure. As discussed in Chapter 2, a critical history positions itself as interrogator of self-serving "monumental" accounts that legitimize violence. These earlier accounts are the primary historical understanding that new leaders and civil society seek to dismantle or replace through questioning their accuracy and showing how they created a framework for dehumanization while excluding some citizens from the moral order and the broader constellation of rights. The danger is that an alternative narrative may emerge whose primary function is to legitimize the new regime while doing relatively little to question the past with the necessary care and depth that is required. There is a common pattern here: Elites provide an account that bolsters their actions and beliefs through selective historical references by downplaying problematic or contradictory facts. A common version of this characterizes the previous regime as fundamentally "evil," while the present regime represents a national rebirth (led, of course, by the new leaders).[4] While such an approach does, in its way, deal with the past, it does so on rather convenient and strategic terms: It eschews critical appraisals in favor of simple narratives of redemption, which unsurprisingly give current elites significant symbolic capital and legitimacy for their own political projects. At their worst, these memory strategies provide little impetus for us to take on the obligation to remember, losing their proper normative content and becoming political weapons of new leaders in their ongoing struggles with their opponents and efforts to distance themselves from the past.[5] That the needs and interests of the present help determine how we understand our history makes this danger all the clearer. Nevertheless, this danger is in some ways unavoidable, as Maurice Halbwachs (1992), the great theoretician of collective memory, reminds us. Political society's contributions to reconciliation are only part of the larger project, and thus should not be allowed to define the entire process of social reconstruction. Indeed, what becomes apparent is that political society is a necessary level for reconciliation, but is insufficient on its own.

Political Society, Consensus, and Exclusion

The difficulties surrounding memorials underscore a larger issue concerning political society. Clearly, it is desirable that leaders support peaceful, democratic deliberation and stay wedded to the rule of law.

Nevertheless, elites must remain responsive to civil society, and not only to one another. Elite consensus, however, is frequently attained through exclusion; leaders achieve stability by ensuring that popular sentiments remain marginalized and contained. Elites operating in formal political publics (e.g., parliamentary bodies) must allow input from civil society, and although they are involved with state power and "cannot afford to subordinate strategic and instrumental criteria" (J. Cohen and Arato 1992, ix) of decision making to the open-ended communicative activity of civil society, they must be responsive to the latter. It is not uncommon for both previous and incoming elites to work on establishing rules of the game aimed at stability and self-interest while limiting exposure to and input from civil society. While this may lessen political violence and threats from antidemocratic forces, it can also have damaging consequences for reconciliation and democratic consolidation. The consequences of this for democracy have been discussed extensively (Linz and Stepan 1996; Menéndez-Carrión and Joignant 1999); here I want to point to a specific problem related to reconciliation: Privileging consensus may lessen sustained reflection in favor of superficial acknowledgment of past wrongs. In order to secure legitimacy of the fledgling state, political leaders agree to not look into the past too deeply, or do so only superficially. This is roughly what occurred in Uruguay, when the new leadership agreed to not interrogate past events for fear of upsetting what it considered to be a fragile political order (Barhona de Brito 2001; Weschler 1997). The result was the repression of historical inquiry (and with it, the nonrecognition of victims) in favor of future tranquility, and only relatively recently have public debates about the years of military rule become common, a pattern echoed in Spain and Mozambique. Or, alternately, elites may provide a new history that follows the redemptive narrative discussed above in reference to memorials—that is, they may emphasize the "harmonious" relations of the present by emphasizing past divisions and horrors, with little examination of the exclusions necessary to achieve the present condition.

A critical history must resist attempts at self-serving historical closure—both the narratives used to justify past violations, as well as those employed in the present to establish the legitimacy of the new state (and, by implication, the new leaders); both risk replacing real historical investigation and reflection with the strategic use of truth for political ends. Here, then, we see the danger of normatively overburdening political society. Leaders can undoubtedly help catalyze and frame debates about the past, and their participation is crucial for reconciliation; however, civil society must remain cognizant of the limitations and motivations. This is not to say, of course, that elites act only for strategic ends and are unconcerned with moral issues. Rather, it is to highlight the constraints and incentives in political society that can distort or otherwise mitigate broader moral reflection. The desire to secure legitimacy for the past or the present affects what stories are privileged in the public domain, and thus it is crucial that civil society groups monitor leaders and pressure them to confront difficult and politically uncomfortable truths.

It is vitally important, then, to not assume that elite consensus constitutes reconciliation. Civil society must be able to influence elites and encourage them to face the moral challenges of the past in an adequate manner. As David Crocker (1999) has argued, civil society actors can help raise and define the normative issues that transitional societies face. They can generate public debates about responsibility and guilt that are avoided by elites, and ensure that debate is not preemptively closed or "settled" by leaders. Furthermore, they can pressure the government for accountability for the worst abusers, recognition for victims, and reform of abusive state institutions. Civil society expands and deepens discussion about the past well beyond what elites would prefer. Thus, while leaders should be tasked with engaging histories of abuse, we should be disabused of the thought that their actions are sufficient to achieve meaningful reconciliation. Their political-strategic calculations can limit the possibility of justice and historical reflection and may result in a superficial understanding of the past.

What emerges from this discussion is that political society can contribute to reconciliation in several ways: by promoting a political ethic of deliberation and nonviolence, supporting the rule of law, and publicly raising issues about the past through debate and the creation of memory sites. In the following sections I discuss one particularly popular device: the official apology. A careful analysis of apologies can highlight the symbolic power elites have at their disposal for furthering reconciliation, but also highlight the limits of this power. This analysis also shows how a series of key political and moral aims can come together in normatively complex ways.

Official Apologies

Official apologies for past wrongdoing have become increasingly popular among elites, who see them as an ethically appropriate way of dealing with violations while establishing the grounds for a society to achieve some form of closure. Their popularity is apparent from the number of situations in which they have been employed.[6]

At the very least, an official apology publicly expresses responsibility and regret for serious wrongs, with the ultimate goal of reconstructing badly damaged relations.

In this section, I discuss several normative aspects of official apologies and provide a qualified defense of their use in transitions. While I do not provide anything like a full theory of apologies here (I do so in Verdeja 2009b), I do believe that we can make some general claims of what a normatively satisfactory apology would look like, and draw from this some contributions it can make to broader societal reconciliation.

Conceptualizing Apologies

While apologies are occasionally promoted as an important means for "moving a society forward," they are certainly not without their detractors. Some commentators have dismissed them as an easy way to mitigate feelings of guilt while granting a sense of self-satisfaction for confessing wrongs (Bowman 1998; Leo 1997; Steel 1998; Taft 2000). Indeed, they often seem insincere, given more to the expectation that the past can be left behind painlessly rather than as an attempt at confronting the moral consequences of past violations. An apology may make us aware of mass atrocities, but certainly this is not a complete response, in itself, to such violations. Many survivors of mass violence feel that there is an almost constitutive impossibility of closure on past injustices, that is, one that can be ameliorated perhaps through truth telling, punishment, and reparations, but one that a speech act on its own cannot fully repair.

Nevertheless, neither the danger of insincerity nor their popularity should dissuade us from considering an apology's value. Victims often demand that the state not only publicly acknowledge their suffering but also accept responsibility for it. As such, apologies include elements of truth telling, victim acknowledgment, and—to the extent that responsibility is taken—accountability. But this is not the whole extent of their value. Beyond this, apologies may signal more than mere acknowledgment of past wrongs and provide a way of envisioning a new moral relationship between victims, perpetrators, and bystanders. As such, they involve a kind of deeply symbolic "ritual cleansing," in the words of Stanley Cohen (2001, 236). This transformation is (perhaps unsurprisingly) often associated with religious language, particularly Christian language. As Cohen notes, there is a constellation of closely associated terms that appear when we speak of apologies in the context of massive atrocity: "*expiation*: making amends for previous sins; *exorcism*: expelling evil forces by invocation of the good; *expurgation*: purification by removing objectionable matter; the many variations of *contrition, confession, atonement* and *repentance*" (2002, 174) Echoing Cohen, Nicholas Tavuchis (1991) has shown how the imagery of transformation through atonement and purification is a powerful and suggestive one for victims and (repentant) perpetrators, for it points to the gravity of the crimes (i.e., sins) that require contrition.

In the Christian tradition in particular, the notion of apology rewritten as confession carries a central position, for it is intimately tied to the faculty of forgiveness and the creation of a new relationship between transgressor and victim. Theologian Martin Marty (1998) argues that the apology and forgiveness serve as exemplary instances of the transformative capacity of the spirit, signaling the beginning of a change in the relationship between the transgressor and the victim on the one hand, and a change in the relationship between the sinner and God on the other.[7] Some Christian theologians have argued that such an understanding of apologies could work in the public realm, and call for a transformational notion of apology heavily based on scriptural interpretations of confession and righting of wrongs. Public leaders should fashion their apologies as a sincere confessional act that transcends the bitterness of past conflict in an effort to open a space for a new future (Johnston and Sampson 1994).

The merit of this argument is that it highlights how apologies should be something beyond the mere instrumentalism of "moving on" by requiring sincere reflection and public discussion about past actions. It requires, however, further theoretical elaboration to connect the apology to practical political challenges. Erving Goffman (1971) has offered a secularized version stripped of the more overt ontological requirements of its religious connotation. For Goffman, a proper apology contains several elements: It must express embarrassment or dismay, awareness of knowing what conduct was expected, recognition of the appropriateness of a sanction, rejection of the harm, a commitment to pursue a proper course of conduct in the future, and a commitment to do penance or offer restitution. Missing from Goffman's account is an explicit acceptance of responsibility for the wrongdoing (though it runs through all of his points), and a discussion of official apologies, a point I return to in a moment. What is important about Goffman's account is that while it avoids the deep ontological shift implied by more religious approaches, it retains the crucial normative aspects of apologies: the recognition of the dignity and moral worth of victims; a public expression of remorse and acceptance of responsibility; and a commitment to change future relationships, which may include some form of reparation.

Drawing on these points, we can begin outlining the core elements of an apology. An apology is different from an excuse, which implies the transgression was unintentional, or a justification, which admits only limited culpability by pointing to external conditions that made the violations necessary. Rather, an apology is a speech act that conveys "an expression of sorrow or regret" both to the victim, and where appropriate, to a broader audience (Scher and Darley 1997; Tavuchis 1991, 23). The wrongdoer acknowledges the legitimacy of the rule or norm that was violated, admits responsibility, and expresses genuine remorse for the harm caused to the victim by the transgression. In this respect, an apology is a type of what John Searle (1969, 20) calls "expressive speech acts," insofar as it primarily expresses regret or sorrow for what was done. Furthermore, it signals recognition of the victim's moral claims to dignity and respect. Unwillingness to apologize for a serious wrong conveys that the victim is unworthy of such moral respect, and this could arguably be said to constitute a second wrong (i.e., that of nonrecognition). An apology may not fully restore a broken relationship, particularly one with a long history of violence and mistrust, but it does represent a type of *moral redress* for past actions, as Martin Golding (1984–85) has argued.[8]

A second dimension of an apology is material, or practical. An apology should include a commitment to some form of restitution or compensation that binds the speaker to some set of future actions. I call this the need for *practical redress*. Without a practical component, an apology amounts to little more than a hollow symbolic statement, achieving little real transformation in the status of victims. Apologies with no practical commitment to future change are problematic precisely because an apology carries with it a promise of future reform, even if only implicitly. The recognition of a past act as a transgression implies rejecting such actions in the future.

As a future-oriented component of an apology, the commitment to change behavior creates a promise. A promise, of course, can be broken; it is a normative rather than empirical constraint. It binds the actor to future behavior that *ought* to be followed. Nevertheless, the important point here is that the promise contained in an apology means that the apology is not fully instantiated when it is given; an apology should be understood not simply as an act but as a *process* including a commitment to a future relationship. Issuing an official apology is a brief act but does not exhaust the apology itself; it requires changes to ensure that the past is not repeated.

An apology, then, contains both moral and practical dimensions. It is a first step in recognizing the victim as a moral person with legitimate claims to moral respect, and furthermore implies a promise on the part of the transgressor to make some form of reparation. More generally, apologies are both past- and future-oriented; they direct our attention to a past act (or series of acts) and cast them as wrongs while also drawing our attention to the necessity of establishing a future relationship where such transgressions will not occur.

Official Apologies

An official apology acknowledges state responsibility for a serious moral wrong (or wrongs) that remains salient in current political life. As Ridwan Nyatagodien and Arthur Neal (2004, 470) state, "the [official] apology is an admission that those in positions of authority failed to act when action was necessary, and recognizes that blameworthy behavior was ignored, rewarded, or in some way excluded from normative sanction." Additionally, it attempts to reform the relationship between the government and the population by underscoring a change in future governmental policy (Digeser 2001; Harvey 1995). While there can be numerous motives behind an official apology, it is not uncommon for (at least some) political elites to endorse apologies for moral (i.e., rather than *merely* political-instrumental) reasons. An official apology ought to reflect a sincere future commitment to certain norms and an acknowledgment of past injustices.

Certainly, the deep symbolism of apologies, combined with their quick and easy public dissemination, make them choice tools for political elites seeking a powerful way to respond to complex social issues. What could be easier and cheaper than apologizing? Such a risk of political manipulation remains a serious threat. Some scholars downplay their political instrumentality and prefer to theorize apologies as devices that can recast moral relations between estranged groups or individuals, and thus they play a central role in promoting reconciliation (Casarjian 1992; Couper 1998; Muller-Fahrenholz 1997; Suchocki 1994). I am hesitant to follow these thinkers, however, for the very use of apologies by elites in deeply politicized contexts requires that we identify the relation between their instrumental and moral aims, and focus on whether they can satisfy, to some extent, both moral and political demands.

As an illustration of the uses of official apologies, consider Chilean President Patricio Aylwin's apology for crimes committed by his predecessor, dictator Augusto Pinochet. In 1991, President Aylwin publicly presented the findings of Chile's official Truth and Reconciliation Commission Report and proffered an official apology in Santiago's National Stadium, where many arrests and tortures had occurred during the first weeks of military rule. He chose a location that was symbolically laden, indicating the seriousness with which the new state took the violation of rights. Speaking in his official capacity, Aylwin (1995, 171) referred to disappearances as "executions" by "agents of the state," and forcefully condemned past violence while committing his government to the respect and defense of human rights. The fact that the president, rather than a subordinate, apologized, highlighted the importance of having a speaker with sufficient authority and symbolic stature apologize (a prerogative of elites), and also reflected a reorientation of the main values in the new Chile. Indeed, through his apology, Aylwin signaled to the public the importance of recognizing the moral worth of victims and the need to reflect on society's complicity in the violence of the past.

With this example in mind, we can identify several contributions that official apologies, and elite discourse more generally, can make to reconciliation. Most importantly, apologies publicly affirm the moral status of victims. As noted by Trudy Govier (2002), apologies focus public awareness on victims and communicate to the community the necessity of reframing moral obligations. Such reframing requires that victims be treated as political, legal, and social equals deserving recognition of their moral status. Clearly, apologies do not accomplish this on their own, and Aylwin's apology should not be measured according to this expectation. At best, they can begin a process of moral reframing and repositioning victims as equals; however, this requires sincere engagement and reflection by the community as a whole and encouragement by leaders over a long period of time (Schaap 2005). Nevertheless, drawing public attention to the moral value of victims, as Aylwin did, represents an important first step. This public affirmation of dignity and equal moral worth—of *victim recognition*, in the sense that I have used the term in this book—is perhaps the most important contribution an apology can make, and highlights the importance of elite discourse in promoting reconciliation.

Second, and closely related to victim recognition, an apology raises questions about basic *social norms and values*, and places these in the center of public debate. Under authoritarian or genocidal regimes, harassment, abuse, massacre, and terror are officially sanctioned methods of dealing with certain minorities or political enemies, and society's basic moral grammar is rewritten to cast all opponents of the regime as "deserving" of what they get. An apology helps reframe state actions as wrongs that violate basic social norms, and thereby force a society to confront these abuses and reflect on their consequences for state-society relations and the very conception of national identity. Aylwin explicitly condemned the behavior of the state and reaffirmed the importance of human dignity and respect that had been violated by Pinochet's government. Aylwin also enjoined fellow citizens to reflect on what kind of society they want and which values they hold dear. Obviously, an official apology given by an elite cannot secure the adoption of human rights, national consensus on basic values, or reconciliation. But it can generate public debate about what those values ought to be by recasting the terms of deliberation.

Third, and less directly, an official apology can promote an alternate and *critical* reading of history. Melissa Nobles (2008) has convincingly shown that apologies reshape the meaning of the past by re-situating victims at the center of interpretations of history. While an apology cannot achieve such a critical reorientation on its own, it implicitly redraws the topography of historical truth, and thus redirects public attention to the importance of engaging critically with the past. Aylwin's apology sought to catalyze a discussion about how citizens understood what it means to be Chilean, and the moral obligations they may have toward fellow compatriots. This was, of course, a first step in promoting a historical reckoning, but the apology sought to contribute to a much broader debate about national identity and history.

Elite apologies, then, can perform at least three key tasks. First, they promote the restoration of victims' sense of moral value and represent a first step at integrating them as citizens. Second, apologies can generate public reflection and debate about social norms by refocusing public discussion to their violation and requiring a new consideration of desired relations between the state and society. Third, they can make critical reinterpretations of history necessary by reframing the past and consequently undermining apologist historical accounts. These are real accomplishments, but they are obviously not the same as societal reconciliation. Much more must happen for a society to be reconciled, including commitments to accountability, the elimination of impunity, and the long-term promotion of the norms of respect and tolerance among citizens. Indeed, without real governmental policy changes, skepticism about the efficacy of apologies is appropriate. Apologies should be one part of a broader reckoning with the past.

The Illocutionary Problems Surrounding Official Apologies

While the discussion up to now has been relatively positive in its treatment of apologies, their political uses by elites raise several concerns. Trudy Govier and Wilhelm Verwoerd (2002) have helpfully identified a number of these challenges, but here I focus on a few that specifically confront official apologies. These are tied to their illocutionary status and tell us something about the elites' role in reconciliation.

The first challenge concerns whether survivors consider the apology satisfactory. In personal scenarios, there is an individual who can choose whether to accept the apology. He or she may decide that it was inadequate—it was insincere, it minimized culpability, and so on; regardless, the individual maintains the ability to accept or reject it, and thus retains his or her moral autonomy. Contrary to Minow's (1998, 115) stricture that official apologies should allow for "a stance that grants power to the victims to accept, refuse or ignore the apology," in an official apology there is no identifiable addressee who accepts or refuses it. Certainly, some survivors may come forth as representatives of victims, but the notion that they can accept an apology (much less grant forgiveness) for all victims is morally problematic, for it ignores those victims who may choose to reject it. The absence of an identifiable addressee with the power to accept or reject the apology means that its positive illocutionary force (i.e., the perception that it is a fait accompli) faces little challenge. I purposefully refer to the apology's illocutionary, not perlocutionary, character. While it may seem that official apologies are perlocutionary speech acts—that is, they must persuade or convince the listener and do not simply gain force from the utterance of the apology (an illocution)—the lack of an identifiable addressee means that, practically speaking, once the apology is uttered the speaker can claim that the apology was in some sense "successful" and that it was "accepted" by the victims. This is not to say that there is no perlocutionary component; rather, it is to draw our attention to the illocutionary dangers contained in this particular type of speech act. From the state's perspective, of course, this illocutionary aspect can be politically attractive. A public official can apologize and argue that the apology itself already places the nation on a course toward "reconciliation." The impossibility of total acceptance and the space this provides for political exploitation are ineradicable, constitutive weaknesses of official apologies, at least from a normative point of view.

A second concern is that an official apology instantiates some form of forgiveness, or at any rate mitigates the ability of victims to make future legitimate grievances. Aylwin (1995, 171), for example, asked for "forgiveness from the victims' relatives," and many Chileans considered his apology sufficient for the state to be "forgiven" and allow society to move forward. Official apologies, then, may be construed as already bestowing an element of forgiveness on the speaker and the represented institution, such as the state or some agency of the state implicated in abuses. Citizens who were not victims may argue that an official apology is a sufficient statement of the state's acceptance of responsibility and marks at least a partial clearing of the historical slate. Thus, apologies may be seen by some as carrying a surplus of illocutionary force; not only is the apology itself instantiated when given but it may also imply some degree of forgiveness, or at least the belief that some past actions have been adequately addressed and therefore any additional demands by victims are seen as an attempt at using their position to demand irrelevant and undeserved privileges.[9]

Nevertheless, there is a legitimate counterclaim: If an official, say a prime minister or president, does in fact sincerely apologize and ask for forgiveness from victims, should there not be an obligation or at least a legitimate expectation of forgiveness? Do sincere symbolic gestures that acknowledge responsibility and seek forgiveness require, at a minimum, that victims explain why it is reasonable to continue their resentment?[10] Many theoretical formulations include an assumption that forgiveness should follow a properly sincere apology, and if the apology is sincere, one could plausibly argue that forgiveness can reasonably be expected. Joanna North (1998) and Margaret Holmgren (1993) have both argued that forgiveness following an apology is not only reasonable but in fact signifies the victim's ability to recover his or her self-esteem by expressing his or her agency. As such, the conceptual formulation that connects the apology and forgiveness also includes salutary consequences, namely, the reaffirmation of the victim's sense of self-worth. The problem with such an understanding is that the apology is treated as a discrete act that is complete upon enunciation, with a clear expectation of what should follow immediately thereafter. This, it seems, ignores the apology's future or forward-looking component discussed earlier—that is, that it demands a change in future behavior by the state, and therefore represents the beginning of a *process* rather than a singular event. Insofar as it begins such a process, the expectation that forgiveness should immediately follow an apology is misplaced, for it implies that there has indeed been a change in relations between the state and the victims (and society, for that matter), when in fact this change remains to be seen. Perhaps another way to put it is this: Only if the state makes good on its promise to change, can forgiveness be considered an appropriate response. This change takes time and patience, but it can occur. In any case, an official apology should not be equated with closure. It points toward a commitment to change, but does not exhaust the change itself.

The first two points deal with two interrelated illocutionary pitfalls surrounding apologies: one concerning the risk that some victims will be ignored because of the theoretical inadequacy of an addressee, and the other concerning the very real possibility that an apology may include its own instantiation—forgiveness may be considered to follow the apology almost automatically. In both cases, the inability of survivors to address the apology is at stake. A third and crucial point concerns the status of the speaker who is apologizing.

Many philosophical conceptions of apologies focus on their content and formulation rather than the authority of the speaker. In Goffman's (1971) definition the status of the speaker is not addressed at any length, nor is it in Marty's (1998), except to say that the apology should be given by the person responsible for the transgression. Normally, it is assumed that the person apologizing is authorized to do so and thus the issue becomes whether the apology is properly formulated. Such approaches underplay the crucial contextual aspect of apologies that give them a large part of their symbolic power and illocutionary force. In the case of an official apology, a properly sanctioned authority (i.e., a political elite who is vested with the power to speak in the name of the state), must enunciate it. Indeed, illocutionary acts gain their symbolic power not only from the force of words but also from the status of the speaker. Consequently, an official apology is not merely a freestanding statement with internally generated legitimacy. As Pierre Bourdieu (1995, 107) has argued, "the power of words is nothing other than the delegated power of the spokesperson, and his [sic] speech— that is, the substance of his discourse and, inseparably, his way of speaking—is no more than a testimony, and one among others, of the guarantee of delegation which is vested in him." An apology finds much of its power in the status of the person who gives it—in our case, the political elite who speaks on behalf of the state. The difficulty in transitional situations arises when the apology is given by a successor elite who is not responsible for ordering past crimes, but nevertheless has taken the mantle of authority to speak in the name of the state and thus apologize on the state's behalf. To be credible, the speaker must assume the position of representative of the state, a symbolic move that must resonate with the population. This is largely possible because it is the office (e.g., of the presidency, the prime minister) that is, in a certain sense, apologizing in the name of the state. The individual performs the speech act in his or her official capacity, and thus it is the state that is making symbolic amends for past crimes. Whether this is successful (i.e., whether a particular elite is judged successful in conveying the state's apology) depends not only on whether the apology is well crafted but also on whether the elite is considered a legitimately endowed speaker. This issue of authority also has consequences for the legitimacy of the new state.

Official Apologies and State Legitimacy

The consequences for state legitimacy are well illustrated in the case of Chile. When Aylwin apologized, he explicitly acknowledged the state's responsibility and apologized as president, in the process positioning himself as a uniquely endowed speaker who could acknowledge responsibility to victims, their relatives, and the population as a whole. The official apology offered a measure of acknowledgment and rehabilitation of victims. In doing so, Aylwin gave an important expression of responsibility in transitional contexts, and also provided a remarkable example of the difficulties of successor regime responsibility and the challenges of legitimacy elites face. When a successor regime expressly repudiates earlier state actions through an apology, it is both distancing itself from the previous authoritarian government *and* establishing a link of legitimacy to the past, insofar as its privileged position as *apologizer* (to coin an ugly word and avoid the ambivalence of *apologist*) indicates its authority to speak on issues of the past and pass judgment on state actions. Aylwin (1995, 171), in fact, explicitly spoke "as President of the Republic." Thus, the official apology seeks to establish a continuity of state authority and responsibility while simultaneously stating its rejection of the previous government. This double movement is part of a broader effort at founding a new political order (rejection of the past) while claiming the right to do so legitimately (demanding to be recognized as the legitimate successor authority); as such, successor elites are forcefully making a claim of separation and continuity with the past, with all of the symbolic ambivalence that this entails. In this sense, it shares much with the debates over successor justice and, more broadly, constitution making in transitional settings.

Undoubtedly, apologies do not carry the weight of constitution making and successor trials, but they do highlight explicitly the tensions of both rejecting and embracing a morally compromised legitimacy. While they can symbolize a break with the past, they also underscore the normative ambiguity surrounding elite claims to legitimacy, and thus to their elite status. In order to displace this ambiguity, apologies are given in the name of the state and the authority to perform it is thereby secured. Whether this is successful in practice depends, of course, on whether the population as a whole—and survivors in particular—accept the displacement. In the case of Chile, Aylwin's apology drew public attention to past violations and helped catalyze a public debate about national identity and responsibility. Nevertheless, many victim and survivor groups considered it only a first step toward additional reparations and redress, and remained frustrated with the lack of accountability that followed his apology (Loveman and Lira 2000; Verdeja 2000).

Political society plays a particularly privileged role in reconciliation because leaders command the respect and loyalty of their followers and are thus in a unique position to shape social attitudes and beliefs. A primary contribution they can make is to underscore the importance of a peaceful politics that takes seriously contestation, debate, and the rule of law as well as the rejection of violence to solve differences. "Leaders," Michael Ignatieff writes, "give their societies permission to say the unsayable, to think the unthinkable, to rise to gestures of reconciliation that people, individually, cannot imagine" (1998, 188). This is perhaps too strong a formulation, but he is right to note that without elite support for peace and mutual respect, these values are unlikely to take root in the broader population. The behavior of leaders marks the boundaries of democratic contestation, what is acceptable and what is not, and influences civil society and individuals alike. Elites' expressions of remorse and their affirmation of the rights of citizens make it more likely that these issues will be taken up by fellow citizens, while creating a space for debate about responsibility, complicity, and the legacies of violence.

Such actions, nevertheless, do not guarantee transformations on other levels. While elites can help shape discourse and behavior throughout society—and, in fact, are shaped by them too—the relationship is a complex, dialectical one, as has been argued in this chapter. A more complete understanding of reconciliation is possible only if we move to other levels as well. In the following chapter, I investigate the use of two institutional mechanisms, truth commissions and trials, to promote reconciliation.

4 Institutional and Legal Responses

Trials and Truth Commissions

This chapter explores the use of institutional mechanisms to foster societal reconciliation. Although the vast majority of conflicts in the twentieth century were never followed with prosecutions of those responsible for the most significant violations, and while few authoritarian leaders have faced trial for their abuses, the century also witnessed the emergence of the principle that serious human rights violations should be punished through a legal process, rather than with simple revenge. The development of international human rights law and the establishment of occasional tribunals reflect a change in how nations understand past violations and their legacies. Indeed, considering the devastation of the past one hundred years, it is perhaps not surprising that a global human rights discourse has developed and matured, espousing fundamental ideals of human dignity and respect.

Nevertheless, this development was never guaranteed. The Nuremberg and Tokyo trials following World War II and the UN Genocide Convention (1948) established the principle that perpetrators of crimes against humanity should be tried and punished for their actions, but the Cold War put human rights concerns in a deep freeze for nearly forty years. In the Soviet-American bipolar world, human rights rhetoric was manipulated for political purposes and was rarely if ever the motivating force behind foreign policy (Ball 1999).

Human rights law is today the weakest component of international jurisprudence, certainly much weaker than international business or trade law. Still, there is no doubt that with the end of the Cold War, human rights discourse has gained strength. The past two decades have seen two international war crimes tribunals established, for Rwanda (ICTR) and the former Yugoslavia (ICTY), and additional tribunals have been created in Sierra Leone, East Timor, and Cambodia. The first permanent global criminal court, the International Criminal Court (ICC), came into being in the early years of the twenty-first century. Furthermore, domestic courts around the world have taken up the challenge of prosecuting human rights violators as a way of meaningfully engaging the past and reestablishing the rule of law. "Retributive" justice has become a guiding norm for human rights supporters around the world.

Tribunals have not been the only institutional response offered by human rights advocates. Over the past three decades, there have been increasing calls for the establishment of truth commissions to compile official histories of oppression and recognize victims. Nations around the world have adopted truth commissions, in many guises, as a way to come to terms with painful pasts. Generally eschewing formal trials (often because of political constraints), commissions have focused on restoring the dignity of victims and survivors and producing a definitive historical account by espousing what advocates call "restorative" justice in their quest for societal reconciliation.

This chapter considers how nations have attempted to come to terms with their violent history through the use of tribunals and truth commissions, by assessing their contributions and limitations for reconciliation. This chapter is divided into two parts. Part I discusses the normative underpinnings of tribunals and truth commissions, retributive and restorative justice, respectively. While I find this distinction ultimately unsatisfactory, I begin here (which is how the debate continues to be framed) before moving on to an alternative formulation. I consider the justifications, promises, and limits of both retributive and restorative justice, and assess their contributions to reconciliation. Part II identifies factors that affect the viability of tribunals and truth commissions, and emphasizes the importance of contextual constraints on their implementation and use. I conclude with qualified support for both institutions, arguing that (1) they are not mutually exclusive (either theoretically or practically) but rather often complementary and (2) they are important but by no means sufficient instruments for social reconciliation. I contextualize the importance of this social level by showing the impact that institutional mechanisms can have on societal reconciliation. The importance of this level for the norms of respect, accountability, rule of law, and truth telling is emphasized, but what also emerges is the insufficiency of this level for broad-based reconciliation.

Part I: Normative Foundations

To assess tribunals and truth commissions requires some criteria for evaluation. In Chapter 2, I discussed and defended a plurality of normative concepts that give greater theoretical substance to the idea of reconciliation as respect. In this chapter, I employ these concepts as a measuring device to analyze tribunals and commissions, and to indicate where the former may require additional support to further the goal of reconciliation.

Because the retributive-restorative justice debate is in reality centered on the practical impact of trials and truth commissions, I focus on these institutions in my discussion. This is valid, I believe, for at least two related reasons. First, in practice the debate often shifts between abstract notions of "justice" and their empirical manifestations, indicating that the real discussion to be had must also include a discussion about the institutional mechanisms themselves. Second, the abstract debates in reality are not free-floating but are grounded in the actual exigencies of transitional settings where trials and commissions have played a major role (indeed, the restorative justice model is seen by some as having developed post-hoc to legitimize truth commissions, though this characterization is unfair and historically inaccurate). With this in mind I focus on restorative justice through the mechanism of commissions and retribution through the mechanism of trials.

Retributive Justice and Tribunals

While the modern effort to prosecute human rights violations has its roots in the Nuremberg tribunal following World War II, it is with the democratic transitions starting in the 1970s in southern Europe, continuing through the Latin American transitions of the 1970s and 1980s, and moving into the 1990s in Eastern Europe that trials for serious human rights offenders came to dominate discussions of how to deal with violent legacies of authoritarian rule or civil war. In practically all of these cases trials were seen from a domestic perspective as national responses to national challenges, and international tribunals like Nuremberg were considered unlikely or otherwise inappropriate. Because many of these transitions were pacted and shaped by amnesties, the trials were often limited in reach and scope, and it was not uncommon for prosecutions to start and stop fitfully. These attitudes changed with the end of the Cold War and the massive bloodletting in Rwanda and the former Yugoslavia, which prompted the international community to establish two international tribunals. Arguably, these new courts were partly a chastened response by foreign powers to the fact that they had done little to stop the wars, but although limited in territorial and temporal jurisdiction, these trials have sought to resuscitate the primacy of international law for the most horrible violations. Both tribunals have made significant contributions to international law, giving greater substance and nuance to the definitions of crimes (e.g., genocide, war crimes, and crimes against humanity, and grave breaches of the 1949 Geneva Conventions), the legal understanding of victim group categories, and the concept of intentionality at the heart of genocide. Since their establishment, international human rights law has moved in several slightly parting or at least parallel directions.

First, we have witnessed the creation of so-called "hybrid" tribunals with international backing that combine, to differing degrees, domestic and international jurisprudence and include both international and national judges. There have been a number of these courts, including the Serious Crimes Panels of the District Court of Dili in East Timor, the Special Court for Sierra Leone, "Regulation 64" Panels in the Courts of Kosovo, the War Crimes Chamber of the State Court of Bosnia and Herzegovina, and most recently the Extraordinary Chambers in the Courts of Cambodia. The Iraq Special Tribunal, later changed to the Supreme Iraqi Criminal Tribunal, is occasionally referred to as a hybrid, though its international component is largely American.[1] These hybrid courts have been established where there is little domestic capacity to deal with mass crimes and international technical and legal assistance is necessary for legitimate prosecutions. Unsurprisingly, there is much variation across the courts: While the Kosovo and Bosnian tribunals are firmly entrenched in domestic law, the Cambodia and Sierra Leone courts are based on substantial international cooperation with national governments. The Iraqi tribunal for its part has been largely isolated from international input.

Second, we have seen traditional domestic courts drawing on international law and jurisdiction, however unevenly, with renewed vigor in an effort to bring international norms into a national setting. In Belgium, Argentina, and Spain, to cite a few examples, national courts or investigative judges have sought to employ principles of universal jurisdiction (or expanded versions of national jurisdiction, such as the so-called passive and active personality principles) to try serious human rights crimes. Lastly, a permanent ICC has been created with near universal jurisdiction to try war crimes, crimes against humanity, genocide, and eventually crimes of aggression. Some of the most interesting developments in human rights law have occurred in these international and hybrid fora, and while national courtrooms relying on domestic law will undoubtedly continue to be useful venues for prosecution, the internationalization of human rights law has become particularly important for understanding the possibilities of accountability (Sriram 2005).

These various tribunals and approaches have significant differences but they are all rooted in the principle of retributive justice, which privileges the importance of trying and punishing perpetrators. The line between retributive justice and vengeance, however, can often seem to be a thin one. While vengeance may seem to imply something like proportionality in punishment, it risks degenerating into wanton violence and cruelty. Retributive justice distinguishes itself from vengeance through procedural and substantive requirements that constrain the actions of the prosecutor—or avenger—and provide some protections to the accused. The rule of law, in other words, is the key difference between retribution and vengeance. Retribution in this chapter is used in this sense, that is, as a type of institutionalized, punitive response based on the rule of law. This formulation serves as an important heuristic device and moral ideal to orient our discussion of post-atrocity justice.[2]

Following Minow (1998), there are several criteria that retribution must satisfy if it is to remain within the bounds of the rule of law and not degenerate into vengeance: (1) a commitment to redress past abuses using generalized, codified, preexisting standards; (2) the use of a formal institution characterized by impartiality and transparency with due process protections; (3) the state's commitment to prosecute individuals only in terms of specific crimes for which there is valid evidence; and we could add (4) the power to impose a binding sentence on the defendant that amounts to more than public censure lacking coercive force.

Advocates of retributive justice offer several justifications for trials:

1. Following severe violence, *basic notions of justice demand that violators be punished for their actions.* This notion of retribution is non-consequentialist; it places no emphasis on the social consequences of its actualization and appeals instead to notions of "just deserts" (Kant 1998; Nozick 1981).

2. *Victims are acknowledged* and regain dignity and moral worth when their violators are punished publicly for their crimes. Trials reaffirm the moral status of victims by showing the world that their demands for justice are legitimate (Neier 1998).

3. *Identifying and punishing leaders* of crimes against humanity places individual guilt on key actors and institutions. By identifying individual leaders as perpetrators, claims of collective guilt that associate crimes with an entire ethnic or national group are minimized (Prunier 1997).

4. Trials may mitigate *demands for vengeance* and redirect them into institutionalized and fair proceedings for accountability, minimizing the likelihood of vigilantism (Shklar 1964).

5. Trials create *a public record* of crimes by collecting and questioning evidence (Bass 2000).

6. Tribunals *further the domestic rule of law,* the basis for a democratically stable and peaceful society (Robertson 2000).

7. Trials satisfy *a duty deriving from international law* (both treaty-based and customary) to prosecute serious violations of human rights (Damaska 2008; Orentlicher 1990).
8. Trials *deter future abusers*, signaling to leaders what may happen to them if they terrorize their populations (Roth 1999).

The main purpose of a trial is to assess culpability and punish the wrongdoer if guilt is proven. Although they work to some extent to recognize victims, they are driven by the importance of establishing accountability. They do this by using higher standards of evidence and due process protections for defendants than truth commissions, which are not, after all, judicial organs. Nor should trials be seen merely as revenge. Defendants may be acquitted, as they occasionally are, but what makes a prosecution legitimate is that due process considerations are followed. In this respect, while prosecutions may focus on retribution they do so, ideally, within the framework of the rule of law, and thus contribute to the establishment of a *Rechtsstaat*, or a political order based on law. Trials should be protected from political interference and focus instead on examining mass atrocity through a consideration of relevant norms and rules.[3] Furthermore, by identifying specific persons and agencies as violators, advocates say, tribunals lessen the stigma of collective guilt (e.g., of all Serbs or Germans). Focusing on individuals highlights that mere membership in a particular identity group does not mean culpability.

There are, however, several significant challenges to using trials. The first concern is the *scope of prosecutions*. At best, a judicial system can prosecute only a certain number of violators, which is a significant problem in the face of massive human rights violations like genocide, crimes against humanity, and similar crimes that depend on the participation and coordination of a large number of perpetrators. The normative claim that accountability promotes the rule of law by holding criminals responsible for their actions is thus only partly realizable; these crimes are often too extensive with too many participants to make complete criminal justice feasible. Confronted by this limitation, trials are sometimes used to prosecute high-level intellectual authors of crimes, their immediate subordinates, and those responsible for the most shocking atrocities. The UN ad-hoc tribunals for Rwanda and the former Yugoslavia have largely followed this strategy, though their mandates do not limit them to this. Whom to prosecute is not only a normative concern generally but also a practical challenge for international tribunals: The ICTR has faced considerable criticism from Rwanda for claiming the right to prosecute the main architects of the genocide and trump domestic trials in Rwanda's judicial system. The ICTY, too, spearheaded the prosecution of high-level leaders, including Yugoslavian President Slobodan Milošević (who died in custody) and Bosnian Serb leader Radovan Karadžić, though it has also prosecuted low-level perpetrators like Duško Tadić who committed particularly atrocious crimes. But even if a balance between international and domestic prosecutions is achieved, how far should prosecutions go in principle? As Raymond Aron has noted, the lines are rarely clear, and it is difficult, at best, to distinguish between prosecutable and non-prosecutable individuals. "How far is the search for the guilty to be carried? To what degree are the duties of obedience or national solidarity to be considered as absolving excuses?" (1967, 115). The counter-problem also exists: Rather than having only high-level leaders prosecuted, only a handful of subordinates responsible for an especially horrific crime are tried, as if the extent of violence began and ended with a few vicious, rogue units. In this scenario, trials are rightly viewed as a mechanism benefiting major perpetrators by scapegoating low-level functionaries.

Some of these concerns over scope and individualization have been mitigated through the employment of so-called collective liability principles like command responsibility, which permits the prosecution of military commanders (and in certain circumstances political leaders) for crimes committed by their subordinates, thus expanding the range of legal culpability beyond those who are the immediate perpetrators up to and including their superiors. The focus on hierarchical culpability has been complemented by recent ICTR and ICTY decisions that employ the novel legal doctrine of joint criminal enterprise (JCE). Under JCE, individuals can be found guilty for crimes they did not directly physically commit if prosecutors can show that defendants had a common design or plan to commit a crime, intended the objective of the plan, and participated in the crime in some way (Ambos 2007; Danner and Martinez 2005).[4] The merit of JCE doctrine is that it takes seriously some of the complexity surrounding contemporary mass crimes by moving beyond highly individualized and selective understandings of culpability to encompass the systematic and collective nature of violations typical of modern warfare and genocide. There are, to be sure, concerns with expanding legal culpability in such a way, and assessing responsibility requires a careful forensic reconstruction of events and relations between perpetrators (whether hierarchical or "horizontal"), inference of criminal intent, and other contextually sensitive criteria for assessing vicarious responsibility, all of which are particularly challenging where express written orders or other corroborating evidence are unavailable. Nevertheless, the new openness to more complex understandings of legal responsibility means that modern jurisprudence has attempted to tackle some of the concerns inherent with the extreme individualization of guilt. Some of these theories of collective liability, like command responsibility, have been employed widely in criminal prosecutions and will likely continue to evolve to take into account complex human rights violations. However, even with these advances trials will always have a relatively limited scope of applicability, as they can be expected to prosecute only a relatively small proportion of violators in situations of mass crimes. Their limited scope should give us pause in expecting them to carry the normative weight of accountability for reconciliation.

A *constrained evidentiary scope* places limits on the kinds of narratives that can be employed in trials. Marie-Benedicte Dembour and Emily Haslam (2004) have noted, quite convincingly, that a trial's focus on specific facts of a perpetrator's responsibility may distort historical accounts that would situate particular instances or cases of violence within a larger context.[5] Thus, rather than give us more informed understandings of patterns of violence, trials may artificially separate events from one another. The structure of a trial—of a procedurally just trial, at least—creates this imposition, which is defensible on its own terms but says little about how to connect discrete events to general historical assessments. Moreover, this evidentiary constraint means that only certain types of truth claims are considered admissible—that is, those pieces of evidence that are directly quantifiable or pass a standard of forensic "objectivity" are accepted. Dembour and Haslam note that these types of evidentiary requirements also distort witness testimony, as victim witnesses only occasionally provide information that can easily be subjected to a "true/false dichotomy" (2004, 156). Some major trials such as Adolf Eichmann's have allowed victims to recount their suffering and thus paint a historical picture of the conflict through the lens of personal anguish, but these cases have been heavily criticized for weakened evidentiary and procedural standards (Douglas 2001). The ICC's founding statute (United Nations 1999, art. 43, sec. 6) allows for more extensive victim participation in its trials (as well as reparations), but it is still too early to say how this will look in practice, and in any case the ICC's position represents the exception to the trend. In contemporary tribunals committed to basic due process, witnesses are rarely invited to provide extensive unstructured accounts of their experiences. Their testimonies are sought for the specific purpose of prosecution (or defense), and counsel unsurprisingly use them strategically. As sites for the construction of historical memory, then, trials risk distorting public understandings of the past, for the evidence provided in a courtroom is selected to prosecute particular individuals and not serve as the primary interpretive framework of the conflict.

Regardless of the efforts to ensure that prosecutions are fair, the problem of *political manipulation* is a constant threat. Trials are exemplary rituals insofar as they communicate that certain acts are so terrible that they rise to a level requiring clear and strong moral (and legal) condemnation. Selective prosecutions focusing on these types of violations indicate that these actions will not be tolerated in the future and that the state is committed to new norms of human rights. This is fundamentally a didactic element of prosecutions; they teach the nation the wrongness of certain actions and behavior in a theatrical way (Osiel 1997). But they also signal the limit of judicial mechanisms for achieving justice. And trials as exemplary performances of punishment can be dangerous; the line between legitimate select prosecutions and show trials is a thin one. In transitional settings, courts are not independent institutions immune from political pressures and strategies. Prosecutions are political symbolic acts meant to separate the new regime from the previous one. However, the strategic use of trials to further some other end—be it to establish the conditions of legitimacy for the incoming government, renew social solidarity through the persecution of identifiable enemies, or "teach" a civics lesson about atrocity—carries the serious risk that the rule of law will be usurped.

Consider the Moscow show trials or more recently the Iraqi Shia government's interference in Saddam Hussein's trial and execution.

I doubt the political component of transitional trials can be eliminated—indeed, even the UN tribunals' efforts to use ostensibly neutral language in court proceedings and statements conflict with their commitment to promote the liberal discourse of human rights. Aiming to completely depoliticize courts would probably only result in masking, to some extent, their explicit normative commitments or the interests of the actors who established them. The challenge is to balance the protection of the rule of law and its basic principles of due process and impartiality with the distinctly epideictic and ritualistic aspects of trials as institutions that condemn the actions of perpetrators and affirm basic rights. This problem of politicization is a constitutive problem—that is, it cannot be eliminated at a theoretical level but can only be reduced and mitigated in the practical application of prosecutions.

An additional problem concerns *retroactivity*. On occasion, certain violations may technically have been legal when they were committed. Prosecuting these acts violates the basic legal principle of nulla poena sin lege, so there can be no punishment where there is no law prohibiting an action. Certainly, when confronted with massive violations the ex post facto challenge seems grotesque because it runs counter to basic moral intuitions of justice and responsibility. Nevertheless, it is an important consideration, for the rule of law requires fidelity to basic principles of justice if it is to create a Rechtsstaat. This was one of the challenges raised against the Nuremberg trials, which sought to punish Nazi leaders for some crimes that were not—legally speaking—recognized as such. Indeed, the famous debate between H.L.A. Hart criticizing prosecutions of Nazis and Lon Fuller defending the trials on moral law grounds set the terms of discussion between positivism and natural law in relation to war crimes prosecutions for several decades (Fuller 1958; Hart 1958; Kelsen 1947). But while retroactivity does pose a problem for prosecutions, its importance is, I think, often overstated. Over sixty years after the precedent-setting trials at Nuremberg and decades of treaty and customary human rights law, as well as a significant corpus of case law emerging from the ICTR and ICTY, it would be difficult to argue that genocide, war crimes, crimes against humanity, and the most fundamental violations of human rights can still be legally defended. Indeed, Nuremberg is often cited as establishing that perpetrators can be prosecuted for knowingly committing crimes recognized by the international community, even where no specific laws exist to bar such activities. The development of a robust body of human rights and humanitarian law since the end of World War II, and the existence of a UN convention (1968) specifically rejecting statutes of limitations for grave crimes, all point to the mitigated salience of the problem of retroactivity.

Although these challenges are notable and the first three, at least, are in a certain sense ineradicable, they do not undermine prosecutions so much as indicate their conceptual limitations. Pointing out the limits of prosecutions means that tribunals are important but not sufficient instruments on their own for accountability; they need to be complemented with other forms of accountability at other social levels, such as debates in civil and political society about responsibility and culpability. Nevertheless, trials play an important role in reconciliation, for without prosecutions to punish extensive violence, impunity remains strong and the rule of law remains weak. Combined with adequate due process protections they can serve as legitimate devices for promoting justice in transitional societies, and to this extent we can say that trials form the locus of accountability for reconciliation (I address the problem of amnesty further below).

What then of the relationship between trials and victims? Antonio Cassesse, the ICTY's first president, offered a rather wishful reading of the contributions of retributive justice to victims: "When the Court metes out to the perpetrator his just deserts, then the victims' calls for retribution are met; by dint of dispensation of justice, victims are prepared to be reconciled with their erstwhile tormentors, because they know that the latter have now paid for their crimes" (1998, 3).

Underlying Cassesse's claim about the power of trials is the assumption that victims' moral need for recognition will largely be met through the dispensation of retributive justice, thus encouraging them to forswear vengeance and move toward reconciliation. Trials, in other words, are meant to right past wrongs and return a sense of moral worth to victims. They are an important arena for punishment, but it is far from obvious that prosecutions directly contribute to tempering calls for vengeance or providing victim recognition. A courtroom can function as a public space for victims to tell their stories and their testimony combined with other forms of evidence can forcefully challenge charges that victims fabricated or exaggerated their experiences. Nonetheless, we should be wary of claims that the trials can somehow be "healing." Eric Stover's important ethnographic research at the ICTY shows that victims often risk being retraumatized when confronting their tormentors, particularly during cross-examinations, which can be emotionally overwhelming and ultimately damaging to their self-esteem and psychological health (2005). Part of the confusion here is that a significant body of psychological research shows that victims can receive some therapeutic benefits from recounting their experiences in supportive settings, and prosecution advocates have taken this to mean that courtrooms can further witness healing by allowing victims to accuse their violators directly as part of a personal catharsis. But it is not at all evident that trial testimony has this effect. While it may be the case that testifying may have a short-term cathartic effect for *some* witnesses, psychological and medical anthropological studies show that healing requires more than the emotional abreaction following public testimony in a courtroom (Summerfield 1995). For some victims, testifying may have few detrimental consequences, but for many it can force them to relive painful experiences in a hostile environment where opposing counsel can trivialize or dismiss their testimony while questioning the authenticity of their experiences. Retraumatization is not uncommon and in a confrontational institutional setting like a courtroom victims can feel abused, humiliated, and used. Rather than provide moral recognition, a trial can further devalue victim witnesses unwittingly, especially if there are no additional support structures for witnesses following their testimony, which typically are lacking. This is perhaps the weakest aspect of trials, and underscores the importance of complementing their work with other state initiatives that deal specifically with victims.

However, the very existence of public prosecutions can generate public debate about social obligations toward victims—trials, in other words, both legitimate victims' claims and redirect public attention toward them. In this sense, trials may foster sustained deliberation about the past and a reconsideration of previously held truths about the period of violence, as well as the place of victims in society, well beyond the particularities of a specific court case. Victor Turner calls these types of trials "social dramas," or cultural events that undermine and render problematic general beliefs while demanding reflection on previously given categories for making sense of the past:

> Since social dramas suspend everyday role playing, they interrupt the flow of social life and force a group to take cognizance of its own behavior in relation to its own values, even to question the value of those values. In other words, these dramas induce and contain reflexive processes and generate cultural frames in which reflexivity can find a legitimate place. (2001, 92)

Though Turner's notion of cultural framing is at times rather mechanistic (in no small part due to his reliance on Emile Durkheim), he is right to underscore how prosecutions can create conditions for citizens to think about alternative conceptions of victimhood. Thus, though trials may not address victims directly, they establish and create an intelligible framework that allows for debate to take place about responsibility, complicity, the status of victims, and what is owed to them.

Trial records also create a public account of past wrongs. The Eichmann trial produced a wealth of information on the organization of the Final Solution, and the Auschwitz trials identified the gruesome process of extermination that was paradigmatic of the Holocaust (Douglas 2001; Whitmann 2006). The Raboteau case in Haiti unearthed significant information on the internal organization and operation of the United States–backed Front for the Advancement and Progress of Haiti (FRAPH) death squad, and perhaps most impressively the UN tribunals for the former Yugoslavia and Rwanda have amassed an enormous amount of material on the civil wars in those countries (Concannon 2001). The prosecution of the intellectual authors of crimes should include the investigation of the agencies, bureaucracies, or groups they lead; this in turn can provide some insight into the organization and operation of violence. In this way, tribunals contribute to the larger project of creating a factual account of the past. Nuremberg, for example, amassed a staggering amount of information on the *Schutzstaffel* (SS) and gave historians a rich archival fund with which to reconstruct the Holocaust. Even Arendt, who opposed justifying trials on any grounds other than their retributive capacity, noted approvingly, "Even today, eighteen years after the war, our knowledge of the immense archival material of the Nazi regime rests to a large extent on the selection made for prosecution" (1967, 231). Furthermore, the fact that fair trials have a high standard for admission of evidence has led some commentators to argue that its "truth" carries greater weight than that found in truth commission reports. This depends on the tribunal and commission in question, of course, but the fact that fair trials include high evidentiary standards means that trial evidence may be considered credible.

Nevertheless, as discussed in Chapter 1, the construction of "truth" after mass atrocity is a fraught enterprise, and this is especially the case in successor trials. While truth production in a trial includes a didactic element—trials, after all, signal to the population the *wrongness* of certain actions—it ought to be limited by the strictures of the rule of law: Individual defendants, for example, should be held responsible only for their actions, and not those of others who fall outside their control or knowledge; and only evidence directly related to a case should be presented. This can be hard to accomplish, however, because successor trials always provide a particular interpretation of the past. Ben Gurion, for example, wanted the prosecution of Eichmann to be told against the backdrop of crimes "against the Jewish people," as part of a rethinking of Jewish history (Lahav 1992, 559–561). And the charter of the Tokyo trial stated that "the tribunal shall not be bound by technical rules of evidence [. . .] and shall admit any evidence that has probative value," essentially permitting the introduction of material that may not be specifically germane to the case at hand (Minear 2001, 118). The difficulty lies in drawing a connection between the particular acts of specific individuals and general historical developments, without stating the criteria used for inferring such connections. The problem is an important one that highlights a difficult obstacle faced by trials. It further points us to the importance of looking at other complements in other mechanisms and at different social levels.

Truthful accounts in reconciliatory processes should be rooted in facts, but all facts must be interpreted. Clearly, we should oppose trials that merely paint perpetrators as evil without stating actual charges or without backing them with relevant evidence. But framed by the requirements of the rule of law, courts can identify hidden cases of abuse and identify those responsible for them. These public records are not only factual but also political, as they shape public deliberation about responsibility and collective norms. This is desirable because trials re-affirm basic values that were violated in the past. We should demand the most convincing and reasonable interpretations of events and responsibility in any particular case, and encourage civil society to turn to the evidence in constructing and debating new understandings about the past. The hermeneutic aspect of truth formation—where particular events delineated in a case help inform broader social understandings of the past—means that trial records contribute to this project because of the legitimacy they carry, but are not the prime locus for it.

Trials may also promote the rule of law by eliminating existing authoritarian enclaves that are holdovers from the previous regime. Through prosecutions of human rights violators who may still have some political protections, trials signal that the new regime is committed to holding all perpetrators accountable. Combating impunity is closely related to the Janus-faced aspect of tribunals; while they face the past through judgment, they also turn to the future by showing the necessity of a new legal regime founded on a respect for rights. This can have an important, transformative effect as trials signal that government power must be held within certain limits and individual rights must be protected from capricious state behavior.

In Chapter 2 I discussed how the rule of law is understood as a normative concept that entails a commitment to the principle of non-violence and the processing of political conflict through legitimate procedures of deliberation framed by a basic rights model. Successor trials inform this by helping creating a space for public deliberation about rights, responsibility, and what it means to live under the rule of law. Nevertheless, transitional regimes are often constrained by amnesties. As such, the retributive impulse of prosecutions is blunted and the rule of law is undermined. Given how common amnesties have become, in the following section I discuss the uses and limitations of amnesties in transitional scenarios.

The Problem of Amnesties

If justice requires accountability, then amnesties—which give legal immunity to persons who should be tried for violations—are nearly always unjust. By limiting prosecutions preemptively, the demand for accountability is undermined and impunity is strengthened. However, amnesties of some sort are a part of many transitions, and their relationship to reconciliation deserves attention.

The difficulty lies in balancing the pragmatic need to secure a stable transition with the normative demand for legal and moral accountability. At their most basic, amnesties are understood as practical compromises with at best no moral weight whatsoever, though in some instances amnesties have been subsumed into the broader search for reconciliation. The South African case is illustrative. As Richard Wilson (2001, 99) and others have noted, "According to the Interim Constitution of 1993, the only function which the TRC had to fulfill in pursuit of reconciliation was to grant amnesty in a spirit of *ubuntu* [humaneness] and understanding, for politically motivated acts within a specific period of time." In such an approach, amnesty is transformed into a tool of social regeneration, blunting the call for destructive vengeance. Accountability, the rule of law, and victim recognition are cast aside in favor of securing some degree of peace. John Dugard (1997, 284) reads the South African case as demanding a coercive form of reconciliation over justice, resulting in a reconciliation that "minimizes the memory of apartheid," and "it is not clear that [reconciliation] takes adequate account of the interests of the victims of apartheid." Dugard is correct, provided we accept such a definition of reconciliation. In any case, though amnesties may guarantee political stability in the near and possibly mid-term, it is not clear that they contribute to reconciliation in the long term. And this is not merely a semantic quibble. Amnesties undermine the rule of law and signal that the interests of victims can be sacrificed for the common good of stability. The issue here may be one of timing: For instance, it may be necessary to defer prosecutions because a new government is too weak to confront powerful violators, as happened in Argentina and Chile. A stronger claim, made by Jack Snyder and Leslie Vinjamuri, is that once amnesties are made, "institutions based on the rule of law become more feasible" (2003–2004, 6). The evidence for this is mixed, however, and while it may be the case that in particular circumstances amnesties are necessary for securing a democratic transition, there is no compelling normative reason why they should continue to be honored when the democratic regime has become more secure. As Argentina, Chile, Peru, and a number of other countries have shown, pursuing prosecutions after democratic rule has been consolidated can be both feasible and morally defensible. At most, amnesties should be seen as deferring justice, not eliminating it.

Given that amnesties may be necessary, is there a way to make them more palatable, or to have them serve the interests of justice? One of the dangers with amnesties is that their distinctly pragmatic nature is often subsumed under a rhetoric of forgiveness, where they are seen as an institutionalized form of forgiveness. By passing an amnesty, leaders may be perceived as saying, "Let us bury the past and begin a new future."

Amnesties, however, are pragmatic devices, not moral responses to injustice, and there is a great deal of differentiation among them. They differ primarily on whom or what they place outside the domain of prosecution. Some are explicitly *act* specific, that is, they protect some crimes, such as murder or terrorist financing, but not torture or kidnapping. Algeria's 2006 amnesty, for example, exempted only those insurgents who had supported or financed terrorism but had not been involved directly in terrorist attacks (it did, however, provide a blanket amnesty for the security forces) (Human Rights Watch 2006). The United Nations recognized only certain acts as amnestied in Sierra Leone's 1999 amnesty, exempting crimes against humanity, war crimes, genocide, and other serious violations of international law (Annan 1999). Other amnesties specify a *temporal* range for protection, indicating that crimes committed during the designated time period are protected from prosecution. This is perhaps the most common way of framing an amnesty and was typical in Argentina, Brazil, Chile, and Mozambique. Nevertheless, even these blanket temporal amnesties may overlook certain crimes: In a novel reading of Argentina's amnesty not intended by its authors, judges ruled that the military's kidnapping of the children of the disappeared constituted ongoing crimes and thus were not covered by the 1986 and 1987 amnesty laws (Verdeja 2009). Other amnesties give immunity to certain classes of *actors* and protect all members of a certain group or institution, such as the armed forces or internal security forces. Peru's (1995) amnesty protected all members of the security forces and civilians (but not insurgents) who were the subject of a complaint, an investigation, a trial, or an imprisonment for human rights violations from the beginning of the war in 1980 to the enactment of the law (Amnesty International 1996). Even here, however, there may be some differentiation such as extending amnesty to insurgent combatants but excluding the top leadership, as happened in the 2000 amnesty in Uganda offered to the Lord's Resistance Army (amnesties were later extended in 2003, 2006, and early 2008) (Ariko 2008). A variant of the *actor* approach is to provide conditional immunity to particular individuals rather than entire groups or institutions, as in South Africa. But South Africa's individualized focus has been the exception: Most amnesties have combined elements from these various approaches, offering immunity to entire groups for a range of crimes committed during a specified time period.

Only conditional, individualized amnesty, I think, can be defended morally to any extent. The South African amnesty provides an important illustration: Amnesty was not part of the collective erasure of memory, as in Uruguay, but was given only to those individuals who confessed their actions completely and truthfully.[6] By testifying for immunity, they publicly incriminated themselves and laid bare the evils of apartheid. Those who chose not to confess risked prosecution, though in reality this was rare. Nevertheless, this conditional component of amnesty helped undermine justifications for apartheid and showed its awful practices and legacy to the South African people. Those who testified had their reputations destroyed and experienced a measure of public accountability and punishment. As Bert van Roermund has written, amnesty served as "a way of covering that uncovers the meaning of what has happened" (2001, 178). In South Africa, amnesty was tied to truth seeking and justice.

Amnesties may be morally defensible if they assist other moral goods, such as truth telling. If granted on an individual basis through public testimony, a conditional amnesty can help the investigative work of a truth commission while also shaming perpetrators who otherwise will receive no punishment. Nevertheless, amnesties, even conditional ones, should be used sparingly, for they also symbolize the state's willingness to trade on the moral dignity of victims by sacrificing it to the interests of stability.

Where amnesties appear fully entrenched, international law and courts become a possible alternative venue for securing retributive justice. International law does not recognize domestic amnesties for serious human rights violations, and the ICC's principle of "complementarity" to national courts allows it to prosecute crimes where the state is either incapable or unwilling to hold trials. Using the ICC or international law, however, is not without challenges; depending on the context, an indictment from an international tribunal may undermine a carefully crafted peace accord or otherwise weaken the likelihood of ending a war. The ICC's recent indictment of top Lord's Resistance Army leaders has arguably pushed back the possibility of bringing the war in Uganda to an end. While amnesties should always be resisted, dismantling them requires a careful consideration of various contextual factors, including the likelihood of the resumption of conflict. The point here is that if amnesties are given they should be conditional, and eventually they should be overturned or rendered legally invalid, either by a domestic court (preferably) or by an international tribunal.

In general, then, we can say that retributive justice, as actualized in trials, focuses on accountability and creating an accurate and credible record of past violations, as well as contributing to the rule of law by rejecting impunity. Restorative justice, articulated through truth commissions, shifts the focus to victims and offers a broader account of the past than that found in trials, thus providing an important complement to the retributive impulse driving prosecutions.

Restorative Justice and Truth Commissions

Over the past several decades, outgoing rulers have created amnesties to protect themselves from subsequent prosecution. In Latin America alone, numerous amnesties have been enacted: Chile (1978), Brazil (1979), Guatemala (1996), Argentina (1986, 1987), Uruguay (1986), Nicaragua (1990, 1991, 1993), El Salvador (1993), and Peru (1995). Where amnesties were passed, truth commissions have been established in lieu of prosecutions. While traditionally commissions served as alternatives to trials, in recent years they have served a complementary role, addressing issues that courts have been unable to handle adequately.

A truth commission is an official investigative body with a mandate to study violations that occurred during a particular time frame in a specific country. A commission normally exists for a relatively short period of time (i.e., a few months to a few years) and produces a final report of its findings that may also include recommendations. Its main task is to create an official account of past

abuses.[7] The techniques for amassing evidence can be varied and
may include forensic anthropological investigations, depositions from
a wide array of persons, and archival research. Furthermore, commissions may include a series of institutional reform and reparations
recommendations in order to help prevent such abuses in the future.
At the core of a commission's work is a commitment to acknowledging victims and restoring their sense of dignity and moral worth.
Thus, advocates argue, truth commissions are seen as paradigmatic
examples of restorative justice.

There are several differences between truth commissions and tribunals. Truth commissions generally lack subpoena powers and cannot
prosecute perpetrators. Justice as criminal punishment is eschewed for
the production of a history that explains violations in the context of
broader social and political processes. Over the past few decades, truth
commissions have become quite popular. Over twenty-five commissions have been established since the early 1980s, and the more successful ones have included prestigious citizens (e.g., authors, public
intellectuals, lawyers) as commissioners, lending greater legitimacy to
the commission's work. Unlike trials, commissions tend to be receptive
to civil society input and often receive information and testimony from
the NGO community and other interested parties, giving commissions
a special place between civil society and the formal state.

Supporters offer several justifications for using truth commissions
and pursuing restorative justice.

1. The primary purpose of such commissions is *to produce an
   accurate public record of a country's past crimes*, through
   archival and forensic truth seeking complemented by inter-
   viewing survivors and perpetrators (Boraine 2001).
2. Advocates point to the *therapeutic benefits* of truth commissions. By providing victims with a sympathetic public
   platform to present their stories, commissions contribute to
   their personal healing and offer a phenomenological or experiential truth that complements archival and forensic
   truth (Krog 1998).
3. Concomitantly, the public presentation of survivors' stories *incriminates perpetrators*, offering a kind of punishment akin to that found in a trial and achieving a powerful

symbolic punishment through the shaming and public stigmatization of violators (Kiss 2001).

4. Public testimonies contribute to societal reflection and,
   ideally, *healing in society itself*, helping restore and affirm
   the democratic values of respect and tolerance, and "repair" the "torn social fabric" (Tutu 1999).

5. Lastly, because of their systematic analysis of patterns of
   abuse and relevant institutions, commissions can *provide
   policy recommendations for institutional reform and restructuring, as well as reparations programs for victims*
   (Crocker 2001).

Truth commissions seek to create an accurate report of past crimes.
They "clarify uncertain events, and lift the lid of silence and denial
from a contentious and painful period of history," in the words of Priscilla Hayner (2001, 25). Because of a combination of investigate techniques, including archival research, interviews, and field investigations
(e.g., unearthing mass graves), commissions are well positioned to present a particularly complex and rich history of abuse. This combination
of numerous investigate methods and access to often secret information can provide a comprehensive macro perspective that is frequently
lacking in transitional contexts. Argentina's truth commission documented the disappearances of nearly 9,000 persons, providing a fuller
picture of the atrocities committed during that country's "dirty war"
(Argentine National Commission on the Disappeared 1986). Peru's
truth commission report documents a twenty-year conflict between
guerrillas and the state that resulted in an estimated 69,000 deaths,
nearly three times the previously estimated number (Peru 2003). South
Africa's Truth and Reconciliation report (1999) detailed thousands of
cases of torture, extrajudicial killings, and other abuses that had remained hidden throughout the apartheid period. These reports can
complement trial records by establishing general patterns of violations
that may be overlooked in prosecutions, and their wider investigative
focus makes them ideal for analyzing the institutions and policies behind systemic abuse.

In certain instances, as Priscilla Hayner (2001) and Mark Freeman (2006) have pointed out, commissions do not uncover crimes so
much as *publicize* what is known but could not be stated openly. By

publicizing atrocities, commissions confront official denial and the culture of impunity that protects violators. A commission's report can encourage debates about responsibility and complicity, and in the process force a society to rethink its obligations to its fellow citizens who were victimized. They do not, of course, offer a finalized account of the past, but they can "narrow the range of permissible lies" (Ignatieff 1996, 113).

A reasonably accurate historical understanding is necessary for the other normative goods to take root. Accountability is impossible if basic facts, including who the perpetrators are, remain hidden or otherwise unknown. Reparations, too, require knowledge of who the victims are if they are to be inclusive and morally defensible. Without a somewhat accurate, empirically based account of the past, there is less likelihood that shared social space can be created, or that former enemies will ever accept alternative histories as any more than lies or willful misrepresentations.

Clearly, amassing facts is not enough; the truth must be publicly disseminated and generate public debate. Because they occupy a unique place between the state and civil society and enjoy significant media attention, truth commissions are well situated to engender debate and are able to legitimize civil society programs about the legacies and challenges of the violence. Both the South African and Peruvian commissions conducted public hearings to gather victim testimony around their respective countries, and they successfully used the media to disseminate their hearings. Commission reports are not final accounts of the past, but rather often serve as an important first step at understanding the history of violations and attendant culpability, and may even spur broader debates about moral responsibility. Researchers continue to add to and modify the commission findings, as the cases of Chile and Argentina show, but this does not detract from their particularly important role in catalyzing debate at all levels of society, from elite politics to civil society to interpersonal relations. They can provide a baseline of historical understanding by identifying primary actors, events, and patterns, and consequently undermine denials.

Truth commissions do, however, face some serious limitations. Though retroactivity is not a problem, *scope* and *politicization* are challenges. The scope of investigation is a particular challenge, as most commissions must consider an enormous range of crimes during their relatively short life span. Given their limited period of operation, normally two years or less, and their often tight budgets, most commissions can investigate only a few hundred cases while briefly mentioning perhaps a few hundred others. Even well-funded and professional commissions such as South Africa's and Peru's are faced with choosing among thousands of violations that bring charges of instrumentalization. Which cases are paradigmatic examples of violations? Which best represent the crimes committed and highlight abusive policies? How were they chosen?

Politicization is equally problematic; it is a concern that emerges with the way in which a commission frames its account of the conflict and the evidence it marshals in doing so. Truth, as we have seen, is inseparable from processes of interpretation and storytelling, and commissions are tasked with presenting—and *re*-presenting—a narrative account that makes sense of the past, given the information they are able to collect. By documenting violations committed by all belligerents they may find that one side is responsible for the majority of crimes, or in any case, a disproportionate number of them. Commissions are not neutral and their normative aspects cannot be suspended by turning to supposedly neutral, non-contextual standards. Nevertheless, political manipulation has remained a problem for many commissions, and only institutional and budgetary autonomy as well as cultivating relations with broad sectors of civil society can provide at least some protection from explicit state interference (Freeman 2006).

The key concern over commissions is whether they provide a satisfactory form of accountability. Some observers remain skeptical about a commission's ability to secure meaningful accountability because they cannot prosecute violators (Llewellyn 1999; Robertson 2000). As products of political compromise, they remain incapable of providing the robust justice found in courts. Undoubtedly, countries have often established commissions when it seemed clear that prosecutions would be impossible due to amnesties. Other scholars, however, have defended commissions' ability to achieve accountability in moral terms, as an alternative to formal retributive justice. Elizabeth Kiss (2001), for example, has claimed that while formal legal punishment may not be a possibility open to commissions, the focus on victims and their suffering effectively condemns perpetrators publicly, bringing some measure of justice. While Kiss may perhaps overstate this point, truth commissions do contribute to accountability in several ways. David Crocker (2001) has noted that they may provide evidence for future trials, shame perpetrators publicly by tying them to abuses, and make well-informed recommendations for judicial reform. Because their work includes the systematic investigation of crimes, the evidence they amass can be useful for prosecutions, and in several cases commissions have provided their files to prosecutors to be used in future prosecutions. In Peru, Argentina, and Chile prosecutions have either followed, or are expected to follow (eventually), the publication of the final report. The Guatemalan Commission on Historical Clarifications (Comisión para el Esclarecimiento Histórico 1999) final report specifically recommended prosecutions in its concluding chapter, and in Sierra Leone and East Timor, trials and commission investigations proceeded together, though there were jurisdictional conflicts over sharing information.

More specifically, the identification of violators in a final report functions as a sort of symbolic punishment by publicly shaming and undermining their self-serving stories of courage and patriotism. The importance of shaming, especially when specific actors are tied to particularly horrendous acts, is certainly a kind of punishment. South Africa's final report powerfully condemned the apartheid regime by drawing on a wide array of archival and testimonial evidence in support of its claims, and those who were associated with the regime's crimes suffered public condemnation and humiliation.[8] Pinochet reportedly remained angry and humiliated until the end of his life over charges that he was responsible for massive crimes, even though he was never found formally guilty. It may be preferable that commissions actually name perpetrators in their final reports, establishing a tighter link to individual responsibility than would be the case with generic references to institutional culpability; commissions in Chad, East Timor, El Salvador, Sierra Leone, and Liberia, among other places, enjoy this authority. This has the benefit of furthering truth telling, accountability, and possibly even victim acknowledgment, since it ties a face to actual atrocities. El Salvador's commission realized that given the existing amnesty, naming perpetrators would be the closest it would come to assigning individual responsibility, and thus published names in its final report. In some cases, however, perpetrators cannot be named but the evidence clearly points to them, achieving something of the symbolic punishment evident above. In settings where trials are impossible because of transitional constraints, humiliation can serve as an important proxy for formal justice. Nevertheless, "naming names" faces some serious drawbacks: Accusations can be made for a number of personal or political reasons and the opportunities to defend oneself publicly and forcefully are few and often inadequate. Particularly where multiple sides committed violations in a civil war or where a large part of the population was complicit in state domination (e.g., as in Eastern Europe), naming risks overemphasizing the responsibility of some while allowing others to avoid unwelcome publicity.

Finally, commissions can give helpful recommendations for judicial reform by identifying corruption and politicization that can facilitate—and legitimize—further abuse. In Peru, El Salvador, and Guatemala, commissions have pointed to compromised judiciaries as key agents for human rights violations. Their work in identifying judicial co-optation and recommending comprehensive reforms is important for accountability and the rule of law. Commissions, of course, cannot replace trials as the locus of accountability but they can function in a complementary relationship with courts. Rather than seeing them in conflict—an increasingly anachronistic and simplistic view I discuss further below—they should be understood as potentially compatible.

Since the mid-1990s, a number of commissions have followed South Africa and incorporated public hearings, welcomed by scholars as a primary device for extending recognition to victims.[9] Much recent scholarship has extolled the supposed social healing dimension of victim testimony by arguing that allowing victims to recount their experiences will strengthen social relations and contribute directly to reconciliation. The dynamics of public social catharsis are strongly disputed, and it is not at all clear that public hearings have such a directly positive impact on either victims or society (Fletcher and Weinstein 2002). Part of the difficulty in this debate appears to be the assumption that commissions are the *only* locus of victim recognition. Framed in such a reductive way, it is unsurprising that complete victim recognition is not achieved through the brief public testimony of some survivors before commissioners. A more realistic view sees commissions as an initially central location for victim recognition that provides a public and protected space where they recount their stories and experiences. But victim testimony gives concrete, emotionally charged perspectives on lived suffering, and may generate public debate and reflection on the past. Furthermore, public testimonies demand that victims be recognized as bearers of moral worth (and legal rights)—people who can no longer be ignored or marginalized in the interest of stability. Thus, public testimony may draw the attention of an uninformed or skeptical public and begin a difficult process of social reexamination and reflection, but its actual benefits for victims is significantly less clear. In any case, while a trial may draw on victim testimony, its focus on prosecutions means that victims at best serve an ancillary capacity in that forum and meaningful victim recognition there is unlikely.

Commissions may also recommend reparations for victims and their families. As discussed in Chapter 2, reparations can take a number of forms: They can be symbolic or material, and collective or individual. They may, for example, give individuals medical or psychological assistance, or provide them with financial compensation for physical harms and destroyed property and goods. Although reparations cannot give a morally complete answer to abuse they can positively affect the livelihood of victims and clearly signal the state's acknowledgment of its responsibility for crimes. A number of commissions have recommended reparations, and in South Africa, Argentina, and Chile they were provided with precisely these goals in mind (Hayner 2001; Verdeja 2006). Nevertheless, reparations face a number of problems that speak directly to the issue of victim acknowledgment. For example, do individual material reparations address the need of survivors for moral recognition? It is difficult to give an answer in the abstract, so instead we must to turn to the recipients themselves. Here, the responses are often contradictory, with some recipients arguing that reparations qualify as a form of moral redress and others rejecting payments as a crude form of self-exculpation on the part of the state (Verdeja 2000). While welcoming just compensation, victim groups often fear the state will use individual payments as an excuse to ignore victims in the future, arguing that they have been adequately compensated for their suffering. Rather than use reparations as a strategic measure to neutralize public debate or isolate victims, they should be crafted to express the state's awareness of its responsibility and contribute to developing public trust in government institutions over the long run.[10]

Reparations are legitimate to the extent that they are not perceived as merely cheap responses to violence but rather recast compensation as a form of moral recognition by the state. A truth commission's endorsement of reparations can help generate public awareness of the depth of violence and its symbolic and practical legacies, while forcing a reticent population to reflect on its obligations to its fellow citizens.

Commissions are significantly less successful, however, as institutions promoting the rule of law. The rule of law is most clearly promoted in the judiciary, through fair and transparent trials that systematically uphold existing laws and norms. Truth commissions, of course, do not guarantee substantive or procedural due process protections or other defendant rights, and for these reasons they should not (and do not) serve as venues for prosecution. They can further the rule of law only indirectly, by recommending reform of problematic state institutions, prosecutions of abusers, removal of corrupt or otherwise unqualified justices, and strengthening individual legal rights. Because these can only be recommendations truth commissions have no binding power to carry out these policies—they must depend on the will of political leaders, which is often a despairing thought.

I discussed earlier the importance of truth for reconciliation, since without an understanding of who did what to whom any possibility of reconciling former enemies is likely to fail. In this, truth commissions can undoubtedly play an important role. On occasion it is argued that commissions are crucial if society is to overcome the deep divisions of the past. The strength of this argument is difficult to gauge: Reconciliation is a long, uneven process that may benefit from a truth commission but it also requires reconciliatory efforts at political, social, and interpersonal levels. Provided that commissions not be normatively overburdened—provided, that is, that we do not expect them to achieve all of the goals of reconciliation alone—they may contribute in the long run to societal reconciliation by recasting issues of responsibility, victim recognition, and accountability against the background of historical evidence of atrocity. Their position between the state and civil society may allow them to function as facilitators for long-term reconciliation.

Tribunals and truth commissions, and retributive and restorative justice more generally, share a number of goals: They seek to uncover past atrocities, hold perpetrators accountable, acknowledge victims, and promote the rule of law. They differ, however, in emphasis: The retributive approach promotes accountability over victim acknowledgment, while restorative justice endorses the importance of recognizing victims and rebuilding social relations over the prosecution of perpetrators. This does not mean that they are essentially contradictory; on the contrary, they may be compatible, and it may be in fact desirable that they operate together under certain transitional contexts. Vasuki Nesiah (2006) has argued that it may be best to stagger their implementation to avoid contradictory aims, beginning with commissions and then focusing more narrowly on legal approaches. The benefit of this is that broader patterns of violence are identified and publicized before pursuing individual cases of wrongdoing, thus mitigating the possibility of highly particularized accounts of wrongs that displace our understandings of the systemic and institutional dimensions of repression and violence. Commissions provide a wider context for understanding the actions of individual perpetrators and chains of command, and trials can devote their resources to the most extreme cases and their orchestrators.

Staggering may indeed be beneficial. However, when prosecutions and commissions work concurrently, as in East Timor and Sierra Leone, sharing information can bring with it a host of practical and normative problems. The Sierra Leone Truth and Reconciliation Commission ([SLTRC] 2004) and the Special Court for Sierra Leone ([SCSL] 2003) were established separately with the expectation that they would work to address the country's violent legacy. The commission encouraged violators, witnesses, and victims to speak in public hearings as part of its mandate to create "an impartial historical record" and promote national reconciliation. The commissioners saw their work as fundamentally different from, but in harmony with, the SCSL:

> The Special Court is also in search of the truth, but the Court's truth will necessarily be limited to the criminal responsibility of the accused. . . . The Special Court and the TRC [Truth and Reconciliation Commission] have essentially different, although complementary, roles to play. Whereas the TRC cannot replace judicial investigations into the criminal responsibility of those that [*sic*] bear the greatest responsibility, the Special

> Court is not as well suited for a broader inquiry into the causes, nature and circumstances of the conflict. (Sierra Leone Truth and Reconciliation Commission 2004, vol. 1, ch. 3, para. 11)

This institutionalized division of labor, however, did not work very well in practice. Many Sierra Leoneans were concerned that self-incriminating testimony given before the commission would later be used in the SCSL's prosecutions, and numerous ex-combatants refused to participate in the hearings. The two institutions also disagreed over the use of amnesties and whether the court's subpoena power would extend to the commission's files (Schabas 2004). Many hearing participants remained confused about the differences between the court and the commission and were unclear about what was expected and permitted in commission testimony. Tim Kelsall notes that these confusions and fears produced testimony that was "rarely able to get beyond detached, factual statements on the part of victims and half-truths, and evasions and outright lies on the part of perpetrators" (2005, 380). This is not, however, merely a case of institutional clashes. Rather, it shows how the institutionalized pursuit of two differing normative goals—truth and accountability—can come into conflict. The SLTRC's legitimate commitment to truth telling was hampered by the court's legitimate desire to amass evidence for prosecution, thus affecting and ultimately distorting the testimony at public commission hearings and satisfying neither the truth nor accountability. Any move to broaden the historical understanding of the civil war would invariably require particular information about individual combatants and their actions, but in a conflict with mass atrocities and the likelihood of prosecution, many people were unsurprisingly unwilling to participate in public hearings. The result was a process of strategic truth telling that was heavily shaped by the threat of trials. Can these competing institutional aims be brought into harmony in future settings? Perhaps, but this requires answering some difficult political questions that have consequences for truth and accountability. Who should mediate the relationship between the institutions? Who prioritizes goals when they clash, and how should they be prioritized? Should commissions name alleged perpetrators in their final reports, even when courts fail to prosecute them on narrow technical or procedural grounds? Doing so risks producing two competing historical accounts and differing (and possibly contradictory) assessments of individual responsibility; if the procedural protections and evidentiary requirements of courts are taken seriously it would be highly problematic, at the very least, to discard acquittals in favor of a lower commission standard based on more flexible testimonial rules. And what if a commission has confidential evidence conclusively showing an individual's culpability or innocence? Should it share this with the court, even if not explicitly requested by the court? These are not merely technical questions about jurisdiction and mandate; instead, they pose fundamental challenges for the types of truths and accountability that are ultimately produced. Staggering these institutions may mitigate in the short term some of the concerns about information sharing and insulate the commission from public perceptions that testimony will be used in trials, while at least maintaining the possibility of future prosecutions.

Even if these institutional clashes can be lessened, complementarity is not always easily achievable. There are a number of other factors that constrain the use of truth commissions and tribunals and affect their ability to promote reconciliation.

Part II: Practical Constraints

The previous section identified the theoretical issues at stake in employing tribunals and truth commissions in post-atrocity societies. But the options available to transition architects are not so extensive; they must work within specific political, social, and economic parameters that constrain their choices. In this section, I consider several factors that play a critical role in assessing the viability of tribunals and commissions, and, more importantly, help us calibrate their contributions and limitations to reconciliation—and how this level is both necessary and insufficient for larger reconciliation.

Degree of Institutionalization and Legitimacy of Previous Regime

The degree of institutionalization and legitimacy of the perpetrating regime affects the likely success of efforts to seek legal recourse for political crimes. Institutionalization means at least three things: (1) the regime rules through the use of formal and bureaucratic mechanisms, so that different aspects of governance are managed and coordinated by various departments; (2) it has penetrated civil and political society systematically and deeply; and (3) it seems stable and durable.[11] Institutionalized perpetrator regimes are essentially Janus-faced: They assemble complex legal justifications for their actions, bureaucratize violence, and generally rationalize repression, yet also engage in extralegal terror against political opponents and the broader population, particularly through the use of secret police, death squads, disappearances, and massacres.

Institutionalization is normally accompanied by an increase in legal justifications for crimes through the emergence of a large body of state-security law, and in this sense we can say that a perverted "rule of law" exists. Here, rules, edicts, statutes, executive orders, administrative decrees, and legislation all work to justify what is essentially a terroristic regime, giving a kind of legal patina to an otherwise despotic state. Concomitantly, the state employs its military and security apparatus to violent ends, often working outside (but in harmony with) the established legal framework. The upshot may be a large body of law and archival evidence identifying the organization and systematization of state-sponsored violence. The more institutionalized and centralized the terror, the more likely it is that a significant body of documentation delineating the coordination of bureaucracies and security forces will exist. Of course, the peculiarities of a negotiated transition may make acquiring this information difficult, particularly if the perpetrating institutions manage to retain some degree of autonomy. In Chile and Argentina, the armed forces were fairly successful at retaining control of records on their "dirty wars," though what has emerged indicates that in both instances the state's violence was highly rationalized and bureaucratized. In South Africa, the armed forces and national police destroyed many of their records of death-squad activity, and the militaries of Central America have simply refused to hand over damning internal documents.

Nevertheless, systematized state terror complemented by a robust body of documentation can facilitate the truth seeking and prosecutorial goals of tribunals, and thus institutionalized regimes make good candidates for trials. Strong and well-documented links between superiors and subordinates illuminate hierarchies of legal (and moral) responsibility, making it more likely that prosecutions will be successful.

But institutionalization poses obstacles as well. Complex, multi-layered systems of repression complicate the criminal-legal under-standing of responsibility (i.e., normally understood as predicated on individuals and not institutions). If the perpetrator regime were highly institutionalized, with a wide web of repression implicating numerous bureaucracies and agencies (e.g., as in South Africa and Eastern Europe, in different ways) and enjoying widespread support or at least acquiescence—and thus arguably legitimacy—then prosecution of individuals can be vulnerable to charges of selectivity: Only some violators face prosecution, while the majority (i.e., normally the higher-echelon violators) will escape justice. Where these considerations hold, a commission may offer an important complement to prosecutions by illuminating how repression entails the cooperation of numerous coordinated institutional actors.

Independence and Fairness of the Judiciary

In some transitions, the judiciary remains an enclave of the past regime, significantly limiting the ability of victims to obtain redress. In these instances, trials are unfeasible, and truth commissions may be the only viable domestic institutional response, at least until (or whether) the judiciary is reformed. Nevertheless, there are alternatives: regional or international fora, such as the Inter-American Court of Human Rights and the ICC, and, under certain conditions, case-specific tribunals assembled by the United Nations. This latter approach requires UN Security Council support, which in turn poses numerous practical obstacles. The apprehension of some major powers, particularly the United States, toward the expansion of universal criminal jurisdiction impedes the success of the ICC, though as mentioned earlier the hybrid tribunals like the SCSL may be viable.[12] Regardless, the reconstruction of the national judiciary remains the best hope for domestic accountability and a crucial prophylactic against future impunity. Eliminating impunity requires an independent and well-run judiciary. Because accountability is situated at this level, a weak judicial system can fatally undermine the likelihood of reconciliation, thus leaving authoritarian enclaves intact.

Extent of Perpetrator Population

In some instances, there exist relatively few overt perpetrators and many "beneficiaries," or persons who benefit from the political circumstances without actively participating politically. In South Africa, for example, apartheid benefited all white South Africans, regardless of their political affiliations or relations to the state. The apartheid government enjoyed the tacit support of much of the (Afrikaner) white population, although many were not active oppressors. Other cases are markedly different. The political terror of the Hutu Power regime in Rwanda included the active participation of many Hutu civilians—thus, the perpetrator population was high relative to the number of beneficiaries. The same can be said of Cambodia. Although the Khmer Rouge ruled through terror and did not enjoy wide-ranging support outside their own ranks, there were few beneficiaries of the regime who were not implicated in gross human rights violations.

In all of these cases, tribunals can offer an important, though limited, contribution to accountability. Where there are relatively few overt perpetrators and many beneficiaries, the latter cannot be held legally accountable; however, it would be misguided simply to ignore their moral responsibility. A truth commission can serve as an important complement to trials by highlighting that complicity and responsibility go well beyond the narrowly understood notions of criminal liability that are characteristic of criminal prosecutions. In South Africa, the commission investigated the role that business, legal, medical, religious, and other professional communities played in supporting the apartheid regime. Investigations of this sort illuminate the wide support that some terroristic states enjoy by morally implicating beneficiaries and countering claims that the latter were ignorant of the state's violence. Nevertheless, even this is insufficient; a robust public sphere open to critical reflection is an important resource for ensuring that state institutions like the judiciary or commissions do not wholly determine complex normative issues of responsibility and perpetrator definition. As the following chapter makes evident, civil society actors can raise many of the difficult questions of responsibility, such as the moral status of bystanders and beneficiaries, in ways that are not possible through trials and even truth commission investigations.

Mode of Transition

A key element in assessing what type of institutional response to pursue is the mode of political transition between regimes. While I discussed this earlier, some points bear repeating: Where the transition is achieved through a complete victory in war or other radical break with the past, successor elites have the political capital to impose trials with little concern for the desires of their enemies. The Tokyo and Nuremberg tribunals, as well as the domestic successor trials in Rwanda, underscore the wide latitude that victors have in pursuing retribution. Where the transition is tightly "pacted," or negotiated, trials are less viable politically. Previous elites may still retain enough power to trump the possibility of trials, either through the creation of an amnesty or the threat of renewed violence. Here, truth commissions have been offered as an alternative response to the past, investigating elites' actions and shaming them through the publication of a truth report identifying their crimes.

Material, Financial, and Personnel Resources

Both trials and truth commissions are expensive, and poor countries emerging from a conflict with a devastated infrastructure and weak economy may be unable to pursue these expensive institutional responses, at least not without significant foreign support. Tribunals, in particular, are especially costly. A trial of a high-level perpetrator can cost millions of dollars, making numerous trials difficult to justify from a strictly budgetary perspective, particularly when a country is faced with myriad other pressing humanitarian concerns and some of those funds could be used to alleviate the plight of survivors and others. International funding is often difficult to secure, and there may be few qualified personnel to carry out a trial. The Rwandan genocide left only a handful of lawyers in the country, creating a seemingly insurmountable obstacle to formal domestic prosecutions (indeed, Rwanda turned to the use of *gacacas*, an alternative, allegedly "native" legal system that could process the accused in quicker succession). With a shortage of attorneys to prosecute—much less defend—suspects, the likelihood of fair trials is seriously diminished. It would be a mistake, of course, to choose commissions over trials simply on budgetary grounds. To do so would make a mockery of the principle of a moral response, thus delegating the moral calculus to the rather profane level of financing. Nevertheless, budgetary constraints *are* constraints. South Africa spent approximately $18 million a year on its commission, a sum unmatched by any other similar body, and commissioners nevertheless felt their work was underfunded. So, too, with the UN-sponsored truth commissions in El Salvador and Guatemala (Lester 2000).

Closely related to the above resource factors is political will. Does the successor regime have the will and commitment to actually pursue and sustain a rigorous, institutional response? Human rights advocates have often found a great deal of rhetorical governmental support for their ambitious projects, only to realize later that the regime has no interest whatsoever in matching its words with deeds. The lack of interest is, unsurprisingly, reflected in the lack of money and resources available for tribunals and commissions. Uganda assembled two commissions—in 1974 and 1986—that were duly ignored by the state, and Ecuador's 1996 commission ended inconclusively after five months, without producing a report of its findings. Zimbabwe's 1985 state-sanctioned commission, investigating state repression in the Matabeleland, never released its report; the government quashed its publication, claiming the findings would unleash "ethnic conflict" (Freeman 2006; Hayner 2001). Political will and sufficient resources are crucial if institutional responses to the past are to succeed. Otherwise, they will amount to nothing more than empty promises.

Possibility of Future Social Unrest through the Use of Trials and Truth Commissions

There exists the very subjective factor of predicting—*reckoning* may be a more appropriate term—whether tribunals or commissions will contribute to the resumption of violence, be it through coup, civil war, or revolution. Political elites must engage in a delicate calculus to ascertain whether certain kinds of institutional responses may lead to a renewal of violence. Highly pacted transitions tend to result in authoritarian enclaves in politics, the economy, and occasionally the armed forces, thus reducing the possibility of trials. Truth commissions may offer the only possibility of a moral response without resulting in renewed conflict and retributive efforts will have to be pursued in the international arena, with all of the great-power pitfalls that entails, or be pushed into an uncertain future. But negotiating the straits of pacted transitions does not entail the abandonment of justice. Rather, it requires the espousal of novel forms of accountability, truth seeking, and victim recognition as a means of promoting the process of reconciliation. It also points to the importance of civil society in promoting reconciliation.

Salience of Specific Cultural and Religious Discourses for Furthering the Cause of Reconciliation

Trials and truth commissions should draw from particular local discourses that can strengthen their legitimacy. Archbishop Tutu (1998) often turned to Christian notions of forgiveness as a primary virtue in dealing with perpetrators, and local leaders frequently called for a collective spirit of ubuntu, roughly meaning "humaneness," to emphasize the importance of reestablishing just and meaningful social relations. These notions and others offer a deep discursive source that can feed broader efforts at encouraging mutual respect. Drawing on local discourses can help ensure that reconciliatory efforts will have greater resonance in the population. One novel approach has been to draw on traditional practices of conflict resolution to bring communities together.

Traditional Justice Mechanisms

This chapter focused on the role of former trials and truth commissions, which represent two of the primary institutional responses to mass atrocity in post-conflict settings. Nevertheless, responses have also taken a decidedly autochthonous turn, especially in sub-Saharan Africa, and here I say a few words about these important recent developments. My comments are limited because there still remains relatively little ethnographic and comparative scholarly work on these developments. In Burundi, Mozambique, Rwanda, Sierra Leone, and Uganda, state

officials and local leaders have encouraged traditional practices to reintegrate former combatants and rebuild social relations. These practices
are quite varied but are based on complex rituals that aim at social healing and truth telling and include extensive community participation.
They often include some component of accountability, such as the requirement of a confession, community labor, or reparation, but with the
exception of Rwanda's gacaca do not rely on formal punishment per se,
such as a prison sentence. Their primary point in common is that they
eschew the formal rational legalism typical of international and Western human rights law for informal communal traditions that are highly
ritualized. The use of traditional practices stems from a common concern that formal courts are incapable of addressing the full extent of
atrocities and their social effects, and consequently alternative approaches are needed. International courts like the ICTR and the ICC
are often perceived as remote, expensive, and largely irrelevant, and do
not speak to the concerns of affected societies. Even domestic trials,
many argue, may have little impact on the immediate needs of survivors
and communities or are otherwise incapable of handling the enormous
number of persons implicated in the violence. Truth commissions may
appear less remote, but a commission rarely gives sustained attention to
any one locality; its interest is in producing a report on national patterns
of violence, not necessarily micro-level reintegration. Ideally, these traditional approaches focus on preexisting local or regional customs for
resolving conflict and maintaining (i.e., reestablishing) social solidarity
on morally acceptable grounds. Some of these practices, such as the
Ugandan ritual of having child soldiers step on an egg, dramatically
capture particular cultural rituals of social repair (Baines 2007). They
are also all communal: They depend on the participation of the entire
community, as the assumption is that the violence has harmed not only
individuals but the community as well. The question, naturally, is "How
successful are these approaches for promoting reconciliation, and are
they more effective than courts or commissions?"

It seems to be too early to tell, largely because these traditional
approaches are so different from one another and have not been employed systematically over long periods of time in any one place. Indeed, many of them are hardly traditional: While all appeal to tradition
as a source of legitimacy, some are significantly different than their
predecessors though they remain at least partly rooted in traditional

practices, such as the modern *mato oput* ceremonies in Uganda or the *magamba* rituals of Mozambique, but others represent fundamentally new institutions, like the Rwandan gacaca. Nevertheless, the ethnographic work on these institutions show mixed results (Huyse 2008).

In Mozambique, for example, the government did not pursue explicit reconciliation or retributive policies following the civil war, but communities in the central part of the country drew on local practices and customs to develop their own reconciliatory approaches centered on the magamba (spirits of dead soldiers returning to the land of the living to seek justice). These highly ritualized ceremonies require that the perpetrator accept responsibility for wrongs before the magamba and the community, and after a show of contrition, village priests, or *curandeiros*, drive away the magamba and begin the process of restoring social bonds. By taking responsibility and explaining their actions, perpetrators help return dignity to their victims and repair badly damaged communities. The magamba ceremonies appear to enjoy popular legitimacy, and recent ethnographies show that many family members of victims have responded positively to the reintegration rituals and accepted that the contrition shown by ex-combatants represents at least a modest form of moral recognition for the deceased (Igreja and Dias-Lambranca 2008).

In Rwanda, the response has been significantly different. The original Rwandan gacacas were village-based institutions meant to settle community disputes including theft and property damage (and possibly manslaughter), but not mass murder. They were presided over by local elders held in high esteem, the *inyanga-mugayo*, and their decisions carried the weight of customary authority. In 2002 the Rwandan government established modern gacaca to process the enormous number of perpetrators in jail after the genocide, and the program was implemented nationally in 2005. These new gacaca hear cases involving common killers, torturers, and looters, but not rapists or the architects of the genocide, who instead are tried in domestic courts or by the ICTR (Rwanda 2008). Like their predecessors, modern gacacas meet in a public setting where perpetrators are confronted by victims and other accusers in a relatively free-flowing exchange, and community leaders mete out a punishment (including prison) and call for reparation. But the differences between the two types of institution are profound, and a number of observers point out that the contemporary gacaca enjoy little connection to their predecessors. Indeed, the claim that they are "traditional" appears to be an effort by the government to enhance their legitimacy; they were essentially developed from the top down and imposed on local communities. Modern gacaca judges rarely enjoy the authority of elders (a sizeable minority of whom have been implicated in the genocide), and the extensive violence seems to have destroyed the legitimacy of many traditional customs and institutions, including the legitimacy of the gacaca themselves (Ingelaere 2008; Kirkby 2006). Furthermore, many victims risk retraumatization in gacaca hearings and face the prospect of having to live next to their tormentors after the latter have paid what is often considered a relatively small reparation or served a brief period in prison. Many accounts indicate that in these sessions victims are often ignored or disparaged and rarely receive meaningful recognition, and there are few programs in place to support their psychological needs after testimony, though a national fund for victim support has been established. Recent studies also show that in many cases gacaca hearings have increased intracommunal conflict (Waldorf 2006).

One of the primary difficulties facing these community justice mechanisms is the scale of the violence, which they are ill-equipped to handle. This is, of course, also a problem for formal judicial systems, but these traditional mechanisms often developed to handle significantly lesser transgressions where the background cultural norms remained intact. The scale of violence, however, can tax the norms on which these institutions rely for legitimacy. The complicity of local leaders in the violence also weakens the traditional authority structures at the center of the reconciliation ceremonies, thus leaving many participants angry, dismayed, and skeptical of community justice.

International human rights organizations such as Human Rights Watch (Roth and Desforges 2002) and Amnesty International (2002) have criticized some of these traditional approaches for their weak commitment to accountability and failure to employ explicit and codified due process criteria. Some of this is misplaced: All of these approaches contain an element of accountability. In the magamba ceremonies perpetrators are required to accept guilt for their actions, and in the gacaca punishment can include prison sentences of several years. In Burundi, the *bashingantahe*, a traditional conflict-resolution ceremony, explicitly requires acceptance of responsibility. Nevertheless, because few of these institutions have codified rules of procedure, explicit evidentiary criteria, or formal protections for the accused, they seem to lack the due process protections of formal trials. Even the gacaca, which have formal rules, suffer from undertrained judges and assistants and significant participant confusion on the process and expectations of the hearings. Some of these accountability problems may be mitigated over time, as the specifically practical and institutional challenges that traditional approaches face are better understood.

A more pervasive limitation concerns their appropriateness in ethnically diverse societies. The traditional practices in Mozambique, Sierra Leone, and Uganda are quite culturally specific, and do not translate well into other cultural milieux in their respective countries. This is partly a source of strength, as their cultural specificity means that they may resonate strongly with particular communities and thus (potentially) enjoy enhanced legitimacy, but it also points to their inherent limitations; different communities have different traditional conflict-resolution rituals and may not be able to deal with intercommunal conflicts. Indeed, the wars in Sierra Leone and northern Uganda crossed national borders and ethnic groups, but traditional mechanisms have not been very effective in dealing with intercommunal violence (Alie 2008; Ojera 2008).

A final point relates directly to the issue of recognition. A primary focus of these institutions is to provide meaningful recognition of victims. To the extent that survivors are included as active participants in these ceremonies, their experiences and claims to dignity can be acknowledged. Unlike formal trials, many of these institutions focus primarily on the suffering of the community and the need to rebuild it, and thus emphasize traditional restorative justice rather than legalistic retribution. Nevertheless, many of these tradition-based institutions are male dominated, and indeed at least part of their legitimacy comes from the authority of male elders. Women and youths are often marginalized in hearings, both as victims and as witnesses, and older male testimony is often given greater weight than women's testimony (Burnet 2008). Some of this has changed recently, with women enjoying more authority in Sierra Leonean and Rwandan hearings, but ensuring greater participation for and acknowledgment of women and younger participants requires rethinking some of the primary gender assumptions at the root of traditional justice.

In any case, it seems too early to know definitively how successful these traditional approaches will be.

What then, can we say about moral respect and institutional responses to the past? The centrality of moral respect in reconciliation demands that institutions be used to protect rights, promote the rule of law, and acknowledge the injustices committed against fellow citizens. Trials promote respect by combating impunity and showing the public that individuals retain claims of moral worth and dignity that cannot be abandoned for some higher, common "good." Through prosecutions, the importance of a rights culture is reaffirmed and unaccountable power is challenged. More importantly, through prosecutions trials publicly express the inherent moral value of victims, indicating that it was wrong to turn them into instruments of some "higher" purpose by using them to achieve some other ends. The centrality of individual moral value, and the concomitant rights that translate that value into legal discourse, are captured through human rights trials.

Nevertheless, it is clear that trials may create more instability and more hatred in the short term. They forcefully distinguish between wrongdoers and victims, and undermine the central claims of perpetrators by showing the consequences of their beliefs and actions. Under such conditions, it is unlikely that social relations will be harmonious, or that former enemies will embrace one another, certainly not in the sense given by Tutu and others. But without remaking the political and moral landscape, as contested and painful as this may be, no significant reconciliation is likely. Reconciliation, after all, is not about a deep moral embrace; it is a state of affairs where erstwhile enemies accept one another as moral beings with legal standing, including the right to participate freely and equally in political and social life without the fear of violence and coercion. Trials can contribute to this precisely by returning some degree of dignity to victims and curtailing impunity.

Truth commissions, perhaps more than tribunals, can refashion public views of victims. Public testimonial spaces provide the opportunity of rehumanization while offering alternative stories that indict misleading historical accounts. Of course, much like trials, commissions may be divisive, as well. They re-situate actors in our historical imaginary and moral understanding, placing formerly admired leaders and their subordinates in the camp of moral, if not legal, opprobrium. This instability carries with it very real risks, but seems necessary if a community is committed to respecting all of its members and recognizing the wrongs of the past. The idea of reciprocal moral recognition that is at the heart of respect becomes worthless if parts of the population remain marginalized and devalued—cast out in the interests of others. Commissions carry some of the difficult load of reconciliation by placing victims at the center of discourses of the past, forcing a society to rethink its obligations to its fellow citizens, and sharply contesting given and unexamined public truths.

These institutional responses are important for the reconciliatory project, but they cannot achieve moral respect on their own. Indeed, none of these goals is possible without elite support. As discussed earlier, elites must show a willingness to engage the past, discuss responsibility and complicity, and show the political leadership necessary to reconcile a pained nation. By adopting a politics of debate and reflection over a politics of violence and fear, elites can signal the population about the importance of reflecting on the findings of trials and commissions. Through their words and their actions, they can give greater legitimacy to the work of these institutions. Civil society, too, must foster respect. Respect and the rule of law require a transformation of the thin notion of accommodation into a thicker conception of mutual recognition; this is something that commissions can encourage because of their special position between the state and civil society. They represent a powerful call for continued public deliberation and reflection, though of course such engagement often falls outside of a commission's control. Indeed, as I have discussed in this chapter, commissions—and to a greater extent, trials—provide closed histories of the past, as reports must eventually be published and judges must eventually reach a judgment. However, these documents may deepen the process of moral reflection in civil society, and catalyze further public engagement over responsibility, justice, and what it means to recognize fellow citizens as moral equals. Individuals, too, must find ways of addressing complex personal issues of responsibility, revenge, forgiveness, and moral transformation, and ultimately adopt principles of mutual respect if the bitterness of the past is to be left behind in some morally defensible way. Institutional responses may not be able to secure reconciliation or achieve respect—indeed, there is often a danger of expecting too much from them too quickly—but the imprimatur of the state that they enjoy provides these institutions with an added legitimacy that can positively shape the social imaginary. For both approaches, respect can be secured only in a political order that recognizes all members of society as moral equals, as recognized bearers of moral worth and dignity; as Mamdani puts it, the boundaries of inclusion are "life itself" (1998).

5 Civil Society and Reconciliation

Political scientists have traditionally studied democratic transitions from the perspective of political elites by focusing on their abilities to promote stability and governance while protecting peace from the spoiling tactics of disaffected opponents. The four-volume work *Transitions from Authoritarian Rule* (O'Donnell, Schmitter, and Whitehead 1986) oriented much of the subsequent work written on analyzing elite fragmentation and its consequences. Civil society received attention only after significant divisions between elite "soft-liners" and "hard-liners" became insurmountable. Along these lines, political scientists have examined the contributions of elites in fostering reconciliation as a process of balancing civil society pressures and maintaining social stability by strategically using trials and truth commissions to promote moral and political ends while securing the legitimacy of a fragile new state (Gill 2000). Scholars have focused less on civil society actors' roles in promoting reconciliation and their interactions with elites and the state in these struggles.

Nevertheless, the role of civil society in reconciliatory efforts is not merely incidental or epiphenomenal, but is fundamental. Civil society can expand the domain of political contestation and ask difficult questions that leaders may prefer to ignore, while forcing elites to address fundamental issues and challenges. Although the state apparatus is, of course, crucial for implementing retributive measures, providing formal recognition of victims through redistributive and other programs and maintaining the rule of law, civil society is also important for reconciliation politics. Civil society is necessary for publicizing past atrocities and generating public discussions about them, publicizing state complicity, promoting moral recognition, and contributing to the broader normative goals of rule of law and mutual respect among citizens.

Some political scientists have begun to focus on the importance of civil society. In her comparative analysis of justice policies in Chile and Uruguay, Alexandra Barahona de Brito argues that the different outcomes in the two countries can be explained by the strength of the human rights movement and the Catholic Church, and their ties with political parties. Whereas in Chile the Church enjoyed significant moral capital and allied itself with the cause of human rights groups early on: "In Uruguay there were no state-autonomous institutions such as the Church, or powerful rights organizations capable of successfully challenging party inconsistencies. The human rights organizations were too weak to press for a different outcome" (1997, 193). Barahona de Brito's work points to the importance of civil society for transitional politics, an importance best understood as part of a dialectical relationship with the state—one not equal in terms of power (for obviously the state maintains coercive capacity in most circumstances and is, in any case, the locus of formal power)—but nevertheless very real and important for reconciliation. This relationship will become evident in the following pages.

In this chapter, I discuss the role of civil society in reconciliation in several steps. First, I outline three important conceptions of civil society and discuss their respective strengths and weaknesses for understanding the peculiarities of societal reconciliation. Using one of these as a normative-analytical tool, I then turn to an analysis of the role of civil society actors in the public sphere and delineate how they can promote reconciliation by influencing political discourse and action at the institutional and political society levels. Next, I discuss some broader normative contributions civil society can make through the promotion of mutual respect, recognition, and the rule of law. Finally, I note several difficulties that emerge when advocates rely too heavily on civil society for reconciliation: (1) the problem of an over-politicized, oppositional civil society that undermines the efficacy of state consolidation and rule; (2) the problem of internal differentiation and authoritarian enclaves in civil society (and the retrograde impulses this can engender); (3) a civil society that loses its critical potential and becomes eviscerated of any communicative or influential power; and (4) the broader problem of normatively overburdening this social level for attaining reconciliation. In keeping with my general thesis that reconciliation must develop across four social levels, I discuss how civil society is strongly connected with developments elsewhere, and thus is a necessary but insufficient element of reconciliation.

Theorizing Civil Society

The concept of civil society has a long, complex pedigree. For early thinkers through the seventeenth and nineteenth centuries, it meant all social life outside of state institutions (Keane 1988; Ehrenberg 1999; Hodgkinson and Foley 2003). In particular, it referred to the institutions, groups, and activities that were mostly autonomous from state regulation. Market relations, for example, were traditionally at the center of the idea of civil society, and this understanding still represents a particularly influential and powerful model. Today, however, many political theorists and scholars view civil society and the associational life it encompasses as distinct from both the economy and the state, though the actual definition of the term is widely contested (Walzer 1995; Fullinwider 1999).

For my purposes, civil society refers to a space of social relations autonomous from the state where groups and movements create new alliances, further their interests and views, and engage with one another to shape public and elite opinion with the aim of influencing state policy and public discourse. Civil society is also where more universalistic bonds of solidarity are created and recreated, remaining in tension—sometimes productive, sometimes not—with particularist identities and claims that resist the construction of a broader social "we," as Jeffrey Alexander has argued (2006, 42). It is, ultimately, a domain of public participation in debates over issues that are important to society as a whole as well as a space for the creation of identity and meaning, and while civil society actors do not exercise formal power, they can nevertheless mobilize the public and ultimately affect social policy. As this is not an uncontested conceptualization, I sketch three relevant views of civil society:[1] (1) a liberal interest-based view, defined by competing groups seeking to influence the state and further their own sectoral interests; (2) a participatory/oppositional model that emerged during the period of oppositional social movements in communist East Europe and authoritarian Latin America, referred to as a "self-limiting" revolution by Adam Michnik and Jacek Kuron, two of its greatest elaborators; and (3) a "discourse theory" model, which sees civil society as distinct from the state but nevertheless serving as an important sphere of deliberation and influence that can inform state policy. Although these are not completely distinct models of civil society, they highlight different perspectives on its role, with different consequences and expectations as to the ultimate function of civil society.

Liberal Civil Society

The classic liberal model of civil society emphasizes the importance of freedom from the state. In this view, life is divided into two spheres: one public, characterized by the state and its attendant coercive capacity; and the other private, where we exercise freedom and pursue our (pre-social) interests. The latter sphere is civil society, which is largely the same as the private market domain. For the liberal, the public and private spheres are largely incompatible, and to the extent that the former encroaches on the latter, liberty disappears. The currency of the state is power; the state can at best enforce certain limited, basic conditions for individual flourishing (e.g., guaranteeing peace, contracts) but unchecked it can easily move beyond its legitimate domain and restrict the freedoms of individuals. There can be no profitable relations between the two spheres in such a view, and thus the only desirable social arrangement requires carefully restricted state power.

Furthermore, society is broadly understood as a series of binary relations: freedom and power, people and the state, and market and the government, with each element in opposition to the other. Because freedom is located in the private sphere, individuals find self-actualization and happiness there by pursuing their needs and interests with as little interference from the state (and others) as possible. To the extent that the state may be engaged, it is to promote particular interests of certain sectors of society (i.e., interest groups); no general public interest or common good is articulated or even considered necessary. It follows that relations in civil society are contractual relations, which allow individuals to secure the goods they want and satisfy the needs they have through mutually beneficial contracts. Relations between civil society and the state are also largely contractual; the state may, in some instances, be able to provide certain services that cannot be secured in the private domain. The market is seen as the primary arena for the distribution of goods and services due to its superior efficiency but the overriding danger of unchecked state power requires individuals to remain wary of government promises to provide too much, as this is the first step on the short road to serfdom.

Such a radically binary view of state-society relations requires a strong scheme of individual rights to protect people from government power. Unsurprisingly, then, the interest-based model has often included the strongest defense of individual liberties possible by presenting them, at least in one formulation, as trumps against the utilitarian policies of the state (Nozick 1974). But what is particularly important for our purposes is how this framework conceives of the individual as largely an economic being, *homo economicus*; one who equates freedom with the unhindered possibility of pursuing economic interests with little concern for fellow citizens. While this may represent freedom in a Hobbesian sense—the lack of "impediments" means liberty—it results in a very impoverished notion of civic life with little if any concern for social cooperation, collective action, or solidarity. The idea of citizens having a stake in society or having an interest that transcends their narrow individual desires is largely absent here. Even the more attenuated version of liberalism found in Robert Dahl's theory of polyarchy, which identifies the bedrock of democracy as the institutionalization of formal representation through periodic voting and the separation of governmental powers, remains skeptical of any conception of civil society that considers public will beyond interest-based politics. Indeed, in this formulation, civil society consists of a network of polyarchic relations and transactions that are shaped and legitimized by an existing party system, which help achieve something like a "general advantage" (1991, 295). Policy making is the result of negotiation and accommodation between different groups. For Dahl, the key is to ensure that civil society actors, promoting their interests, can shape and influence policy outcomes.

The liberal conception of civil society replaces sociability and publicness with the pursuit of private interest. As the citizen becomes a solitary and "autonomous" consumer, issues of shared concern cannot be thematized from a broader perspective that includes the well-being of society as a whole. Indeed, at best, one is left with citizens who seek to maximize their interests and preferences, and politics is reduced to instrumental relations.

Civil Society as a "Self-Limiting" Revolution

Some analysts view civil society in a more Gramscian sense, one that consists primarily of popular social movements standing in opposition to the state. Here, civil society opposes the state's coercive power and creates and sustains a domain where individuals, acting collectively, further social solidarity and their conceptions of the common good. Civil society can certainly play this role in transitions to create a space free from government repression where subordinate groups can contest official power. This view was widely endorsed in the Latin American civil society movements of the 1970s, 1980s, and early 1990s. Carina Perelli (1992) has documented how youth movements in Uruguay confronted the authoritarian state first through small acts of disobedience and later, as their temerity lessened, through rallies and publications that made explicit their antagonism toward the military regime. While the youth movement was never able to maintain significant links with other groups in a broad front, it is nevertheless epigrammatic of this conception of civil society. In Chile, too, civil society became organized and politicized beginning in 1983. In May of that year a series of large demonstrations were begun by labor groups, and grew to include a variety of youth groups, religious associations, leftist political organizations, women's groups, and even some organizations representing middle class interests (Martínez 1992). These demonstrations failed to remove Pinochet, but fundamentally altered the political landscape, eventually leading Pinochet to hold a referendum in 1988, which he lost. The movement's refusal to countenance any negotiations with the regime reflects the politicized divide between state and society at the center of this approach (a position that was, alas, reciprocated by the government).

This popular, confrontational approach gains its most theoretically careful elaboration in the work of Polish activist Adam Michnik. Under the category of "new evolutionism," Michnik conceptualizes civil society in radical opposition to the state, and speaks of the necessity for an "unceasing struggle for reform and evolution" based on a "steady and unyielding stand" against the government (1985, 142–143). Michnik draws on the importance of creating links with a host of civil society actors, including the Catholic Church. Civil society, in his estimation, should be a repository of transformational and horizontal relations between non-state groups, but it should be restrained, or "self-limiting"; that is, civil society actors do not seek formal power but remain in permanent relations of contestation with the state in the process democratizing the regime and society more broadly (1985, 144). This conception of broad opposition is useful insofar as it identifies the importance of social struggle against a repressive state—one that is unlikely to begin reform and expand civil liberties on its own initiative. It is rooted in contesting the legitimacy of authoritarian governments through self-limiting but forceful action. In present day Zimbabwe, the Movement for Democratic Change (MDC) and social movements like the Women of Zimbabwe Arise have continuously pressured President Robert Mugabe to recognize civil rights, hold fair elections, and share power with opponents, all the while eschewing violence or revolutionary struggle (Zimbabwe Human Rights Forum 2008). The fact that Mugabe agreed to a power-sharing arrangement with the MDC speaks to the power, but also significant limitations, of civil society in that country and oppositional politics more generally (Human Rights Watch 2008).

This perspective is certainly helpful for contexts where an oppressive regime is in power. Unlike the liberal model presented above, it is not primarily private in orientation; rather, it emphasizes the importance of continued engagement and popular pressure on the state through broad social mobilization, while maintaining and cultivating a social space unencumbered by state interference. It is less useful, however, for understanding transitional situations and theorizing what future relations between society and a reformed state should be. Civil society cannot be only oppositional; it must maintain selective links with the state if it is to maintain any influence and deepen democratization. In democratic transitions, the new regime distinguishes itself by its commitment to the rule of law and democratic responsiveness, and requires new state-society relations based on principles of trust that emerge naturally over time. The crucial point, however, is that while popular mobilization may be necessary in response to an authoritarian regime, civil society actors must transform themselves during the transition as well, for otherwise important links with the state will fail to develop and democratization may not occur. This model provides few insights for rethinking new relations and risks reducing itself to either a depoliticized liberal-pluralism that emphasizes personal autonomy and little social engagement (as Vaclav Havel did in the mid-1990s), or a confrontational stance that remains wary of any state action.

The "self-limiting" revolutionary model underscores the importance of broad-based social mobilization, making social solidarity the primary desired norm. It shares with liberal-pluralist views skepticism toward the state, while it rejects the liberal demotion of collective action in favor of the private pursuit of satisfaction. Neither approach, however, satisfactorily explains how civil society actors can shape state policy and historical understanding in transitions. A more fruitful approach, I think, is found in the discourse theory model, which draws our attention to the importance of the deliberative force generated in the public sphere by civil society actors, and its influence on state practice and social discourse.

The Discourse Theory of Civil Society

In the discursive approach, civil society is conceived as a "network of associations that institutionalizes problem-solving discourses on questions of general interest inside the framework of organized public spheres" (Habermas 1996, 367). Through open-ended, public engagement with one another, myriad social groups form (or re-form) public opinions that shape and influence political elite behavior and state action. There are numerous mediating institutions (e.g., radio, television, newspapers, magazines, the Internet) that promote the proliferation of public opinion. The crucial contribution of this model is its theorization of the "public sphere." This is a domain in which civil society actors operate and is neither a formal institution nor organization, but rather a network where citizens (in a non-official capacity) can communicate information and contest differing views on issues of common interest, with the goal of ultimately shaping public doxa. A well-formed public sphere allows for the greatest possible participation and resists political and economic pressures that can disrupt free discourse, while privileging argumentation based on basic principles of status parity among participants. Importantly, any public issue is open to discussion. "Public discourse," argues Jean Cohen, "also has the important political purpose of controlling and influencing the formation of policy in the juridically public institutions of the state" (1999, 70).

The discursive approach is concerned only with those issues that are of distinctly public relevance; as such, civil society "refers to the structures of socialization, association, and organized forms of communication in the lifeworld to the extent that these are institutionalized or are in the process of being institutionalized" (J. Cohen and Arato 1992, ix). With its privileging of the public sphere, this model emphasizes the communicative power that flows from public deliberation. Unlike the liberal conception, however, the discourse model does not conceive of deliberation as the result of preformulated aggregate individual or group interests; its content is broader, and includes rethinking and debating basic social norms and ways of reckoning with the past. In this sense, then, it is also transformative of the participants. They must subject their opinions and beliefs to public scrutiny and debate, justify them in ways that appeal to common interests, reframe them as new criticisms, and then raise counterarguments. With these transformations, participants move toward achieving some degree of consensus on issues of public concern.

While this model has much in its favor, we should be wary of some of its rationalist pretensions. Critics have argued that cultural pluralism, economic inequality, institutionalized status differentiation, social conflict, and a highly contested social public sphere make the idea of consensus through public reason at best chimerical. In the context of transitional settings, where material and status differences can be more pronounced, the idea of an open public sphere seems even more vulnerable to these criticisms. We can draw some important lessons from the discursive approach, however, if we loosen some of its requirements. First, we should acknowledge that the theoretical distinction between "rational" and "emotional" speech, central to much rationalist deliberative theory (especially Jürgen Habermas's [1996]), is empirically unsustainable and normatively problematic. The elevation of rationality and demotion of affect not only misrepresents the nature of actual deliberation but assumes that the latter contributes nothing of value to discourse. By privileging "rational" modes of communication at the expense of other forms that may employ emotional appeal or rhetoric, this approach risks delegitimizing interlocutors before they can even participate in collective deliberation, thus circumscribing the domain of appropriate debate arbitrarily (Young 1996; Streich 2002; Dryzek 2005). Furthermore, the assumption that rational debate can result in uncoerced consensus rests on a suspect teleology; that is, an end goal that is particularly unlikely where collective identities are deeply divided and groups disagree not only about current interests but even basic moral orientations and historical understandings. Where there is so little in common, except perhaps for a shared mistrust, robust rational consensus of the kind endorsed by Habermas is probably unattainable.

A discourse model of civil society requires a more participatory model of discursive exchange that allows for other forms of communication, particularly if it is to retain relevance in deeply divided societies. Rather than require, or expect, rational deliberation through epistemically robust norms of argumentation and decision making among free, equal, and purely rational actors that would result in substantial consensus, we can use the discursive approach from a different vantage point; one that offers us a way of rethinking the importance of drawing attention to and debating the most important political and normative issues that transitional societies confront. That is, deliberation is ultimately the primary legitimate means of engaging one another over concerns of deep political importance: It is the sine qua non of democratic life. The discursive model draws attention to the centrality of a public sphere as the proper domain for formulating, assessing, and contesting concerns. One of the strengths of such a model is its insistence on the open-ended nature of public discussion, and the expectation that long-held beliefs be "tested" in a public forum and even transformed through continuous critique. The ultimate aim is to reach normatively acceptable compromises on the most contentious issues of public concern; that is, political compromises that recognize the importance of accountability, commit actors to presenting accurate accounts of past violence, include victims in deliberations and acknowledge them as fellow citizens of equal moral worth and dignity, promote mutual respect, and further the rule of law. In this sense, the

deliberative approach sketched here seeks to replace a politics of violence with a politics of discourse, but a public discourse that retains a
normative edge precisely through its commitment to these normative
concerns.

Jean Cohen and Andrew Arato have argued that the discourse
model emphasizes the importance of having associations whose internal structure is democratic. To the extent that civil society groups are
internally democratic, civil society as a whole becomes more democratic and processes of democratization become better anchored. Here
I wish to loosen this requirement, as it is clear that although internally
democratic organizations are desirable, their necessity is less clear. As
I discuss further, some organizations, like the Catholic Church in parts
of Latin America, have played extremely important roles in promoting
human rights and condemning abuse while remaining internally hierarchical. The correlation between internal structure and the institution's values is not as linear as Cohen and Arato argue. Nevertheless, it
is clear that, broadly speaking, social movements and civil society organizations represent a key element of "a vital, modern, civil society
and an important form of citizen participation in public life" (1992,
19). Particularly in transitional settings, what is needed is a civil society
constituted of myriad groups that are committed to principles of accountability, the recognition of the moral status of victims, investigation of the past, and the basic norms of democracy and the rule of law.
Thus, operating as "counter-hegemonic blocs of social movements," to
take a term from Nancy Fraser (1997, 86), these groups can serve important roles in resisting collective amnesia or revisionist, self-serving
histories.

The discourse model is sympathetic to Michnik's concern about
"self-limitation" (1985, 65). Civil society should not replace the market
nor the state as the sole domain of human activity. However, it breaks
with Michnik in rethinking civil society not as permanently opposed to
the state but instead connected to it through a series of mediating
spaces, such as political society, through which civil society can influence social dynamics and processes. Civil society actors and the state
become strongly oppositional when "these mediations fail or when the
institutions of economic and political society serve to insulate decision-
making and decision makers from the influence of social organizations,
initiatives and forms of political discussion" (J. Cohen and Arato 1992,

ix–x). Certainly, civil society cannot resolve fundamental social problems; hence the need to establish and maintain robust mediations with both political leaders and the state. But from the perspective of a theory of reconciliation, the public sphere ideally serves as the location for citizens to thematize and contest basic social values and policies related to the past. Habermas (1996) argues that through unconstrained communication (i.e., a public sphere with no limitations on rights of access and participation) a collective will forms, with civil society serving as a critical bulwark to state power and the legitimacy of (possibly limited and self-serving) norms that the latter promotes. Public will, reframed as public opinion, seeks to influence state action by identifying those issues that concern collective life. While Habermas's view perhaps sets a normative ideal that is too high for transitional contexts, we can argue that civil society has a democratizing role to play in transitions insofar as the formal deliberative institutions with decision-making power, such as the legislature, can be influenced by public discourse.

The discourse model emphasizes groups that are internally democratic, a point about which I have raised some concerns. Nevertheless, it shares with the oppositional approach a focus on a domain where citizens feel they have a stake in issues concerning the common good. Because plurality is a fact of modern political and social life, shared world views can no longer be taken for granted—a situation particularly pronounced in transitions—and norms of reciprocal respect and tolerance must play important roles for generating and maintaining social cohesion while also expanding the opportunities for meaningful recognition. The main point here, however, is that the multiplicity of groups must be committed to resolving differences through deliberation, and that civil society cannot substitute for the power of the state but rather should remain autonomous from the state while helping to shape elite policy.

Civil Society and Reconciliation

Using the somewhat reconstituted discourse model sketched above, we now turn to a discussion of the role civil society can play in fostering reconciliation. If civil society is to work positively under such fragile circumstances, that is, where the threat of a return to violence often seems likely, its participants must espouse an ethics of deliberation, respect, and tolerance without sacrificing the commitment to critically interrogating the past. Here I draw attention to several contributions civil society actors make before moving on to some limitations.

The most important contribution civil society can make to reconciliation is to foster public deliberation, a point central to thinkers such as David Crocker (1999). Civil society actors can move political discourses based on exclusion and threats of violence away from reductionist, zero-sum argumentation. Although J. Cohen and Arato do not explicitly link rational discourse with reconciliation and broader social regeneration in this manner, their notion of communicative activity and its theoretical presuppositions are conducive to the development of respect, mutual recognition, and rule of law. A politics based on argumentation and criticism at the very least rests on minimal respect, as it places limits on the kinds of strategies admissible in political debate. It requires, for example, that one give reasons for one's beliefs and arguments, rather than resort to the threat of force to "convince" an opponent. Deliberation rests on the assumption that one's interlocutor enjoys at least some basic rights that cannot be abrogated. J. Cohen and Arato stipulate more stringent requirements: A commitment to deliberation necessitates certain procedural safeguards such as ensuring that participation is as inclusive as possible and free from "deformations of wealth, power and social status" (J. Cohen and Arato 1992, 186) and that arguments be justified by reasons that can in principle be addressed to all. Thus, decision-making processes produce collectively authored results. While I have argued for flexibility in the rationalist strictures of this approach to deliberation, the core argument—that a commitment to reciprocally endorsed norms of contestation are central to civil society—is important in several respects. It moves us toward achieving *respect* among citizens, since open deliberation is fundamentally inclusive of everyone who could potentially be affected by the outcome, and at the very least accepts their claims to participation. Additionally, deliberation includes within it a defense of *tolerance*, since public deliberation is always about debate and contestation, and differences of opinion must be tolerated (i.e., not censored or suppressed) if deliberation is to be sustained, though of course they can be criticized and repudiated through further debate. Indeed, in a deeper sense, deliberation can promote a form of public moral education by teaching the importance of values like democracy, basic human rights, how to listen to others with whom we disagree, and how to accept deep moral disagreements without turning to oppression. By engaging with others we partly rehumanize them and come to see aspects of them that we see in ourselves; that is, we extend a kind of moral recognition. Moral education is based in ongoing practice and can be reinforced though deliberation and mutual engagement. Without sustained engagements with others and without learning how to listen to contending voices, moral development is unlikely to occur.[2] Deliberation also means a respect for the *rule of law*, as it rests on legitimized procedures for fair and open participation that are the scaffolding for vigorous but peaceful political life. Respect and tolerance among citizens and respect for the rule of law strengthen one another over time. Respect and tolerance are reciprocal norms (i.e., all participants must endorse them for their actualization), and institutions of the rule of law become firmly anchored only when citizens and elites endorse public deliberation, with its attendant expectations of renouncing violence, as the primary mechanism for resolving disputes.

Second, civil society can inform the *definition of categories* of victims, perpetrators, and bystanders. Political violence leaves behind numerous victims, but disagreements about who is and is not a victim can persist long after the violence is over. As I discussed in Chapter 1, the issue of victim recognition works along several axes: material-symbolic and individual-collective. Legally, a victim is anyone whose rights were violated; that is, the law constructs and categorizes victims according to its own internal logic of rights, duties, and remedies. Although this is certainly a political-interpretative process insofar as some persons are interpellated as victims while others are not, the issue becomes significantly more complex as we move from individual victims to family members (or even entire communities) who may or may not be considered victims, to the various consequences that flow from this. For instance, if an entire group is defined as a victim, such as an ethnic group, we are highlighting some common features that give salience to their victim status, aside from the fact of having been violated.[3] Take, for example, the repression of indigenous groups in rural Guatemala. The state instituted a policy of systematic violence against indigenous communities that was framed as part of its anti-insurgency campaign. The indigenous were seen as subversive and treasonous persons who had forfeited their basic rights. In a sense, then, the Maya indigenous community as a whole was a victim of state terror. However, some political leaders have claimed that though violations occurred on a relatively large scale in some areas, this was a result of "excesses" rather than an actual policy. Where authoritarian enclaves persist, and especially in situations where individuals of the previous regime continue to serve in the current government, there is a tendency to reframe past abuses as "excesses," without interrogating the structural and systematic aspects of violence. Rather, past policies (and their consequences) are framed as either necessary or unfortunate but otherwise unrepresentative instances of atrocity. Civil society actors can resist these accounts and work to expand the category of victimization to include those close to them and others who were affected by their loss. Admittedly, this kind of discourse can be generalized to the point of including all of society as the victim, with the consequent loss of real distinctions between actual victims and perpetrators, so that the terms lose their normative content. The risk is that responsibility is shifted away from actors to "history," where persons were "forced" to do what they did. But the importance of civil society lies in its ability to define and elaborate different categories of victims, and thus ensure that those groups who have been marginalized or otherwise ignored are given the *moral recognition* they deserve from the public. Indeed, victim recognition requires more than state redistributive policies; it also necessitates efforts at recasting victims as fellow citizens with moral claims to respect. The state and political elites, of course, play a central role in this; however, civil society can deepen this goal of *victim recognition* by ensuring that victims are not simply ignored or overlooked in official accounts of the past.

Civil society actors can also catalyze debate about responsibility and perpetrators. They can highlight the complexity of this category and show how juridical guilt does not exhaust the category of perpetrator. Groups like the Association of the Relatives of the Disappeared in Peru (Asociación Nacional de Familiares de Secuestrados y Detenidos-Desaparecidos [ANFASEP] 2002) have played crucial roles in ensuring that culpability is not conceived as belonging only to a select few. Rather, they have shown how "perpetrator" should include material and intellectual authors of crimes as well as the members of the bureaucratic apparatus who carried out state terror. In conjunction with other human rights groups, they have initiated campaigns to bring attention to the responsibility of the state and Marxist guerrillas in the perpetration of crimes. The Association for Human Rights (Asociación pro Derechos Humanos [APRODEH] 2009) and the Andean Commission of Jurists (Comisión Andina de Juristas [CAJ] 2009), two other Peruvian human rights organizations, have been instrumental in generating public debate about the extent of violations through workshops, publications and, in the former case, grassroots efforts at informing citizens about the complicity of some elites in violence and the corruption that fostered it. Maintaining a broader conception of who is a perpetrator, one that includes others such as high-level bureaucrats who facilitate the commission of wrongs, forces elites and society in general to confront the past and their place in it. In this respect, civil society can deepen public reflection on responsibility and guilt beyond that found in a juridical setting.

Perpetrator and bystander are not always easily distinguished from one another, however. As we move away from individual juridical culpability we encounter a kind of moral responsibility that is characterized by a "responsibility for inaction," or sin of omission. The Association of the Relatives of the Disappeared in Peru, as well as other survivor groups, have drawn attention to the urban elites' lack of interest in the suffering of poor indigenous peasants during that country's civil war. For some, the fact that leaders were in a social position where they could have publicly denounced state violations against peasants but chose not to underscores their moral culpability. Certainly, it is often difficult to know who is a perpetrator or a morally responsible bystander: If leaders support a war with awful consequences for the poor, does this make them perpetrators or accomplices of some other sort? Often there are substantial numbers of persons who benefited from the violence and chose not to denounce it. They fall outside the normal purview of justice but without their tacit—and sometimes explicit—support, the violence would likely be lessened, in either intensity or duration. How do we understand the responsibility of morally compromised bystanders, those whose guilt extends beyond the juridical, and how do civil society groups contribute to this understanding?

Karl Jaspers uses the term *political guilt*: a kind of guilt that attaches itself to all citizens who tolerated what was done by the state in their name. According to Jaspers's rather strong formulation, everyone "is co-responsible for the way he [*sic*] is governed" (1961, 31), a position echoed by groups as diverse as the Peruvian Association of History and Reconciliation and the Argentine Alliance for Refounding the Nation to emphasize the broad responsibility that all of society carries. While Jaspers attempts to draw some distinctions between different forms of guilt, political guilt is perhaps too expansive and rough, since it fails to articulate how different individuals can be responsible in different ways, and how responsibility at this level may be better thought of on a moral continuum. It levels differences between perpetrators and others by extending responsibility to everyone, thus erasing specific perpetrator responsibility. Used in this way, civil society actors not only misrepresent responsibility but also distort history. However, a focus on the complexity of responsibility and the ways in which it goes beyond juridical conceptualization can open a space for more nuanced—and difficult—reflections on the extent of popular support for previous policies and the moral weight that this carries. Will this promote reconciliation? Clearly, any effort at widening debate about responsibility is likely to be divisive, at least in the short term. It can heighten antagonisms between former enemies and degenerate into political theater meant to tarnish one's opponents, rather than reckon with the past and its place in the present. But in the risks of such an endeavor lie its strengths. Maintaining an open debate about responsibility can shake complacent and self-serving historical accounts by placing those stories—and the population at large—under a critical eye. It reframes debate by resituating moral responsibility squarely in the center of discussion, and redirects attention toward the actual suffering of victims, the violation of their rights, and the moral burdens that society as a whole may carry. Civil society actors contribute to this by keeping alive these debates about responsibility and resist efforts at simplifying culpability. Indeed, the introduction of the bystander as a moral category reduces the ability of elites as well as common citizens to distance themselves from their history and moral obligations.

A third important contribution concerns civil society's ability to *interrogate and resist apologist historical accounts that justify past violations*. Nietzsche (1997) defended the importance of critical historical inquiry as a way of investigating and ultimately destabilizing those histories that are unreflective (i.e., unaware of or uninterested in examining their own assumptions) and serve the interests of power, a point discussed in Chapter 2. The importance of this critical history cannot be overstated. Civil society can critique existing narratives to weaken and even replace elite accounts that mask their own ends and interests. In Peru, the human rights umbrella group National Coordinator for Human Rights (Coordinadora Nacional de Derechos Humanos [CNDDHH] 2009) plays a pivotal role in disseminating information on human rights abuses with the explicit goal of overturning elite interpretations and "raising the consciousness of the population."[4] The CNDDHH has published numerous large reports and shorter, glossy booklets and pamphlets for wide distribution contesting the inevitability and necessity of abuses (an argument often made by combatants on all sides), and articulating an alternate historical interpretation that focuses on human rights abuses and the disproportionate suffering that fell on rural populations. The goal here is twofold: (1) to trace how the Shining Path's crude Marxist philosophy of history and the state's national security doctrine both provided ideological justification for atrocities, and (2) to re-situate victims at the center of discussions about the war, forcing a reconsideration of existing interpretive frameworks that see the conflict as nothing more than a civil war between armed sides. This re-situation provides at least some form of public recognition of victims.

The CNDDHH campaign to discredit past narratives has been echoed in Timor-Leste. The Timorese NGO Perkumpulan Hak (2008) has worked extensively to highlight how Indonesian supremacist ideology gave legitimacy to the state's violent policies. Hak and other NGOs have continued to document how this ideology shaped the perceptions of the Timorese by creating substantial challenges to developing reciprocal moral respect.

Some civil society groups have focused on truth telling by mounting investigative projects to detail and publicize government abuse. In Brazil, Chile, and Guatemala, human rights and church groups catalogued violations and later published their findings. A group of Brazilian investigators secretly worked with the World Council of Churches and the Archbishop of São Paolo to copy hundreds of thousands of pages of judicial testimony of prisoners who were tortured. Smuggled out of the country during the dictatorship, the records became the heart of the report *Brazil: Never Again* (1985), which analyzed the state's use of torture over a decade and a half. During Pinochet's rule in Chile, the Roman Catholic Church's Vicaría de la Solidaridad collected thousands of judicial records on disappearances. Later, these records played a central role in Chile's truth commission report. In Guatemala, the Archdiocese of Guatemala City (1998) created the Project for the Recovery of Historical Memory (REMHI) to document atrocities committed by both sides in the civil war. As Melissa Ballengee (2000) notes, REMHI's work was pivotal in providing additional information and documentation that was missing from the official Historical Clarification Commission (Comisión para el Esclarecimiento Histórico [CEH] 1999), which was hampered by financial constraints and a limited focus. REMHI's final report, *Guatemala: Never Again*, was disseminated widely around the country through public presentations, radio, and print, enjoying a much larger audience than would otherwise be possible in a society with significant illiteracy. The report estimated 150,000 deaths and another 50,000 disappearances during the civil war, holding government forces and their civilian militias responsible for approximately 90 percent of the violations and the insurgents responsible for roughly 5 percent (with the rest undetermined). REMHI was crucial for bringing public attention to the scope of violations and countering the justifications and lies of the military elite. In these and other examples, civil society groups have produced historical accounts that have challenged widely held beliefs and contributed to ongoing debates about complicity, collective identity, and obligations to victims.

Fourth, civil society groups can reframe historical memory by *encouraging the state to establish public memorials about the past*. In an important respect, monuments and memorials are reified memory; they freeze public conceptions about common identity and give meaning to, if not create, a shared past. As markers of political violence and the experiences associated with it, these public works provide a locus around which a society can confront its history. The Argentine civil society group Seré Association for Promoting Memory and Life (2008) has used a former torture center as a synecdoche for the crimes of the previous regime, where the center itself assumes the status of symbol or icon for violations. Focusing on the torture center shows an alternate history of state terror that gives lie to previous official histories that minimized state atrocity and treated victims as traitors. Ugandan groups like the Gulu District NGO Forum (2009) have worked extensively to establish memorial sites for the Acholi people, and in Cambodia, the former torture site Tuol Sleng S-21 (2009) is today a museum documenting the atrocities committed by the Khmer Rouge.

Finally, civil society actors may give *technical and policy recommendations* for restructuring institutions most responsible for violations. As Naomi Roht-Arriaza (2002) has argued, professional groups such as lawyers associations, scholarly institutes, and rights organizations with specific technical knowledge can provide useful assistance to the state in restructuring sectors of the government and achieving institutional reform. Consider the reform of the legal order: Groups such as the Peruvian CAJ have provided detailed recommendations on revamping the courts by instituting stronger chains of accountability to civilian leaders, greater transparency in the operation of the judiciary, and removing the most unfit judges from power. They have worked closely with certain sectors of the government, most notably the Ministry of the Public (in charge of prosecutions and rights violations) to strengthen the rule of law, and have provided technical reports on that country's "antiterrorism legislation," an instrument used by the previous government to facilitate the commission of numerous human rights abuses.[5] Similar professional organizations provide training programs to professionalize members of the judiciary and security forces. In Argentina, the Center for Legal and Social Studies (Centro de Estudios Legales y Sociales [CELS] 2009), has conducted numerous training workshops for the judiciary and published a series of reports on reform that have had an important impact in judicial restructuring. The Santiago-based Commission on Human Rights (Comisión de Derechos Humanos 2009), an NGO founded by attorneys in 1978, continues to give legal advice on restructuring the military and police in Chile. In Sierra Leone, the Campaign for Good Governance ([CGG] 2009) has developed important policy recommendations on security sector reform, which has enhanced women's access to voting and reduced corruption in state institutions. Much of its success has come from its command of technical issues relating to government reform, placing it among a relatively small number of Sierra Leonean NGOs with professional training and experience on complex reform issues. The CGG's combination of technical expertise and ability to publicize instances of state corruption and abuse has made it an influential civil society actor in Freetown.[6]

None of this is to say that these organizations should replace the state in providing services or administering the security apparatus. Rather than promoting the devolution of state power to civil society and the privatization of governmental obligations, civil support for institutional reform seeks to enhance the efficacy of the state and guarantee greater democratic responsiveness and accountability. We should nevertheless avoid placing too great an expectation on the influence of civil assistance: These organizations cannot guarantee state reform or ensure that their recommendations are heeded. Often, their greatest impact stems from their ability to monitor reforms, provide policy recommendations, and watch for continued state abuses. But professional groups can contribute to public deliberation by publicly recommending needed reforms and thereby signaling the importance of state responsiveness to public accountability and input.

Reconciliation and the Challenges of Civil Society

Civil society's contributions to reconciliation are important, but limited. There are a number of limitations that should bring pause to those who identify civil society as the fundamental wellspring of reconciliation. Its transformative role as a site for debate and democratic practice can be hampered by other social dynamics, thus weakening its critical potential and contributions to social change. And it can only *aid* the pursuit of accountability and recognition of victims, as David Crocker notes: "Government has an indispensable role with respect to some forms of prosecution, punishment, investigation, compensation and commemoration" (2001, 390–391). Even civil society's greatest contribution, the promotion of an ethics of deliberation in an open public sphere, has a limited ability to resolve significant problems without state action. The state is necessary for securing these goals, and without elite and institutional commitment it is unlikely that the public will succeed in achieving reconciliation.

Debates over history are rarely polite affairs, particularly when groups have their basic values and very sense of identity riding on the outcome. In such a context, it is not unlikely that exclusivist ideologies will develop within civil society that strategically downplay a complex history and evade responsibility for crimes and in some instances shift the blame on opponents. The very liberties central to a healthy civil society, such as free speech and open debate, can become mechanisms to distort and even dismiss historical facts and experiences. Under circumstances where the public sphere simply becomes a venue for political combat, groups are driven to provide apologist accounts that ignore or minimize the complexity of past experiences and substitute simple narratives for complex events. Simplification, then, is a danger common to not only elite state discourse but also civil society.

Indeed, a civil society fractured by deep differences with radically opposed historical understandings is unlikely to sustain the norms of respect and tolerance that are needed for social stability and cohesion. Without at least some shared understandings of the past (i.e., without some shared narratives) society will remain as torn as it was before the violence, as in Bosnia and Herzegovina today (Verdeja 2007). The old distinctions that played a pivotal role during the violence are rewritten in public debate, with in-groups and out-groups occupying the same positions they did in the past. In some cases polarization can hinder open debate to such an extent that authoritarian enclaves remain in place, ensconced in the same stories that work self-servingly to give them the legitimacy they seek. A recent World Bank (2005) study found that in the aftermath of conflict civil society organizations frequently worked to *reinforce* political divisions and mistrust by manipulating past events to strengthen sectoral interests while ignoring the need to promote open deliberation. This, of course, is surprising only to thinkers who equate civil society with progressive and inclusive politics (one can read Habermas's [1996] stronger formulations in this way). Such a shattered civil society is hardly *civil*, and in any case contributes nothing to a shared exploration of responsibility and reconciliation.

I emphasize, however, that we should be wary of treating opposition as illegitimate. The public sphere, and democratic politics in general, should be as open and inclusive as possible, and this means tolerating groups with whom we strongly disagree. I am not arguing that contestation is permissible only when we agree with the groups involved, as this effectively means tolerance in name only. Rather, we should draw a distinction, at least conceptually, between those groups that are willing to respect democratic and peaceful politics but nevertheless harbor radically different views and may even support the previous regime, and those who reject the very premises of the democratic game and are little more than spoilers who are unwilling to compromise. Spoilers exist at both ends of the political spectrum; they may include those who are unabashed in their defense of the most offensive past policies and those who will brook no compromise (or even the possibility of coexistence) with defenders of the past. Spoilers, in other words, includes the most unrepentant apologists as well as adamant retributive absolutists who view anything short of "full" justice as unacceptable. If politics is to replace violence, then citizens must accept that compromise and coexistence with former enemies are unavoidable. My concern with oppositional spoiler politics is that it does not generate values of respect for the rule of law, tolerance, deliberation, and other norms that are at the core of a functioning democratic order. Under these conditions state authority risks paralysis through its constant confrontations with an oppositional civil society, and the public sphere loses it crucial capacity to nurture debate and reach acceptable compromises. Communicative power and argumentation become tools in the search for the tactical domination of opponents, and the possibility of solidarity or even mutual respect disappears in the face of increasingly virulent discourse. Relations between the state and society, and within society itself, are destroyed.

An alternative possibility is simply that public discourse becomes so drained of analytical and normative potential that apologist doxa remains supreme, and the communicative power of a critically engaged civil society disappears. Rather than sustaining counter-hegemonic discourses, social movements disappear due to lack of public interest and citizens seek a more privatized, less overtly political public order. In such a context, a weakened civil society ceases to try influencing political elites or resisting policies of official forgetting. The critical resources at the center of a deliberative civil society are no longer sufficient to mobilize continued interest in accountability, victim recognition, and truth telling. Tomás Moulian (1998) gave a fascinating, if dispiriting, reading of Chile in the 1990s along these lines, showing how apart from a relatively small group of highly active human rights organizations and pro-military associations, many Chileans preferred to put the past behind them and place their energy in the emerging consumerist culture. This second outcome bears more than a resemblance to the defenses on historical oblivion discussed in Chapter 1. And it faces the same moral challenges. Precisely because the public sphere is such a crucial site for resisting self-serving elite calls for letting "bygones be bygones," civil society's loss to apathy and disengagement is a powerful blow to meaningful reconciliation.

Under either condition of a radically oppositional or politically weak civil society it is not uncommon to find existing enclaves of authoritarian power. In the first scenario, authoritarian blocs are often able to stall or derail efforts at historical reckoning or accountability, whereas in the latter situation authoritarian leaders may step into the vacuum left by an engaged civil society and make compelling public cases to simply "move on." Under the former condition, however, it unlikely that mutual respect will gain much support, precisely because a significant portion of the population refuses to engage in morally relevant issues. In the latter condition, of course, victims will continue to encounter forms of misrecognition and continued authoritarian power that will hamper democratic governance.

These points underscore the fundamental difficulty of normatively overburdening civil society. What is clear is that civil society can contribute to reconciliation, but its fragility means that we should not expect more from it that it can achieve. It is a necessary, though insufficient, level for reconciliation. Its importance stems from its potential for generating communicative power with which to pressure the state to address past wrongs and push for greater recognition of victims. Furthermore, it is in civil society that the general normative concepts of rule of law and mutual respect are nurtured and deepened. It is here where a politics of deliberation can replace a politics of violence, citizens can learn through practice the importance of human rights, and where they can embark on the difficult project of achieving a just reconciliation. If reconciliation is to occur, it must be deepened at this level.

6 Interpersonal Reconciliation

Societal reconciliation is, in its most basic sense, about reconciling *individuals*, thus any theory of reconciliation must at some point face the difficult task of how to connect social and institutional processes of reconstruction with the personal dynamics between individuals. At this level, issues of repentance, acknowledgment, forgiveness, pardon, and vengeance occupy the moral space between victims, bystanders, and perpetrators. We are tasked with identifying which responses are morally legitimate, which are not, and (in a more theoretical-reflexive sense) what the limits of such an inquiry are. There is a danger here: A model of reconciliation should not reduce itself to the proposition that achieving broad-based social reconciliation requires every individual to reconcile him- or herself with the past and fellow citizens. It is not only empirically impossible but it is illiberal to ask for a degree of mutual acceptance that is achievable only through ideological coercion, and if so, it would most likely be a superficial reconciliation. Such an approach also represents a kind of reductive functionalism that places all possibility of reconciliation on individual behavior while downplaying its institutional, political, and social aspects. It is not the case that all individual perpetrators must be stigmatized and held accountable and all victims recognized individually for reconciliation to take root.

Consequently, any discussion of reconciliation at this level is complex, for it requires a noncoercive understanding of social life that distances itself from both vengeance and an imposed forgiveness. It requires a great deal of sensitivity to the issues of individual transformation of all the actors involved—many of these affected by the specifics of personal experience with violence—without dismissing the importance of other social levels. In this chapter, I trace several types of interpersonal relations that can occur at this level, drawing on my interviews with survivors in Chile and Bosnia-Herzegovina as well as the extensive literature on this topic, and ultimately I defend one type of interpersonal relation based on reciprocal respect.[1] Because this is a normative discussion I do not cover in any systematic detail the broad social psychological literature on what victims feel and desire, since what they seek may not necessarily be morally defensible, even though it is understandable. In a recent study, for example, researchers found that even if perpetrators pay reparations and accept guilt for their actions, many victims continue to feel insulted unless violators publicly express self-abasing shame. Here, *guilt* is associated with acceptance of the wrongness of an action and may lead to an apology or reparation while *shame* involves the perception that "one's core self is bad" and is thus a significantly stronger expression of self-abasement (Giner-Sorolla et al. 2008; Smith et al. 2002). While resentment, anger, and similar emotions are not morally empty—a point I address below—these findings suggest that what survivors want may sometimes be morally problematic, and thus any account of morally acceptable interpersonal reconciliation must rest on a set of justifications wider than particular victim desires, though these should of course be taken seriously.

Three Views

We can discuss three general views, or paths, that relations between perpetrators and victims may take. They range from the notion of forgiveness to vengeance, with the latter understood as the morally justified action that identifies punishment as a necessary and prime integrative mechanism for achieving peace among former enemies. I endorse an alternate satisfactory notion, one that is characterized by mutual respect, yet understood in a particular manner. As I hope to show, this middle conception is not merely a mitigated synthesis of

forgiveness and vengeance but rather a distinct alternative. I then outline the relation of this level to the others by indicating how it is an
important element for broader reconciliation.

Vengeance and Resentment

Revenge is often understood as little more than a perverse, irrational
emotional reaction to harm (C. Lewis 1957). Jonathan Glover (1970,
145) has remarked that many see it as an immoral union of "hatred and
pleasure," and Robert Nozick (1981, 366) acknowledges its status as
the "primitive view" of justice. Following mass violence, however, survivors may consider revenge appropriate for a variety of reasons, including the basic sense that perpetrators "deserve" to be punished
for their crimes. Indeed, when we demand revenge, we are demanding
that a violator be punished for some harm done. Jeffrie Murphy captures the intuitive sense of moral appropriateness encapsulated in vengeance: "I believe that most typical, decent, mentally healthy people
have a kind of commonsense approval of some righteous hatred and
revenge" and that "common morality" sees revenge as morally appropriate (1995, 136).[2] For Murphy, revenge is at its core tied to punishment: It gives perpetrators their just deserts for the unjustified and
willful harms they inflicted on others.

The driving forces of revenge are the emotions of anger and
resentment. Part of the difficulty here is that these emotions have become morally suspect and are often perceived as irrational or otherwise damaging to those who hold them (and in any case incompatible
with reconciliation, "moving forward," "letting the past go," and so on).
This has it roots, I think, in Nietzsche (1989) and Scheler's (1973)
highly influential accounts of *ressentiment* as a form of self-obsession
and pity animated by spite and malicious envy toward those of higher
social status, which often reflects an irrational obsession with the past.
This reading of resentment has effectively collapsed any sense of morally defensible outrage into indefensible feelings of hostility, reflecting
moral stuntedness. This is unfortunate, as resentment can tell us much
more about a person—and about morality—than Nietzsche (1989)
suggests. A much more sensitive and insightful understanding has been
put forth by Thomas Brudholm (2008, 11), who centers resentment not
on how one feels but in the ways in which these feelings are articulated

in terms of "injustice, injury or violation."[3] To the extent that resentment reflects a concern for one's moral value, holding on to it and refusing to forgive one's abuser is not categorically irrational or morally blameworthy; it may be morally defensible. While in Chile, I met Cristina H., a torture survivor who for many years sought to defend her right not to forgive to her family and friends. She went through terrible experiences and was insulted by the notion that the burden was on her to forgive her violators. "How can I forgive those people who harmed me? What they did to me was inexplicable, indefensible! To forgive them would be to say that it is OK, that I can move beyond the injuries. It would be to say that I don't take myself seriously and they can do whatever they want. I am a person, with rights, and they should be punished for harming me!" A resentful person need not be crazed with vengeance or obsessed with the past. While Cristina still undergoes therapy, she has also become a successful businesswoman with a family and finds numerous ways to channel her impressive energy and intellect. But she refuses to equate "moving on" with forgiveness and is adamant that her resentment is a reflection of her self-respect. Indeed, to be a person, morally speaking, means seeing oneself at least partly as an end in oneself, and resenting moral injuries and their perpetrators is a sign that one takes this moral status seriously. To relinquish the desire for punishment for a serious wrong is to deny one's own value as an agent with moral status; such relinquishment indicates that one neither considers oneself worthy of moral respect nor a bearer of rights. In a somewhat similar, though non-deontological vein, Aristotle also tied the feelings of resentment and vengeance to a proper sense of self, arguing that

> the man who is angry on the right occasions and with those he should and also in the right manner and at the right time and for the right length of time is praised. . . . The deficiency, whether an inirascibility of a sort or whatever it might be, is blamed. For those who do not get angry on the occasions they should and in the manner they should, and when they should, and with those they should, are thought to be fools; for they are thought to be insensitive and without pain, and since they do not get angry, they are thought not to be disposed to defend themselves. But it is slavish for a man to submit to be

besmirched or to allow it against those who are close to him. (1984, 1125b–1126a)

For Cristina, Brudholm, and Aristotle resentment and the desire for vengeance it animates are neither inappropriate nor irrational; rather they are understandable and legitimate moral expressions. Robert Solomon goes so far as to locate it at the center of justice. "Vengeance is the emotion of 'getting even,' putting the world back in balance." Justice "begins not with Socratic insights but with the promptings of some basic emotions, among them envy, jealousy, and resentment, a sense of being personally cheated or neglected, and the desire to get even" (1990, 293). Solomon may be correct to claim that resentment and desires for revenge may be at the center of demands for justice, though the danger of justice degenerating into cycles of "righteous" violence should give us pause in endorsing the moral appropriateness of vengeance. Solomon holds nothing back when he states that "if resentment has a desire, it is in its extreme form the total annihilation, prefaced by the utter humiliation, of its target—though the vindictive imagination of resentment is such that even that might not be good enough" (1990, 266).

The desire for revenge following mass violence is, of course, expected. Victims understandably want to see their tormentors punished.[4] More importantly for our purposes, I think resentment and the desire for revenge can be, at least in principle, morally defended. Here, however, I distinguish a bit further between two different conceptions of punishment, echoing an earlier discussion in Chapter 2. There is institutionalized punishment, bounded by clear rules, procedures, and protections, and the wild justice carried out by individuals that can quickly degenerate into reciprocal violence. The point here is not that the desire for revenge—much less the expression of resentment—is necessarily immoral or uncivilized, because the desire itself stems from the recognition that moral injuries should be punished and the moral worth of victims require acknowledgment. I agree with this as far as it goes. The point, rather, is that placing justice in the private domain (that is, taking justice into one's "own hands," so to speak) reduces the morally defensible response of punishment to little more than the reactionary infliction of pain. Without laws and procedures limiting it, the demand for vengeance can become unyielding and escalate into open violence. As Solomon states, "If resentment has a desire, it is in its extreme form the total annihilation" of the opponent (1990, 266). Even short of the desire for total annihilation, revenge can easily degenerate into violence. One person I spoke with in Sarajevo, Mahir P., told me about how his Muslim family had been violently driven from Mostar during the war by Bosnian Croat forces. It was clear from speaking with him that the war still consumed him, and he spent much of his time thinking about private vengeance against Croats—any Croats. Mahir said, "I am furious every day. I hate the Croats. I recognize that this is unhealthy, in some way, but I can't let go. I simply hate these people who did this to us, and I doubt I'll ever change. I think of hurting the first Croat I see all of the time." Not only is this psychologically unhealthy, but under certain circumstances Mahir and others like him can act on these attitudes by carrying out new violence against real or perceived enemies (the generalization to "the Croats" is typical; broad negative stereotyping is a necessary component of mass violence). It is interesting to note that Mahir actively speaks of vengeance, whereas Cristina accepts that more violence will not bring her any peace. What she means to hold onto is a sense of justified resentment, not the right to seek out her abusers and personally harm them. She accepts that the courts are the proper space for accountability, and though she admitted to despairing over whether her perpetrators will ever see a courtroom, Cristina recognized that allowing individuals to carry out their own private justice reproduces the lawlessness of the previous regime, with victims now the victimizers.

Forgiveness

What, then, of forgiveness? Forgiveness means many things to many people, and I am unconvinced that there is a "true" objective form that holds for all societies and situations. The proliferation of theories on the concept seems to bear this out (Walker 2006). There are, however, certain elements that are shared across understandings including the emphasis on overcoming resentment, bitterness, and anger, and forswearing vengeance and laying the ground for a new future sworn of violence. In its most traditional Christian formulation, for example, forgiveness is understood as a duty, as Jesus commands one to forgive "till seventy times seven" (Matthew 18:22). Forgiving not only allows one to let go of pain and recast future relations; it also reinforces the idea of fraternal love that is at the core of Christianity. Indeed, some theologians such as Martin Marty (1998) and Desmond Tutu (1999) have presented forgiveness as a principle ethos of the Christian faith (Botman and Petersen 1997). It is a righteous practice that promotes the love of one's enemies. Others, such as Jacques Derrida (2001), argue for a secular forgiveness that is both unconditional and noninstrumental; one can forgive only what is unforgivable and it should be done for no extrinsic reasons (Verdeja 2004). Psychologists Robert Enright, Suzanne Freedman, and Julio Rique understand forgiveness as "a willingness to abandon one's right to resentment, negative judgment, and indifferent behavior toward one who unjustly injures us, while fostering undeserved qualities of compassion, generosity, and even love toward him or her" (1998, 46). They claim that "The offended may unconditionally forgive regardless of the other person's current attitude or behaviors toward the offended, because forgiving is one person's volitional response to another" (1998, 47). Such an understanding clearly rests on the transformative power of forgiveness, with its emphasis on the qualities of "compassion, generosity, and even love." In fact, it is remarkable for its insistence that the offender's repentance and apology are not even necessary.

Forgiveness is often cast as a more fundamental embrace of one's enemy, or "positive mutual affirmation," in the words of Donald Shriver (1997, 8). The objective is to combine "realism with hope," which emphasizes the distinctly practical relevance of forgiveness in a world torn asunder. Indeed, forgiveness is eminently of this world, and not an abstract concept for philosophers or saints.

While there are some differences among them, all of these approaches share several key points.[5] First, they conceive of forgiveness as the abandonment of resentment and hatred toward one's violator. Second, forgiveness becomes the primary way for achieving a fundamental transformation of both victim and perpetrator, allowing for the emergence of a new relationship between the two that is no longer anchored in the past. It is a transformative faculty. And not only is it transformative; it is morally superior to mere tolerance, indifference, or resentment because only forgiveness provides the possibility of a shared future that does justice to memory while eschewing vengeance. Finally, all of these thinkers emphasize the practicality of forgiveness.

Rather than placing it solely in the province of theologians, forgiveness should play a central role in political and personal life, especially following mass violence.

How extensive is forgiveness likely to be? Without doubt, some persons will forgive even the most awful acts committed against them or their loved ones. Indeed, we should not declare a priori when survivors can and cannot forgive. Suleyman L. explicitly forgave the murderers of his family, who were killed outside of Bihać in northwestern Bosnia, telling me, "It is necessary that I forgive these soldiers, for this is the proper thing to do. I realize that they have not come forth to seek my forgiveness, but I do so anyhow." Maria Helena C.'s brother was tortured by the Chilean military, and while she knows the perpetrators and they have not asked for her forgiveness, she forgave them anyhow, stating, "I am a Christian, and thus I must forgive. It is hard, very hard. But my faith directs me to do so, and I believe that by forgiving them someday they will come to see the wrongness of their actions." Some will forgive unconditionally, moved by a deep faith or other moral resource, others will demand certain conditions such as a show of contrition, and yet others will refuse to forgive under any circumstances. Forgiveness is ultimately the decision of the individual. But the likelihood of forgiveness becoming a generalized practice in transitions—at least forgiveness of the deeply transformative type discussed above—is probably rather low. Many survivors do not want to forgive but rather seek recognition, truth, and (often) retributive justice, if not outright revenge. A more satisfactory normative approach would leave open the possibility of forgiving while identifying other responses that are compatible with moral respect. Indeed, the real problem is not with forgiveness as such but with the problematic way in which these discussions are often formulated; that is, pitting the moral superiority of forgiveness against vengeance as if there were no other defensible alternatives. Berel Lang imagines a world without forgiveness as "less than human—one where resentment and vengeance would not only have their day, but would also continue to have it, day after day" (Govier 2002, 42). Tutu shares this, arguing, "Forgiveness is an absolute necessity for continued human existence" (1998, xiii). But is this truly the case? Again, this partly depends on what is meant by forgiveness, whether it is requires substantial inner transformation or simply a recognition of the need to let go of poisonous feelings of anger. For Lang, as for Shriver, Tutu, and others, forgiveness is more like the former, leaving us with two fundamental choices: (1) commit oneself to the difficult process of forgiveness with the ultimate goal of securing a deep transformation of both victim and perpetrator, or (2) risk falling into paralyzing despair or obsession with vengeance. But this overlooks the variety of forms of interaction that are short of forgiveness yet significantly deeper than mere coexistence and which are morally defensible. It also establishes a rather substantial requirement for reconciliation because if interpersonal forgiveness is part of a *theory* of reconciliation, we risk placing an immense burden on all citizens.

Many victims may feel that their violators should not be forgiven and they argue this sentiment morally. Cristina H.'s passionate defense of not forgiving shows how rejecting a hasty forgiveness is a moral claim, thus signaling to society that she sees herself as a moral agent with self-worth and dignity. But she is also clear that she has been able to move forward with her life and has renounced any interest in seeking personal payback. Nevertheless, Cristina bristles at the idea that she should forgive for the sake of society, stating that "those who want us to forgive for the sake of everyone are hardly speaking for victims; they are often the killers, or at least were complicit in supporting Pinochet." Of course, many people calling for forgiveness are simply trying to articulate the need to avoid a return to violence; they are not necessarily apologists for dictators. But it is also clear that expecting a victim to overcome resentment and "leave the past behind" for the sake of solidarity does little to convince survivors that society takes them seriously.

We should pause before accepting forgiveness—at least transformative forgiveness—as the prime way of securing reconciliation. Embracing it as the fundamental moral response to violence disregards legitimate anger and resentment while placing a burden on victims that they may find inappropriate. Victims may become instruments for some broader good without taking into account their desires or needs. Civil society can suffer, too, because if reconciliation comes to mean an imposed harmony with dissent and contestation suppressed, and disagreement is tarnished as the forerunner of political instability, then legitimate politics itself risks disappearing. We should be wary of treating any alternative to forgiveness as dangerous. Doing so robs us of the potential of distinguishing theoretically between acceptable disagreements and even legitimate resentment from personal revenge.

A weaker formulation of forgiveness seems to me both normatively defensible and practically attainable. This certainly has a utilitarian edge to it, insofar as it recognizes the need to give up debilitating feelings of anger that would otherwise continue to harm the victim in some way. Uma Narayan, for example, defines forgiveness as abandoning a right to a "sense of grievance" that the violated may otherwise continue to hold. A victim may still desire punishment or compensation, but has effectively repudiated the legitimacy of continued anger and resentment (1998, 172). By forgiving, the victim acknowledges that these emotions are no longer appropriate, even though they may resurface. This sense of letting go, then, is a recognition that while anger is unlikely to disappear it cannot continue to define relations and some alternative form of living together without violence is necessary. Here, forgiveness is not so much about moral transformation on the part of victims, perpetrators, and bystanders but rather is about forswearing violence and coming to acknowledge the basic moral status of former enemies. This weaker conception of forgiveness, which I call a *partial pardon*, is closer to what I have in mind below, where I sketch an account of mutual respect among individuals. A partial pardon is not particularly transformative in individual ontological terms but it does require a substantial change in social relations.

An Alternative: Mutual Respect

Vengeance and transformative forgiveness face a number of challenges for establishing personal reconciliation. An alternative would allow for a certain skepticism toward some of the stronger claims of forgiveness while remaining morally satisfactory, yet reject the danger of revenge. This steers clear from a concern with repentance and instead argues that a pardon may be partial and offer a kind of acceptance of the perpetrator as an equal for the purposes of social coexistence without any requirement of deep ontological transformation on the part of victim and violator. Such a "partial pardon" includes several elements, and in no way absolves a perpetrator of responsibility. Rather than springing from the principles of "love," "fraternity," and "pity" toward one's enemy, this approach seeks to establish interpersonal relations on the principles of mutual respect. It is not set in opposition to substantive understandings of forgiveness—as I have said, these are morally praiseworthy—but remains a considerably thinner articulation while including elements that are more demanding than either forgetfulness or vengeance.[6] In order to make the distinction sharper, I first discuss what is meant by respect and tolerance interpersonally, and then turn to the idea of a partial pardon.

Tolerance assumes both disagreement (and even strong disapproval) with the beliefs or actions of others and a willingness to not impose oneself on those with whom one disagrees. As the long history of liberal social thought has argued, tolerance assumes that disagreements are a given part of social life and they can be eliminated only through an indefensible demand for uniformity. Especially in post-conflict conditions, disagreements can run deep. Nevertheless, tolerance also assumes that we remain in a relationship with those whom we are in conflict; we recognize the necessity of maintaining more than merely temporary relations. Tolerance emerges from the recognition of a shared fate or a sense that we are part of a larger community with a common past and future in which we are invested (or the very least from which we cannot escape), and thus we are tasked with establishing morally acceptable grounds for living with one another. This point of a shared fate, or of the awareness that we must live with those who harmed us and whom we harmed, underscores the importance of finding ways to live together peacefully and justly.

Tolerance, then, means simultaneously accepting fundamental disagreements and the importance of reciprocal moral recognition. How this occurs in practice depends on the case at hand and various available strategies. We cannot deduce the full spectrum of the means for securing tolerance solely theoretically (though a commitment to the rule of law is indicative of at least one aspect of this, as I have discussed). The central point, however, is that tolerance is not simply unilateral; it is premised on establishing and nurturing relationships over time, even where conflict and differences are still part of the social background. Such an understanding of tolerance is based on the notion of respect. Respect is the recognition of the value of others, not because of their political views or identity but because of their status as beings carrying moral rights that we have an obligation to recognize. Interpersonal relations that privilege respect and tolerance establish the necessary conditions for the emergence of future social trust. The powerful dynamics of violence, which neatly divided everyone into one category or another, are weakened to allow for the development of alternative political identities over time; former enemies establish new alliances and identities that overlap with earlier, conflict-era identities. This requires, at a minimum, that former adversaries realize that in politics negotiation and compromise do not signify defeat. Victory does not mean absolutely vanquishing the other side. Similarly, views and beliefs about others must be transformed so that others are seen as worthy of respect—that is, that enemies become opponents. Another way to put this is to say that interpersonal moral respect reflects several things: The overcoming of dehumanizing hatred that is typical of relations between hostile groups, a rejection of personal claims to vengeance, and finally the rehumanization of the other, so that we come to see former enemies in human and individual terms, rather than stereotypical examples of an out-group. This is deeper than mere coexistence because it implies recognition of the humanity of the other and of recognizing in others individualizing qualities that are familiar to us. To some extent, this also means a capacity to entertain, if only briefly, another's perspective and views and give them serious consideration, even though we may ultimately reject them. Most importantly, however, is the notion of acknowledging former enemies as beings whose status as moral agents make claims, or demands, on us that we must respect. What then can facilitate the emergence of respect and tolerance between individuals?

First, consider the status of the perpetrator. There is always the possibility that perpetrators may not be held accountable and society instead "chooses" to forget. Here, reconciliation is highly unlikely because victims do not receive the recognition they deserve. But even if accountability is pursued, there is no guarantee of reconciliation. The perpetrator must reflect on his or her actions critically and accept several conclusions: (1) the moral criminality of his or her actions, (2) a sense of personal responsibility for those actions, (3) the injured party as a victim of those actions, and (4) a commitment to a new, inclusive political and social order that recognizes the moral status of the victim. Now, the perpetrator *may* indeed begin a profound process of self-examination, culminating in repentance and possibly a plea for forgiveness. But more common is the example of Petar L., a Bosnian

Croat who fought during the war with a small guerrilla group that frequently engaged Bosnian Serb forces near Brčko in present-day northern Bosnia. While he was unwilling to go into detail about what he did, he made it clear to me that he participated in "what you would probably call criminal attacks" against civilians, though Petar gave little indication that this troubled him. "Do I regret what I did? Of course not. It was a war and they attacked us, and the only solution was to fight back, even if that meant attacking their people. They are dogs." During our conversation, Petar made it clear that he saw all Serbians in essentially the same terms, that is, as violent thugs who deserved no quarter and with whom he could not live. It is hard to know whether he was radicalized prior to or during the conflict but the depth of his animosity was striking, and his refusal to even accept that perhaps some of what he had done was wrong was disconcerting. With such an outlook, nearly fifteen years after the end of the war, it is unlikely that Petar will ever come to see his enemies in human terms.

Say a perpetrator not only acknowledges responsibility but undergoes some type of moral transformation and seeks forgiveness, as Tutu (1999) encourages; ought the victim forgive? Again, this depends on the victim. Forgiveness is a moral action and while it may be desirable, it should not be taken for granted. It can be an impressive example of moral agency, as Maria Helena showed, but I believe it should be given only if it strengthens the person's dignity. Regardless, I think there are ways of theorizing perpetrator acceptance into the same political and social (and possibly moral) spheres without relying on a substantive conception of forgiveness. A survivor may forgive his or her tormentor and thus close or at least lessen the moral chasm between them, or instead may offer a diminished or partial pardon; that is, a recognition that accepts the necessity of rejecting vengeance without offering full acceptance of the violator. Such a pardon, oriented toward mutual respect and tolerance, is satisfactory, if only because it would be problematic to expect forgiveness to serve as the only or primary way of reaching reconciliation. Nevertheless, a partial pardon is more robust than the thin coexistence discussed in Chapter 1, because even to consider pardoning there must be some acknowledgment of past wrongs and recognition of victims. The pardon is premised on the belief that any stable and just future must focus on creating a common moral, political, and social space for former enemies.

A partial pardon should also be understood as emerging over time. It is rarely if ever "given" in one moment, like a self-executing speech-act. It does not create a new relationship ex nihilo, for new relations take root only through continued and sustained interactions between former adversaries working together on common enterprises as they slowly learn that they can trust one another. This is a complex endeavor occurring over years or perhaps generations, unlike some understandings of forgiveness that occasionally downplay the importance of time. Indeed, respect among individuals is unlikely to result from a unified, collective will but rather emerges from new personal relations, from changes in attitudes and behavior, and from a willingness to accept others as moral equals, though not necessarily as friends or intimates. One example that comes to mind is the case of Juan Carlos L., a Chilean office worker I met in Santiago whose father was tortured by the security services during the dirty war, and passed away six years after Pinochet stepped down from power. Juan Carlos was adamant that he did not forgive the people who harmed his father. "I don't forgive them, since that would be absurd. But I do recognize that we need to learn to live together, and that not everyone who was a supporter of Pinochet is evil. In fact, I work with some right-wingers, and while we don't agree on many things, we get along. We have some things in common, like sports and even some social issues, and sure I wouldn't call them friends, but we can have conversations and feel OK around each other. We've even gone out for drinks together. They also understand where I'm coming from, and realize that what happened to a lot of us was unjust."

Juan Carlos's comments are important for several reasons. First, he makes clear that for him and many like him, forgiveness for those who harmed them or their loved ones is out of the question. But second, he acknowledges that many people who hold opposing political views can nevertheless be decent human beings, and through sustained daily interactions he began appreciating this. He has, in other words, begun a process of rehumanization, recognizing that political opponents are like him in some ways. Furthermore, this has been a reciprocal process where he and his coworkers have come to recognize each other as individuals, while trying to understand each other's political perspectives. Juan Carlos may not come to embrace them in any deep sense, but he has accepted that they can live together. Marisela P., an older

Chilean businesswoman who is suspicious of "leftists and students" and supported Pinochet, has come to a somewhat similar position from the other end of the political spectrum. She acknowledges that Pinochet "did some bad things, and certainly many innocent people suffered during the dictatorship." Like Juan Carlos, over the years Marisela has come in close contact with persons holding opposing views, at work and in social gatherings. She realizes that many of the beliefs she once held were grossly reductive and dehumanizing and treated anyone who opposed the junta as traitors who "deserved what they got." She has gone through a long change, coming to recognize that her old views contributed to terrible crimes, and she has sought to reach out to other Chileans who suffered during military rule. What is interesting is that she couched this essentially in terms of recognition and respect:

> For a long time, I didn't even see [leftists and liberals] as human, as having any rights at all. I didn't accept that they could have legitimate complaints, or that violating their rights to defend the country meant treating them like nothing, like trash. With the [Truth and Reconciliation] Commission report and later getting to know people who suffered then, I realized the extent of what happened, and the importance of not letting this happen again. I've had a lot of discussions about this, a lot of arguments, which changed my mind. I still am suspicious of liberals, but I realize that they are Chileans, too, and we have to learn how to work things out. And I feel terrible about the years of the dictatorship and the fact that I supported it.

Marisela notes the importance of broader events, like the publication of the commission report and the ways in which personal interactions have given her a new perspective on the past. She later mentioned the ways in which general public debates framed for her how she thought about individual experiences she had heard, and also how personal accounts of suffering and fear made sense in the larger historical context that emerged during the transition. Furthermore, she has moved to extend a kind of moral recognition to survivors by acknowledging the wrongness of what was done to them and accepting at least some responsibility.

These are all examples of the ambiguities between acceptance and rejection. The complexity of this process means that a society will not move in tandem or smoothly toward new relations or reconciliation because individuals have myriad ways of responding to suffering and violence. Some, of course, may follow Tutu, Shriver, and others and choose to forgive those who harmed them, while others may remain embittered and feel that only vengeance is satisfactory, as does Mahir. Others like Marisela will change enough to acknowledge the moral standing of victims and extend something like moral acknowledgment and respect to them. With time, hatred and resentment may become dulled, and respect and tolerance may slowly replace the animosity of the past. "In some ways," says Jasmina I., a Bosnian Muslim whose brother and father were killed outside of Sarajevo during the war, "we need to figure out how to move on. I have finally come to realize that the other side suffered too, that they are people too, who suffered enormously at our hands. It has taken me a long time to accept this, that they could be our neighbors, that we can eventually work together and live next door to each other again and do things together as Bosnians. I don't forgive the people who killed my family, but I do understand that Bosnian Serbs are Bosnians, like me. We can't keep demonizing each other. We need to see each other as humans, as individuals." Of course, time is not enough. Victims must feel that the future holds more than a fragile peace or continued impunity, for without some likelihood of improvement—of hope in the future—the sources of violence are not removed but only contained. Juan Carlos was clear that Chile's impunity throughout the 1990s and the ever-present threat of a second coup made it practically impossible to speak of peace in any substantive sense. If hope in a better future is to be secured, there must be a sense that former enemies are willing to work together and address the deepest causes of conflict. Furthermore, political institutions and the rhetoric of politics must change, so as not to emphasize differences but instead a unity that is based on justice and respect. To the extent that these changes resonate among individuals, respect and tolerance may take hold and will be stronger if individuals experience these changes in their everyday lives. Respect and tolerance must be practiced in everyday life.

Perhaps a different way to express this is to say that people must see themselves as contributing to social change where exclusivist ideologies are replaced by values that emphasize inclusiveness and re-spect. Survivors, in particular, must be brought back into the political and social life of the community, perhaps by creating spaces where their personal experiences can be retold publicly and connected to larger narratives about the past. In Chapter 1 I introduced the notion of phenomenological truth, which concerns personal experiences and suffering as well as their expression. Survivors express these experi-ences through narration, specifically by tying their personal experi-ences to collective stories that provide both empirical and normative context. Of course, it is not surprising that the kinds of experiences we are dealing with here (that is, terrible suffering and seemingly mean-ingless violence) often may not fit comfortably with broader narratives, and so there remains an aporia between public versions of the past that may be shot through with stories of redemption and overcoming, and horrible personal experiences.[7] We should not expect that personal stories will connect perfectly with general accounts but instead that these stories will bring an immediacy to the present that helps others understand the terribleness of the past, and the need to change for the future.

Linking personal stories and broader social narratives also pro-vides moral recognition to victims. Survivors are rehumanized as moral agents when new, critical histories reframe history and bring the sto-ries of individuals to the fore, thus drawing attention to the importance of human rights and the dignity of victims. Days of commemoration, memory sites, and other public endeavors strengthen this reframing, and draw a powerful connection between individual experiences and social reflection on the past. Certainly, moral reframing does ease the burdens of suffering and the changes that this may engender can assist in combating the impunity and marginalization that often accompa-nies victimhood. In addition to symbolic moral recognition, we should add that material reparations are equally necessary where victims con-tinue to live in poverty that is a legacy of violence. Individualized repa-rations provide greater personal autonomy, for they permit individuals to address their own needs as they see fit. This matters only, of course, if the reparations are substantial enough to affect their lives, and not merely token responses with the aim of ultimately neutralizing or si-lencing them.

This leads us immediately to note that any form of recognition is only partial, since the most terrible experiences cannot be completely communicated to others. This representational gap is a product of the nature of the experiences we are dealing with here. Broad patterns of repression, locations of mass graves, and institutional hierarchies of authority can be understood using traditional research and forensic techniques, but individual experiences are difficult, if not impossible, to represent and communicate, and serve as a terrible burden and source of loneliness for survivors. This gap is evident when a survivor of the Armenian genocide says, "My spirit is blinded. That is the point I have come to. Nothing will come of me, because I have been defeated by life" (Miller and Miller 1999, 172). His experiences lived on long after the violence ended and haunted him for the remainder of his life. Survivors "inhabit a world that has been made strange through the desolating experience of violence and loss" (Das 1997, 23). Such radical separation, and the attendant difficulty of representing personal experiences of suffering and grief to those who were protected from violence, give us a sense of the limited expectations we should hold for interpersonal reconciliation. While some individual survivors may succeed in placing the past behind them and leading meaningful lives, others may not be able to do so, and so we should be sensitive to the limited possibilities for reconciliation that are available in these contexts.[8] The idea behind the partial pardon is the recognition that a certain distance from the past is necessary, and while any future will carry the weight of the past, it is incumbent to create a space where new relationships can take root. The pardon is skeptical of the radical change at the heart of substantive accounts of forgiveness, and instead emphasizes fostering the values of respect and tolerance, as well as practices that promote cooperation among former enemies. We should seek to lessen resentment and fear, foster respect, and bring adversaries together into the same moral sphere, which is a significant accomplishment on its own.

In the end, it is individuals who must adopt the principle of respect and accept the importance of reconciliation. The nature of interpersonal relations means that here reconciliation will have its own dynamics, far from the publicity of official apologies and truth commission hearings, or the excitement and anger generated by high-profile trials. Citizens must learn to negotiate the complexities of the past in ways that are acceptable but not too disruptive, and to navigate between the temptations of vengeance and the impossibility, for some at least, of forgiveness. As enemies become neighbors and face the prospect of living together, everyday interactions take on a new cast. Certainly, change may occur more slowly here than in civil society or in the law. A report may signal the end of a truth commission's work but it is only the beginning of personal change. Victims may welcome a successful prosecution but it may also have relatively little direct impact on their everyday lives. The variety of personal histories and ways of coping with the past means that in some respects this level is only loosely connected to political, institutional, and social developments.

None of this is to say that interpersonal reconciliation is separate from what happens in the rest of society. The interpersonal is connected to public reconciliatory developments, even if only in a highly mediated fashion; however, individual reconciliation is unlikely where there are no efforts at institutional reform, where elites continue to disparage survivors, and where civil society turns away from the needs of the suffering. Without these broader developments, it is unlikely that reconciliation will develop, for there will be little reason to trust the state or believe that survivors and their loved ones will be safe or treated with respect. Impunity in the law reveals itself as fear among individuals. Without transparency in the workings of the state and robust methods of accountability citizens will continue to feel vulnerable to arbitrary violence, and may, under certain circumstances, demand private vengeance. Cristina H. argued that while Pinochet maintained impunity and power after stepping down, any talk of reconciliation was largely a sham—a way of using moral language to cover up difficult political compromises that in her opinion had sidelined victims. Accountability is important not only as a way to strengthen the rule of law but also because it signals to the population what values should be protected in the new society. Leaders can change the contours of debate and encourage individuals to confront the past, both in their public and private lives. Reparations, apologies, and similar strategies can further respect by showing that the state is concerned with the plight of victims and that the population should reexamine its own responsibility. And to the extent that the rule of law is reinforced institutionally and accepted individually, its role as a regulative normative ideal will thus be strengthened. Consequently, interpersonal changes are sensitive to developments at other social levels.

The success of interpersonal reconciliation requires an understanding of its possibilities and limitations. Too strong a conception of reconciliation may be unachievable, but forgetting and vengeance are so deeply problematic that they should be resisted. The idea of a partial pardon speaks to both of these concerns by seeking to establish the groundwork for a defensible mode of morally satisfactory coexistence while not foreclosing the possibility of deeper instances of forgiveness. Its success depends in part on the achievements made by elites and institutions, and in civil society, but it requires at its most basic a commitment by individuals themselves to live within a shared moral sphere with their former adversaries.

7 Conclusion

In the aftermath of political violence and oppression, a society is tasked with the difficult challenge of moral and material reconstruction. This is a complex process that involves many moral goals, actors, and institutions. I have sought to show how reconciliation in a society emerging from a period of significant violence is shaped by a number of normative goals that operate across diverse social spaces, and I have sought to provide a theoretical framework for understanding such processes that differs from prevailing approaches. The understanding of reconciliation provided here attempts to ground a realistic, critical account of what is feasible by using a set of normative criteria that can work to gauge its success.

As I have argued, there are five key concepts at play: (1) public dissemination of the *truth* of past atrocities, as well as a critical interrogation of ideologies supporting the violence, (2) *accountability* of perpetrators, (3) public *recognition* and acknowledgment of victims, (4) a commitment to the *rule of law*, and finally, (5) the development of *mutual respect* among erstwhile enemies.

Respect is the core principle here. Reconciliation is ultimately a condition of mutual respect between former adversaries that necessitates the reciprocal recognition of moral worth and dignity. We can speak of reconciliation when earlier, conflict-era identities are no

longer the primary fault lines in politics, and citizens have new identities that cut across earlier identifications. This requires moving away
from estrangement and distrust toward tolerance and respect of others, especially former enemies. The emergence of respect takes time
and is unlikely to develop when the other normative concepts have not
been adequately addressed. Respect develops partially in tandem with
these other norms but also in the wake of their successful actualization. It is only then, after erstwhile adversaries can come to see each
other as moral beings (even if politically at odds), that the goals of tolerance and respect can be said to take root.

I have sketched a conception of reconciliation as respect that emphasizes reciprocal recognition between equal actors. It emphasizes
the recognition of the inherent moral value of others, while accepting
that basic worldviews and political ideologies may often remain at odds
and disagreements will persist. Reconciliation is primarily a public
relationship that differs from both esteem (which recognizes some exceptional aspect or attribute in a person) and liminal conceptualiza-
tions of thin coexistence, because reconciliation rests on the possibility
of discussion, deliberation and, in short, politics. Furthermore, it falls
short of the deep acceptance, or willful embrace of the "other," that
some have argued is the essence of reconciliation. The disagreements
that pull us apart are balanced by a commitment to a sustained, significant relationship.

Mutual respect is intimately tied to the other normative concepts
presented earlier. Lies and half-truths about the past signal that victims' experiences are considered unworthy of public attention, and require truth telling efforts to resist. Some accountability, too, is necessary, as continued impunity effectively means contempt for all citizens
and their basic rights. In a similar vein, survivors will not be respected
if there are no efforts to recognize them morally. Under these conditions, they will likely remain marginalized and ignored. The protection
of the law and the commitment to democratic practices are also necessary to deepen principles of respect.

These normative concepts allow us to see how reconciliation develops across social space. The fundamental difficulty with previous
approaches like legal minimalism or maximalism based on forgiveness,
as I indicated, is their univalent origin. What the model presented
here has attempted to show is the necessity of each social level for

broad-based social reintegration. Each level on its own is both necessary and insufficient to achieve reconciliation. Such an approach
highlights how reconciliation is fundamentally disjunctured and uneven, occurring across social space in different ways and susceptible
to different challenges. The complexity and disjuncture of the process
come from the fact that actors at different levels are influenced by different factors and that no one level is sufficient to guarantee reconciliation. The different levels are, in effect, engaged in a complex relation where developments at one level may affect the others.

For example, political society can contribute much to reconciliation, especially if elites commit themselves to endorsing and defending
values like deliberation and the rule of law and rejecting violence, while
pursuing the reform of key institutions responsible for violations. Leaders can also shape popular historical understanding by calling for sustained reflection on the past and establishing memory sites that rewrite
shared historical narratives. And yet elite-driven reconciliation carries
risks, particularly because they are typically concerned with the immediate needs of stability and legitimacy, rather than extensive public reflection or moral discourses about responsibility. Pacted transitions further constrain the opportunities available to leaders and are likely to
focus elite attention on establishing basic ground rules for politics, even
through amnesties, rather than embarking on morally challenging and
politically fraught challenges to injustices. Substantive justice claims
like reparations and apologies can fall by the wayside under these conditions. Reconciliation among elites does not indicate societal reconciliation but only that they have settled on rules and procedures for solving
differences (no small accomplishment, of course). Achieving this may
mean avoiding the complex issues of responsibility, guilt, and the burdens of memory. For leaders, the need to strengthen state legitimacy
and efficacy may sideline a commitment to deepen reconciliation.

Trials and truth commissions may also play important roles in reconciliation but they, too, are only part of the puzzle. To be sure, fair
prosecutions show the state's commitment to fight impunity and return
to the rule of law. Indeed, prosecutions can change the expectations
citizens have of the state by highlighting the importance of protecting
rights and bringing violators to justice, as well as by developing a
record of violations that can inform public debate. Truth commissions
can play a somewhat similar role. Their official status and public nature,

coupled with the publication and broad dissemination of a final report, means that commissions are particularly well suited for furthering public debate. As important as trials and truth commissions may be, however, they can only contribute to public discourse; neither prosecutions nor commission hearings can address the host of complex issues confronting transitional societies. Trials must contend with the difficulty of selecting whom to prosecute and the danger of misrepresenting patterns of abuse by individualizing guilt. Furthermore, we should be wary of overemphasizing the democratizing effects of trials (as Osiel (1997) sometimes does). While fairness is crucial, trials are likely to have a deeper impact if they confirm popular expectations of guilt. Nevertheless, acquittals may be legitimate if they are reached through fealty to procedural and substantive norms, though popular support is likely to wane in the face of too many acquittals, however appropriate. For their part, commissions can provide, at best, only a general history of violence and responsibility since they lack prosecutorial (and often even subpoena) powers. Their final reports are best thought of as provisional though important histories rather than a final truth. It is not uncommon for evidence to emerge after a commission report that can deepen or even change important findings. In any case, strong advocates of truth commissions often promise a sea change in social relations—or even reconciliation—following a report; something that is exceedingly unlikely.

Civil society plays an important role as well, for it is here where more critical and nuanced historical understandings can counter statist or elitist accounts while encouraging greater recognition of victims. Most importantly, perhaps, is the contribution civil society can make to developing modes of public deliberation that take contestation seriously without collapsing into conflict. But exclusionary discourses may undermine this, or civil society may simply be so weakened that there are few resources or little interest in rebuilding social relations.

Finally, I have argued that reconciliation must develop among individuals. While interpersonal relations are shaped by events in public, reconciliation between people follows a different path, for most individuals are at least partly shielded from public attention and are much more responsive to the immediacy of everyday experiences and demands. Through sustained and personal interactions with former enemies—at work and in our neighborhoods—we slowly rehumanize them, we individualize them in ways that are impossible when collective identities trump individuality. Through this process, fraught as it often is with distrust, anger, and fear, respect can develop over time, though it may take years. Forgiveness may not always be possible but mutual respect can serve as the cornerstone of new relations. The complexity of these dynamics highlights how interpersonal reconciliation remains somewhat detached from broader social and political developments, yet responsive to the everyday experiences of individuals.

I have shown that reconciliation requires development across these different social levels. We cannot be certain of the success of any of these strategies in reconciling former enemies, for as Andrew Schaap notes, reconciliation—and politics more generally—is constituted by risk and we must "maintain an awareness of the frailty and contingency of community" (2005: 150). It is unlikely that reconciliation across levels will unfold smoothly in practice. But by sketching a multivalent theory I have shown how various developments can shape, for better or worse, the possibility of reconciliation, as well as highlight the main normative issues that transitional societies confront.

Placing respect at the center of reconciliation may appear like the abandonment of loftier aims. Some may feel that this view of reconciliation, which ultimately sees new relations and identities as a form of success (and perhaps the most we can expect), gives up on the need for deep personal transformation and reflection. This may be so, but we should be aware of the challenges that post-atrocity societies face. The period following conflict is frequently marked by bitterness, recriminations, and the threat of more violence. The challenges—emotional, material, political, and social—are often so staggering that any discussion of peace or justice appears fanciful to the jaded and harmed. These conditions limit the kinds of expectations we should hold. Charles Villa-Vicencio and Wilhelm Verwoerd (2001: 290) turn to the poet William Merwin to capture the difficulty of rebuilding what has been irreparably broken. Merwin's short piece, "Unchopping a Tree," begins:

> Start with the leaves, the small twigs, and the nests that have been shaken, ripped, or broken off by the fall; these must be gathered and attached once again to their respective places . . .

> . . . the time comes for the erecting of the trunk. By now it will scarcely be necessary to remind you of the delicacy of this huge skeleton. Every motion of the tackle, every slight upward heave of the trunk, the branches, their elaborately re-assembled panoply of leaves (now dead) will draw from you an involuntary gasp.

Finally, there comes the moment when one must step back and see whether the tree will stand on its own.

> The first breeze that touches its dead leaves. . . . You are afraid the motion of the clouds will be enough to push it over. What more can you do? What more can you do? But there is nothing more you can do. Others are waiting. Everything is going to have to be put back. (1970, 85)

How does one unchop a tree? Which pieces go where? Will they grow together in strength or collapse with the first soft wind? And how does one rebuild a shattered society? The delicacy required of the endeavor, so perfectly captured in Merwin's piece, reminds us of the fragility of remaking what has been destroyed. Like Merwin, citizens are enjoined to rebuild something that has suffered devastating harm, and do so while carrying their own burdens of trauma, pain, and fear. It may be impossible to return the tree to its prior self, just as it may be impossible to reconcile fully following terrible events, but the belief in a healthy tree, strong in its foundations and confident in its branches, gives hope to the possibility of a better future.

Notes

Chapter 1

1. On the former, see Schaap 2005, Lederach 1999, and Amstutz 2005. On the latter, see Moon 2008, Norval 1998, and Short 2008.

2. In 2005 the right was affirmed by the UN Commission on Human Rights in *Resolution 2005/66 "Right to Truth."* Also see Linden 1994. Nevertheless, though moral arguments in favor of a "right to truth" can certainly be made, it is less clear that international humanitarian law has given a cogent legal argument in its favor; thus to call it "emerging" seems a bit premature. The traditional source cited for this norm is Van Boven 1993, which is understood implicitly to include a right to the truth, since otherwise no reparations would be possible. More explicit is the argument put forth by UN Special Rapporteur Louis Joinet, who writes, "Full and effective exercise of the right to the truth is essential to avoid any recurrence of [gross human rights violations] in the future," and "[a] people's knowledge of the history of their oppression is part of their heritage and, as such, shall be preserved by appropriate measures in fulfillment of the State's duty to remember. Such measures shall be aimed at preserving the collective memory from extinction and, in particular, at guarding against development of revisionist and negationist arguments" (1997).

3. Human Rights Watch's "Policy Statement on Accountability for Past Abuses" states that there is "a duty to investigate" and that "the most important means of establishing accountability is for the government itself to make known all that can be reliably established about human rights abuses" (1995, 217). Amnesty International's "Policy Statement on Impunity" states that "there should be a thorough investigation into allegations of human rights violations" and that "the truth about violations must be revealed" (1995, 219).

4. A variation on the argument in favor of forgetfulness does not focus on political constraints; rather, it embraces a triumphalist understanding of the power of forgetting, claiming that the will to forget, to maintain an "as-if-not" attitude toward transgression, reflects the will to power of "noble morality." In *On the Genealogy of Morals*, Nietzsche argues that the demand for retribution is reactive because it remains shaped by the transgression and limits both victim and perpetrator to a logic of vengeance. He then traces how forgetfulness can be a positive act, representing a sovereign disregard for just deserts (a kind of noblesse oblige, one suspects). He writes, "To be incapable of taking one's enemies, one's accidents, even one's misdeeds seriously for very long— that is the sign of strong, full natures in whom there is an excess of power to form, to mold, to recuperate and to forget (a good example of this in modern times is Mirabeau, who had no memory for insults and vile actions done him and was unable to forgive simply because he—forgot). Such a man shakes off with a *single* shrug many vermin that eat deep into others; here alone genuine 'love of one's enemies' is possible—supposing it to be possible at all on earth" (Nietzsche 1989, 39). Remarkably, Nietzsche rejects forgiveness in this passage as reactive, implying that both punishment and forgiveness are opposites of forgetfulness. The question is whether the as-if-not attitude is morally defensible. I think not. It is morally indefensible to treat a rapist as if the rape had never occurred, and to the extent that the violator may be admitted back into society, it should happen once certain conditions have been met: for example, that he be identified as the rapist in question, that he morally distance himself from the act and show sincere regret and remorse, that he receive some form of punishment (which can include the moral censure that accompanies being outed), and so on. It is difficult to see how letting perpetrators avoid facing the consequences of their actions is a sign of self-actualization for the victims rather than a further illustration of the injury inflicted upon the victims.

5. The term is used in Schreiter 1997 (21). Also see Helmick 2008 (24–29).

6. Also see Muller-Fahrenholz 1997 (12).

7. Indeed, I use the term "reconciliation" in this book with some apprehension, as it contains within it these serious internal tensions that elide its distinctly political aspects. Nevertheless, it has become common currency for discussing processes of social change following violence or authoritarianism, and so I employ it for the sake of convention.

8. The terms are used often in Dawson 2001 (219–243).

9. Though one could argue that the sovereign is also a "victim" of mass atrocities insofar as its mandate to ensure law and order is violated, this misses the point, since frequently it is precisely the sovereign state that commits many of these crimes, and thus to annul its responsibility through pardoning itself offers little consolation or acknowledgment for its victims. Even Hegel, while acknowledging that only the sovereign has the right to pardon, confuses

it with the notion of forgiveness: "The right to pardon criminals arises from the sovereignty of the monarch, since it is this alone which is empowered to actualize the mind's power of making undone what has been done and wiping out a crime by forgiving and forgetting it" (1967, par 282).

Chapter 2

1. This distinction is captured in Darwall 1977 (36–49). Also see Bird 2004 (211–215).

2. For a detailed discussion, see Van Boven 1993 (16–34). Also see the UN Human Rights Council (2008) affirmation of the right.

3. The term is taken from Arendt 1993. Also see Crocker 2000 (100) and South African Truth and Reconciliation Commission 1995 (vol. 5, ch. 4, sec. 1).

4. Also see Szymusiak 1999 and Ung 2000.

5. Note that, broadly speaking, justice need not ignore the value of recognizing victims and providing them with some form of compensation. This is clarified below.

6. I use *bystander* in a moral sense and thus do not include persons who were incapable of acting meaningfully to denounce or oppose abuses. *Bystander* includes some sense of agency, though this is often highly constrained.

7. For this reason, some commentators prefer the term *survivor* to *victim,* for it connotes greater agency. Nevertheless, I use *victim* and *survivor* interchangeably throughout the book, with the explicit understanding that both should include a strong sense of agency.

8. Honneth (1995, 249–254) identifies three forms of disrespect that endanger healthy identities: (1) at a very basic level, the injury to self-confidence caused by loss over one's physical integrity (e.g., through torture or rape) and the consequent devastating destabilization of personal identity and predictability in the world, (2) the type of disrespect following the denial of rights enjoyed by other citizens, and (3) the damage done to self-esteem through the pronounced and repeated denigration of one's way of life.

9. It is important to emphasize that while I use *recognition* in Fraser's sense of status parity to include both redistribution and recognition, I restrict it to the necessities of transitional societies. Broader social justice issues that she analyzes require slightly different theorization, since they engage long-term problems of both transitional and consolidated democracies and thus extend beyond the situation under discussion. One problem with conflating redistributive measures in consolidated and transitional democracies is that victim recognition becomes an issue of social policy, and the particular moral content that restitution includes is diluted into broader debates about redistributive justice. Victim recognition in these transitional settings should be seen as largely but (because of the unique burdens transitional societies face) not completely reducible to a particular moment within general social justice debates.

10. The importance of this approach is evident in a number of notable works, including Herman 1997, Scarry 1987, Summerfield 1995, and Orr 2000.

11. The state may, for example, claim that certain infrastructural improvements such as repairing roads or building schools in historically poor areas that experienced violence constitute reparations, and many inhabitants would certainly welcome these developments. But urban, middle-class victims will already enjoy access to roads, sanitation, education, and a number of other "benefits" that they see as the entitlements of citizenship. Indeed, for them, material aid should focus more on psychological support. Are the state's economic development efforts, then, really reparations or simply part of citizen rights relabeled through the discourse of victim recognition? See Roht-Arriaza 2004 (189).

12. The goal here is not, however, to offer a programmatic menu of reforms or required policy initiatives. The interested reader should consult the overview in the 2006 World Bank report by Samuels.

13. It includes more than this, of course. In additional to criminal law, reform initiatives often tackle commercial law (particularly because economic and political corruption often go hand in hand) and broader constitutional issues, insofar as they concern core human rights protections and the division of power among government branches. See, for example, Domingo and Sider 2001, Menéndez-Carrión and Joignant 1999, and Lawyers Committee for Human Rights 2002.

14. For a broader account, see Sen 1999.

15. Also see Laclau 1996 and 1990 and Lefort 1986 (307–319).

16. Also see Manin 1987 (338–345) and Nino 1996 (67–106).

17. I realize that much legal theory equates the rule of law in transitional settings with prosecutions. Since here the specific issue of prosecutions is a few degrees separated from the principle of non-violence and respect for law in question, this discussion is better left to the section on accountability.

Chapter 3

1. To be clear, I mean political culture in the sense of the broad attitudes and values that most of the population has toward the political system (democratic, authoritarian, and so on). See Diamond 1995.

2. Robert Post (1993, 654) has argued that the deliberative model overemphasizes unfettered deliberation at the expense of basic procedures of exchange. This is a rather unfair characterization, and in order to avoid facing the same accusation, I underscore the importance of having some basic ground rules for deliberation as the sine qua non of discussion.

3. In discussing the usefulness of deliberation as a regulative ideal, James Johnson (1998, 161–184) has argued that proponents of deliberative politics underplay the extent to which political actors seek to challenge one another

not at the level of reasons, but rather at an existential level. While this may be true, and it is certainly more pronounced in transitional settings, Johnson underplays the point made by deliberative theorists, which is normative (as in a prescriptive principle) and not necessarily descriptive.

4. This kind of narrative of rebirth was common in both South Africa, where black leaders were unwilling to delve too deeply into black-on-black political violence during the apartheid regime, and France, where after World War II Charles de Gaulle's government effectively redrew the extent of fascist collaboration to include only a few high-level members of the Vichy regime. See Golsan 2000 and Paris 2001 (74–121).

5. See Hartman 1994 (6). National memory is a fickle thing, and debates around the Berlin Holocaust memorial show that even its greatest advocates can remain insensitive to the present even as they genuflect over past crimes. A memorial always risks serving the interests of the offending group more than those of victims, for it may speak directly to a shallow sense of guilt that remains narcissistic and indifferent—whether deliberate or not—to survivors or their claims to recognition. An anamnestic culture, one that remembers rather than forgets the past, is obligated to reflect not only on its history but also on the meaning of solidarity in the present, lest it simply reproduce the separation and estrangement of victims through a self-absorbed commemoration of its own culpability. See Moses 2007 (263–284).

6. Roy Brooks (1999, 3) has referred to this as "the age of apologies." Also see N. Smith 2008. On transnational apologies, see Gibney and Roxstrom 2001. On historical injustices, see Barkan 2000.

7. Undoubtedly, there is no historically uniform Christian understanding of the relationship between apology and forgiveness, especially since the Reformation. Nevertheless, the basic understanding is similar among the major divisions. See Albrecht Ritschl's important (1900) three-volume work, *The Christian Doctrine of Justification and Reconciliation*, especially volume 3. Also see Mackintosh 1927 and Lehman 1986 (233). Forgiveness as *teshuvah* ("return") has a long pedigree in Judaism as well. See Dorff 2001.

8. Golding discusses how making moral amends speaks directly to the resentment held by the victim: "One of the main functions of other-oriented regret, in the interpersonal situation, is the negation of the justifiability of the injured party's resentment" (1984–1985, 133). Also see Govier and Verwoerd 2002 (69–70).

9. This concern was raised when then-President of Argentina Néstor Kirchner apologized for disappearances and torture during the Dirty War, and several victims' groups refused to accept the apology on the grounds that to do so would constitute forgiveness and would thus result in a loss of public and official attention to the era of military rule.

10. I thank J. Donald Moon for raising this important point. Also see Buruma 1999 (4–9).

Chapter 4

1. On East Timor, see UN Transitional Administration in East Timor 2000. On Sierra Leone, see the Special Court for Sierra Leone Web site at http://www.sc-sl.org. On Kosovo, see UN Interim Administration Mission in Kosovo 2001. On Bosnia and Herzegovina, see The Courts of Bosnia and Herzegovina on the Bosnia and Herzegovina Web site at http://www.sudbih .gov.ba/?jezik=e. On Cambodia, see Task Force for Cooperation with Foreign Legal Experts for the Preparation of the Proceedings for the Trial of Senior Khmer Rouge Leaders on the Cambodia Web site at http://www.cambodia. gov.kh/krt/english/ and Law on the Establishment of Extraordinary Chambers in the Courts of Cambodia for the Prosecution of Crimes Committed during the Period of Democratic Kampuchea on the Cambodia Web site at http://www.pict-pcti.org/courts/pdf/Cambodia/Cambodia_052203.pdf. On Iraq, see Supreme Iraqi Criminal Tribunal statute on the Iraq Web site at http:// www.ictj.org/static/MENA/Iraq/iraq.statute.engtrans.pdf; see also Rassi 2006– 2007, 219–235). All Web sites accessed September 18, 2008.

2. Note that this formulation is not meant to defend a positivist notion of law, where any determination of what is just is achieved through looking at extant law. An adequate response to a violation, as discussed in Chapter 2, must be a just response, and morality, and not merely positive law, should inform the relationship between crime and punishment. While the normative status of accountability was raised in Chapter 2, it bears repeating: Punishment is intimately tied to the respect and autonomy of the victim, for it signals that a violation of such respect and autonomy is a moral wrong and should be addressed accordingly.

3. Arendt takes this position to the extreme, arguing for a strong division between legal and extralegal issues. While I sympathize with this to an extent, I take exception to her strong formulation. She writes, "The purpose of a trial is to render justice and nothing else; even the noblest of ulterior purposes—the making of a record of Hitler's regime which would withstand the test of history— can only detract from the law's main business: to weigh the charges against the accused, to render judgment, and to mete out due punishment" (1963, 233).

4. But see the decisions in *Prosecutor v. Krstić* 2004 and *Prosecutor v. Blaškić* 2004. For a strong critique of these broader understandings of legal culpability, see Nersessian 2001–2002.

5. Some of the related technical problems are discussed in Dipardo 2008 and Bassin 2006.

6. Specifically, they had to show that their crimes were committed for "political" reasons, not for personal gain or from personal malice. Establishing motive proved quite difficult in some cases. See the excellent 2007 book by Du Bois-Pedain.

7. The best discussions of truth commissions can be found in Mark Freeman 2006 and Hayner 2001.

8. This can occur even when a report does not completely detail a perpetrator's actions. A dramatic instance is found in the South African Truth and Reconciliation Commission's findings on former president F. W. de Klerk. By means of a last-minute court injunction, he successfully stopped the commission from publishing its findings on him. The final report includes a section devoted to de Klerk with the entire text blacked out. See South African Truth and Reconciliation Commission 1995 (vol. 5, ch. 6, sec. 104).

9. See, for example, Humphrey 2002.

10. These issues deal with the effectiveness of restitution. Pablo de Greiff (2006) has highlighted a second set of normative issues that consists in how to measure harm when dealing with individuals: How is compensation assessed for the loss of limbs or mental and emotional harms? Should reparations be highly individualized or part of a "package" (which minimizes administrative costs)? What if the same harm to different people has different effects? Should recompense be tailored accordingly? These complex questions have both practical and moral consequences.

11. Precisely how long is an issue for case study, and it cannot be ascertained a priori. In part, it concerns the degree to which the state has succeeded in convincing the population as a whole that it is institutionalized and permanent and thus not likely to disappear anytime soon.

12. Victims may also turn to foreign national courts to seek redress. The 1992 U.S. Torture Victim Protection Act has served as a vehicle to prosecute foreigners domestically for violations of "the law of nations," and this manner of tort redress is gaining popularity as universal jurisdiction becomes more widely accepted in national jurisprudence. Criminal trials in foreign courts are also gaining acceptance, even if the support is far from firm; Belgium sentenced four Rwandans (including two nuns) for their role in genocidal killings, though its broader "universal jurisdiction" legislation was significantly curtailed as a result of U.S. pressure. And the impact of international trials (particularly tort cases) on domestic politics is uneven; in some cases, such victories have had little impact domestically (Macedo 2006).

Chapter 5

1. David Crocker (1999, 374–401) has presented a somewhat similar triptych of civil society in his work, distinguishing between "anti-government," "associational," and "deliberative." Since it is more relevant to well-established democracies, I do not discuss the most important American contribution to the civil society literature, Robert Putnam's neo-Tocquevillean "associational" model (see Putnam 1995 and Edwards and Foley 2001 [1–16]).

2. Indeed, deliberation and engagement may promote social learning of this sort. See Volkhart 2001 and Vergara 1994.

3. Obviously, everyone who suffered a human rights violation is a member of the group "everyone who was violated." And this may become a politically

salient group if its members, or some of them, organize around that shared experience. But at this point, I am simply discussing people who were in a politically or socially recognized group before the violations occurred and where that group was targeted as such.

4. See the Web site of the Coordinadora Nacional de Derechos Humanos (2009) at http://www.dhperu.org/Index.html.

5. In Peru, the ombudsperson's Office of Human Rights also plays an important consultative role in restructuring the judiciary.

6. Their work is available on the Campaign for Good Governance, Sierra Leone Web site at http://www.slcgg.org/. Also see Baker 2005.

Chapter 6

1. I spoke to survivors and others both in Chile and in Bosnia and Herzegovina about the violence their societies experienced. In Chile, I met with not only individuals but also members of a number of groups, including CODEPU, Comité ProPaz, Agrupación de Familiares Detenidos Desaparecidos, FASIC, and the Fundación Jamie Guzmán. In Bosnia, I met with individuals who were unaffiliated with other groups. These conversations are not meant to reflect the whole range of responses or reactions to past experiences, but they do reveal various attitudes of victims and others. In the pages that follow, I draw on a few of these conversations to elucidate my points: In Chile, I conducted interviews with Cristina H. (July 24, 2000), Maria Helena C. (July 15, 2000), Juan Carlos L. (August 17, 2000), and Marisela P. (August 3, 2000). In Bosnia, I conducted interviews with Mahir P. (July 6, 2007), Suleyman L. (July 6, 2007), Petar L. (July 5, 2007), and Jasmina I. (July 7, 2007).

2. Margaret Walker similarly states, "To coerce in any way a person already harmed or disrespected by a wrong into relinquishing her own need to grieve, reproach, and make demands may itself be harmful or disrespectful" (2006, 179).

3. Also see Murphy and Hampton 1988 (18) and Hill 1973.

4. Charles K. Barton takes this position further: The pleasure that victims receive from the suffering of the perpetrator is "not morally objectionable"; rather, it "is most plausibly identified as satisfaction in justice being done" (1999, 13).

5. Indeed, the literature espousing this approach is rather large. The classical formulation is given by Bishop Joseph Butler (1971 [1726]), especially Sermon VIII, "Upon Resentment," and Sermon IX, "Upon Forgiveness of Injuries." For important modern statements, see Enright and The Human Development Study Group 1994, Downie 1965, Holmgren 1993, Horsbrugh 1974, Lewis 1980, and Richards 1988.

6. It is worth distinguishing this approach from another common one. Some liberals, such as Bruce Ackerman (1992), recommend that we avoid dealing with interpersonal relations after mass violence. They argue that the

better alternative to forgiveness (or even accountability) is social forgetting. This strategy may seem superficially similar to what I argue; however, my approach emphasizes moral recognition, engagement with the past, and a commitment to accountability. Without these, such tolerance is morally impoverished. Their approach would bury likely feelings of mistrust and lingering resentment under the rubric of "tolerance."

7. Such a gap is often evident in the personal memoirs of survivors; they struggle to explain experiences to readers who may have had no direct connection to the violence. See Delbo 1968 and Langer 1991.

8. Compare, for example, "Part II: Stages of Recovery" in Herman 1997 with Scarry 1985 (especially chap. 3, "Pain and Imagining").

References

Ackerman, Bruce. 1992. *The Future of Liberal Revolution*. New Haven, CT: Yale University Press.

Alden, Chris. 2001. *Mozambique and the Construction of a New State: From Negotiations to Nation-Building*. New York: Palgrave.

Alexander, Jeffrey C. 2006. *The Civil Sphere*. Oxford: Oxford University Press, 2006.

Alie, Joe A. D. 2008. "Reconciliation and Traditional Justice: Tradition-Based Practices of the Kpaa Mende in Sierra Leone." In *Traditional Justice and Reconciliation after Violent Conflict: Learning from African Experiences*. Ed. Luc Huyse and Mark Salter. Stockholm: Institute for Democracy and Electoral Assistance.

Ambos, Kai. 2007. "Joint Criminal Enterprise and Command Responsibility." *Journal of International Criminal Justice*, 1–25.

Amnesty International. 1995. "Policy Statement on Impunity." In *Transitional Justice: How Emerging Democracies Reckon with Former Regimes*. Ed. Neil Kritz. Washington, DC: United States Peace Institute, 3 vols., 1: 219–221.

———. 1996. "Peru: Amnesty Laws Consolidate Impunity for Human Rights Violations." AI Index: AMR 46/003/1996 (February 23).

———. 2002. "Rwanda: Gacaca: A Question of Justice." AI Index: AFR 47/007/2002 (December 17).

Amstutz, Mark. 2005. *The Healing of Nations: The Promise and Limits of Political Forgiveness*. Lanham, MD: Rowman and Littlefield.

Annan, Kofi. 1999. "Seventh Report of the Secretary General on the United Nations Observer Mission in Sierra Leone." United Nations doc. S/1999/836, para. 1.

Apter, David, ed. 1998. *The Legitimization of Violence*. New York: New York University Press.

Archdiocese of Guatemala City. 1998. "Guatemala: Never Again." REMHI: Project for the Recovery of Historical Memory. Guatemala City, Guatemala.

Archdiocese of Saõ Paolo. 1985. *Brasil: Nunca Mais*. Archdiocese of Saõ Paolo: Saõ Paolo, Brazil.

Arendt, Hannah. 1963. *Eichmann in Jerusalem: A Report on the Banality of Evil*. New York: Viking.

———. 1989. *The Human Condition*. Chicago: University of Chicago Press.

———. 1993. "Truth and Politics." *Between Past and Future*. New York: Penguin Books.

Argentine National Commission on the Disappeared. 1986. *Nunca Más: Report of the Argentine National Commission on the Disappeared*. New York: Farrar, Straus and Giroux.

Ariko, Charles. 2008. "Ex-LRA men get Amnesty." *The New Vision: Uganda's Leading Website* (January 21). Available at http://www.newvision.co.ug/D/8/13/607788. Accessed May 25, 2008.

Aristotle. 1984. *Nicomachean Ethics*. Grinell, IA: Peripatetic Press.

Aron, Raymond. 1967. *Peace and War: A Theory of International Relations*. New York: Praeger.

Asociación Nacional de Familiares de Secuestrados y Detenidos-Desaparecidos de Perú. 2002. "Análisis de la Situación Judicial en el Perú." Lima, Perú.

Asociación pro Derechos Humanos. 2009. Available at http://www.aprodeh.org.pe/. Accessed February 23, 2009.

Aylwin, Patricio. 1995. "Chile: Statement by President Aylwin on the Report of the National Commission on Truth and Reconciliation." In *Transitional Justice: How Emerging Democracies Reckon with Former Regimes*. Ed. Neil Kritz. Washington, DC: United States Institute of Peace Press, 171–172.

Baines, Erin K. 2007. "The Haunting of Alice: Local Approaches to Justice and Reconciliation in Northern Uganda." *International Journal of Transitional Justice* 1, no. 1: 91–114.

Baker, Bruce. 2005. "Who Do People Turn to for Policing in Sierra Leone?" *Journal of Contemporary African Studies* 23, no. 3 (September): 371–390.

Ball, Howard. 1999. *Prosecuting War Crimes and Genocide: The Twentieth Century Experience*. Lawrence: University of Kansas Press.

Ballengee, Melissa. 2000. "The Critical Role of Non-Governmental Organizations in Transitional Justice: A Case Study of Guatemala." *UCLA Journal of International Legal and Foreign Affairs* 4 (Fall 1999/Winter 2000): 477–506.

Barahona de Brito, Alexandra. 1997. *Human Rights and Democratization in Latin America: Uruguay and Chile*. New York: Oxford University Press.

———. 2001. "Truth, Justice, Memory and Democratization in the Southern Cone." In *The Politics of Memory: Transitional Justice in Democratizing Societies*. Ed. Alexandra Barahona de Brito, Carmen González-Enríquez, and Paloma Aguilar. Oxford: Oxford University Press, 127–131.

Barahona de Brito, Alexandra, Carmen González-Enríquez, and Paloma Aguilar, eds. 2001. *The Politics of Memory: Transitional Justice in Democratizing Societies*. Oxford: Oxford University Press.

Barkan, Elazar. 2000. *The Guilt of Nations: Restitution and Negotiating Historical Injustices*. Baltimore: Johns Hopkins University.

Bartoli, Andrea. 2001. "Forgiveness and Reconciliation in the Mozambican Peace Process." In *Forgiveness and Reconciliation: Religion, Public Policy and Conflict Transformation*. Ed. Raymond C. Helmick and Rodney Petersen. Philadelphia, PA: Templeton Foundation Press, 351–373.

Barton, Charles K. 1999. *Getting Even: Revenge as a Form of Justice*. Peru, IL: Open Court.

Bass, Gary. 2000. *Stay the Hand of Vengeance: The Politics of War Crimes Tribunals*. Princeton, NJ: Princeton University Press.

Bassin, Ari S. 2006. "'Dead Men Tell No Tales': Rule 92 Bis—How the Ad Hoc International Criminal Tribunals Unnecessarily Silence the Dead." *New York University Law Review* 81, (November).

Beah, Ishmael. 2008. *A Long Way Gone: Memoirs of a Boy Soldier*. New York: Farrar, Straus and Giroux.

Becarria, Cesare. 1995. *On Crimes and Punishments and Other Writings*. Cambridge: Cambridge University Press.

Benhabib, Seyla. 1996. "Toward a Deliberative Model of Democratic Legitimacy." In *Democracy and Difference: Contesting the Boundaries of the Political*. Ed. Seyla Benhabib. Princeton, NJ: Princeton University Press, 67–94.

———. 2002. *Claims of Culture: Equality and Diversity in the Global Era*. Princeton, NJ: Princeton University Press.

Benjamin, Jessica. 1988. *The Bonds of Love*. New York: Pantheon Books.

———. 1995. "Recognition and Destruction: An Outline of Intersubjectivity." In *Like Subjects, Love Objects: Essays on Recognition and Sexual Difference*. New Haven, CT: Yale University Press, 27–48

Bentham, Jeremy. 1995. *The Principles of Morals and Legislation*. New York: Prometheus Books.

Bhargava, Rajeev. 2001. "Restoring Decency to Barbaric Societies." In *Truth v. Justice: The Morality of Truth Commissions*. Ed. Robert Rotberg and Dennis Thompson. Princeton, NJ: Princeton University Press.

Bird, Colin. 2004. "Status, Identity, Respect." *Political Theory* 32, no. 2 (April): 207–232.

Boraine, Alex. 2001. "Truth and Reconciliation in South Africa: The Third Way." In *Truth v. Justice: The Morality of Truth Commissions*. Ed. Robert Rotberg and Dennis Thompson. Princeton, NJ: Princeton University Press.

Borneman, John. 1997. *Settling Accounts: Violence, Justice and Accountability*. Princeton, NJ: Princeton University Press.

Bosnia and Herzegovina. n.d. *The Courts of Bosnia and Herzegovina*. Available at http://www.sudbih.gov.ba/?jezik=e. Accessed April 23, 2009.

Botman, Russell H., and Robin Petersen. 1997. *To Remember and to Heal: Theological and Psychological Reflections on Truth and Reconciliation*. Cape Town: Thorold's Africana Books.

Bourdieu, Pierre. 1995. *Language and Symbolic Power*. Cambridge, MA: Harvard University Press.

Bowman, James. 1998. "Sorry about That." *New Criterion* (May): 50.

Brilmayer, Lea. 1991. "Secession and Self-Determination: A Territorial Interpretation." *Yale Journal of International Law* 16: 177–202.

Brooks, Roy, ed. 1999. *When Sorry Isn't Enough: The Controversy Over Apologies and Reparations for Human Injustice*. New York: New York University Press.

Brudholm, Thomas. 2008. *Resentment's Virtue: Jean Améry and the Refusal to Forgive*. Philadelphia, PA: Temple University Press.

Burg, Steven, and Paul Shoup. 2000. *The War in Bosnia Herzegovina: Ethnic Conflict and International Intervention*. Armonk, NY: M. E. Sharpe Press.

Burnet, Jennie E. 2008. "The Injustice of Local Justice: Truth, Reconciliation, and Revenge in Rwanda." *Genocide Studies and Prevention* 3/2 (August): 173–194.

Buruma, Ian. 1994. *The Wages of Guilt: Memories of War in Germany and Japan*. New York: Meridian.

Butler, Bishop Joseph. 1971 [1726]. *Fifteen Sermons*. London: Cashew Books.

Cambodia. 2004. "Law on the Establishment of Extraordinary Chambers in the Courts of Cambodia for the Prosecution of Crimes Committed During the Period of Democratic Kampuchea." Available at http://www.pict-pcti.org/courts/pdf/Cambodia/Cambodia_052203.pdf. Accessed September 12, 2008.

———. 2006. "Task Force for Cooperation with Foreign Legal Experts for the Preparation of the Proceedings for the Trial of Senior Khmer Rouge Leaders." Available at http://www.cambodia.gov.kh/krt/english/. Accessed September 12, 2008.

Campaign for Good Governance of Sierra Leone. 2009. Available at www.slcgg.org/Programmes.html. Accessed April 15, 2009.

Casarjian, Robin. 1992. *Forgiveness: A Bold Choice for a Peaceful Heart*. New York: Bantam Books.

Cassesse, Antonio. 1998. "Reflections on International Criminal Justice." *Modern Law Review*, no. 60: 1–10.

Centro de Estudios Legales y Sociales. 2009. Available at www.cels.org.ar. Accessed April 26, 2009.

Chakravarti, Sonali. 2008. "More than Cheap Sentimentality: Victim Testimony at Nuremberg, the Eichmann Trial, and Truth Commissions." *Constellations* 15/2 (July): 223–235.

Cohen, Jean. 1999. "American Civil Society Talk." In *Civil Society, Democracy and Civil Renewal*. Ed. Robert K. Fullinwider. Lanham, MD: Rowman and Littlefield, 55–88.

Cohen, Jean, and Andrew Arato. 1992. *Civil Society and Political Theory*. Cambridge, MA: Massachusetts Institute of Technology Press.

Cohen, Stanley. 2001. *States of Denial: Knowing about Atrocities and Suffering*. London: Polity Press.

Comisión Andina de Juristas. 2009. Available at http://www.cajpe.org.pe/in dex.html. Accessed January 1, 2009.

Comisión de Derechos Humanos. 2009. Available at http://www.cndhch.org .ch. Accessed April 19, 2009.

Comisión para el Esclarecimiento Histórico. 1999. *Guatemala: Memoria del Silencio*. Ciudad de Guatemala: CEH.

Comisión Nacional Sobre la Desaparición de Personas. 1984. *Nunca Más: Informe de la Comisión Nacional sobre la Desaparición de Personas*. Buenos Aires: Editorial Universitaria.

Concannon, Brian, Jr. 2001. "Justice for Haiti: The Raboteau Trial." *The International Lawyer* 35, no. 2 (Summer): 613–648.

Coordinadora Nacional de Derechos Humanos. 2009. Available at http://www .dhperu.org/. Accessed January 4, 2009.

Couper, David. 1998. "Forgiveness in the Community: Views From an Episcopal Priest and a Former Chief of Police." In *Exploring Forgiveness*, Ed. Robert D. Enright and Joanna North. Madison, WI: University of Wisconsin Press, 121–130.

Crocker, David. 1998. "Transitional Justice and International Civil Society: Towards a Normative Framework." *Constellations* 5, no. 4: 492–517.

———. 1999. "Civil Society and Transitional Justice." In *Civil Society, Democracy and Civil Renewal*. Ed. Robert K. Fullinwider. Lanham, MD: Rowman and Littlefield, 375–401.

———. 2000. "Truth Commissions, Transitional Justice, and Civil Society." In *Truth v. Justice: The Morality of Truth Commissions*. Ed. Robert Rotberg and Dennis Thompson. Princeton, NJ: Princeton University Press, 99–121.

Dahl, Robert. 1991. *Democracy and Its Critics*. New Haven, CT: Yale University Press.

Damaska, Mirjan. 2008. "The Henry Morris Lecture: What Is the Point of International Justice?" *Chicago Kent Law Review* 329: 329–368.

Danner, Allison Marston and Jenny S. Martinez. 2005. "Guilty Associations: Joint Criminal Enterprise, Command Responsibility, and the Development of International Criminal Law." *California Law Review* 93 (January): 77–170.

Darwall, Stephen. 1977. "Two Kinds of Respect." *Ethics* 88, no. 1 (October): 36–49.

Das, Veena. 1997. "Language and Body: Transactions in the Construction of Pain." In *Social Suffering*. Ed. Arthur Kleinman, Veena Das, and Margaret Lock. Berkeley: University of California Press.

Dawson, John. 2001. "Hatred's End: A Christian Proposal to Peace Making in a New Century." In *Forgiveness and Reconciliation: Religion, Public Policy and Conflict Transformation*. Ed. Raymond C. Helmick and Rodney Petersen. Philadelphia, PA: Templeton Foundation Press, 67–92.

De Greiff, Pablo. 2006. "Justice and Reparations." In *The Handbook of Reparations*. Ed. Pablo De Greiff. Oxford: Oxford University Press, 451–477.

Delbo, Charlotte. 1968. *None of Us Will Return*. Boston: Beacon Press.

Dembour, Marie-Benedicte, and Emily Haslam. 2004. "Silencing Hearings? Victim-Witnesses at War Crimes Trials." *European Journal of International Law* 15, no. 1: 151–177.

Derrida, Jacques. 2001. *On Cosmopolitanism and Forgiveness*. London: Routledge.

DeVito, Daniela. 2008. "Rape as Genocide: The Group/Individual Schism." *Human Rights Review* 9, no. 3 (September): 361–387.

Diamond, Larry. 1995. *Promoting Democracy in the 1990s: Actors and Instruments, Issues and Imperatives*. Washington, DC: Carnegie Commission on Preventing Deadly Conflict.

———. 1999. *Developing Democracy: Toward Consolidation*. Baltimore: Johns Hopkins University.

Digeser, Peter E. 2001. *Political Forgiveness*. Ithaca, NY: Cornell University Press.

Dipardo, Elizabeth. 2008. "Caught in a Web of Lies: Use of Prior Inconsistent Statements to Impeach Witnesses Before the ICTY." *Boston College International and Comparative Law Review* 277: 277–302.

Domingo, Pilar, and Rachel Sider, eds. 2001. *The Rule of Law in Latin America: The International Promotion of Judicial Reform*. London: University of London, Institute of Latin American Studies.

Dominguez Charneo, and Margaret Lilian. 1998. "La Importancia de la Sociedad Civil para la Transformación Democrática en el Perú." *Análisis* 4: 23–34.

Dorff, Elliot. 2001. "The Elements of Forgiveness: A Jewish Approach." In *Dimensions of Forgiveness: Psychological Research and Theological Forgiveness*. Ed. Everett L. Worthington, Jr. Philadelphia, PA: Templeton Foundation Press, 29–55.

Douglas, Lawrence. 2001. *The Memory of Judgment*. New Haven, CT: Yale University Press.

Downie, R. S. 1965. "Forgiveness." *Philosophical Quarterly* 15: 128–134.

Drumbl, Mark. 2007. *Atrocity, Punishment and International Law*. Cambridge: Cambridge University Press.

Dryzek, John. 2005. "Deliberative Democracy in Divided Societies: Alternatives to Agonism and Analgesia." *Political Theory* 33, no. 2 (April): 218–242.

Du Bois-Pedain, Antje. 2007. *Transitional Amnesty in South Africa*. Cambridge: Cambridge University Press.

Dugard, John. 1997. "Retrospective Justice: International Law and the South African Model." In *Transitional Justice and the Rule of Law in New Democracies*. Ed. James McAdams. Notre Dame, IN: Notre Dame University Press, 269–290.

Edwards, Bob, and Michael Foley. 2001. "Civil Society and Social Capital." In *Civil Society and the Social Capital Debate in Comparative Perspective*. Ed. Bob Edwards, Michael Foley, and Mario Diani. Hanover, NH: University Press of New England, 1–16.

Ehrenberg, John. 1999. *Civil Society: The Critical History of an Idea*. New York: New York University Press.

Elster, Jon. 2004. *Closing the Books: Transitional Justice in Historical Perspective*. Cambridge: Cambridge University Press.

England, Harri. 2002. *From War to Peace on the Mozambique-Malawi Borderland*. Edinburgh: Edinburgh University Press.

Enright, Robert D., Suzanne Freedman, and Julio Rique. 1998. "The Psychology of Interpersonal Forgiveness." In *Exploring Forgiveness*. Ed. Robert D. Enright and Joanna North. Madison: University of Wisconsin Press, 46–62.

Enright, Robert D., and The Human Development Study Group. 1994. "Piaget on the Moral Development of Forgiveness: Reciprocity or Identify?" *Human Development* 37: 63–80.

Etcheson, Craig. 2005. *After the Killing Fields: Lessons from the Cambodian Genocide*. Westport, CT.: Praeger.

Fletcher, George. 2001. *Rethinking Criminal Law*. Oxford: Oxford University Press.

Fletcher, Laurel, and Harvey Weinstein. 2002. "Violence and Social Repair: Rethinking the Contribution of Justice to Reconciliation." *Human Rights Quarterly* 24, no. 3: 586–591.

Fraser, Nancy. 1997. *Justice Interruptus: Critical Reflections on the "Postsocialist" Condition*. New York: Routledge.

———. 2000. "Rethinking Recognition." *New Left Review* 3: 107–120.

———. 2001. "Recognition without Ethics?" *Theory, Culture and Society* 18, no. 2–3: 21–42.

———. 2003. "Social Justice in the Age of Identity Politics: Redistribution, Recognition and Participation." In *Redistribution or Recognition? A Political-Philosophical Exchange*. Ed. Nancy Fraser and Axel Honneth. New York: Verso, 7–109.

Fraser, Nancy, and Axel Honneth. 2003. "Introduction." In *Redistribution or Recognition? A Political-Philosophical Exchange*. Ed. Nancy Fraser and Axel Honneth. New York: Verso, 1–6.

Freeman, Mark. 2002. "Lessons Learned from Amnesties for Human Rights Crimes." *The 3rd Page: The Journal of Transparency International* X, no. 9: 12–13.

————. 2006. *Truth Commissions and Procedural Fairness*. Cambridge: Cambridge University Press.

Fuller, Lon. 1958. "Positivism and Fidelity to Law—A Reply to Professor Hart." *Harvard Law Review* 71: 630–670.

Fullinwider, Robert K., ed. 1999. *Civil Society, Democracy and Civil Renewal*. Lanham, MD: Rowman and Littlefield.

Gagnon, Valére Philip. 2005. *The Myth of Ethnic War: Serbia and Croatia in the 1990s*. Ithaca, NY: Cornell University Press.

Garretón, Manuel Antonio. 1992. "Fear in Military Regimes: An Overview." In *Fear at the Edge: State Terror and Resistance in Latin America*. Ed. Juan Corradi, Patricia Weiss Fagen, and Manuel Antonio Garretón. Berkeley: University of California Press, 13–25.

Gellately, Robert. 2001. *Backing Hitler*. Oxford: Oxford University Press.

Gibney, Mark, and Erik Roxstrom. 2001. "The Status of State Apologies." *Human Rights Quarterly* 23: 911–939.

Gibson, James L. 2004. *Overcoming Apartheid: Can Truth Reconcile a Divided Nation?* New York: Russell Sage Foundation.

Gill, Graeme. 2000. *The Dynamics of Democratization: Elites, Civil Society and the Transition Process*. New York: St. Martin's Press.

Giner-Sorolla, Roger, Emanuele Castano, Pablo Espinosa, and Rupert Brown. 2008. "Shame Expressions Reduce the Recipient's Insult from Outgroup Reparations." *Journal of Experimental Social Psychology* 44: 519–526.

Glover, Jonathan. 1970. *Responsibility*. London: Routledge.

Goffman, Erving. 1971. *Relations in Public*. London: Allen Lane Press.

Golding, Martin. 1985. "Forgiveness and Regret." *Philosophical Forum* 16: 1984–1985.

Golsan, Richard A. 2000. *Vichy's Afterlife: History and Counterhistory in Postwar France*. Lincoln: University of Nebraska.

Goodin, Robert. 1989. "Theories of Compensation." *Oxford Journal of Legal Studies* 9: 56–79.

Govier, Trudy. 2002. *Forgiveness and Revenge*. London: Routledge.

Govier, Trudy, and Wilhelm Verwoerd. 2002. "The Promises and Pitfalls of Apology." *Journal of Social Philosophy* 33, no. 1: 67–82.

Graybill, Lyn. 2001. "To Punish or Pardon: A Comparison of the International Criminal Tribunal for Rwanda and the South African Truth and Reconciliation Commission." *Human Rights Review* 2, no. 4 (July–September 2001): 3–18.

Gross, Jan T. 2001. *Neighbors: The Destruction of the Jewish Community in Jedwabne, Poland.* Princeton, NJ: Princeton University Press.

———. 2006. *Fear: Anti-Semitism in Poland After Auschwitz.* New York: Random House.

Gulu District NGO Forum. 2009. Available at http://www.ugandafund.org/Empowering_Gulu_NGO.htm. Accessed April 24, 2009.

Habermas, Jürgen. 1996. *Between Facts and Norms: Contributions to a Discourse Theory of Law and Democracy.* Cambridge, MA: Massachusetts Institute of Technology Press.

Halbwachs, Maurice. 1992. *On Collective Memory.* Chicago: Chicago University Press.

Hampshire, Stuart. 1989. *Innocence and Experience.* Cambridge, MA: Harvard University Press.

Hampton, Jean. 1994. "Democracy and the Rule of Law." *NOMOS XXXVI: The Rule of Law.* Ed. Ian Shapiro. New York: New York University Press, 13–45.

Harneit-Sievers, Axel, and Sydney Emezue. 2000. "Towards a Social History of Warfare and Reconstruction: The Nigerian/Biafran Case." In *The Politics of Memory: Truth, Healing and Social Justice.* Ed. Ifi Amadiume and Abdullah An-Na'im. London: Zed Books, 110–126.

Hart, Herbert Lionel Adolphus. 1958. "Positivism and the Separation of Law and Morals." *Harvard Law Review* 71: 593–629.

Hartman, Geoffrey. 1994. "Introduction: Darkness Visible." In *Holocaust Remembrance: The Shape of Memory.* Ed. Geoffrey Hartman. Oxford: Blackwell Press, 1–22.

Harvey, Jean. 1995. "The Emerging Practice of Institutional Apologies." *International Journal of Applied Philosophy* 9, no. 2 (Winter/Spring): 57–65.

Hatzfeld, Jean. 2008. *Life Laid Bare: The Survivors of Rwanda Speak.* London: Other Press.

Hayner, Priscilla. 2001. *Unspeakable Truths: Confronting State Terror and Atrocity: How Truth Commissions Around the World are Challenging the Past and Shaping the Future.* New York: Routledge.

Hegel, Georg Wilhelm Friedrich. 1967. *Philosophy of Right.* Oxford: Oxford University Press.

Helmick, Raymond C. 2008. "Seeing the Image of God in Others: The Key to the Transformation of Conflicts." *Human Development* 29, no. 2 (Summer): 24–29.

Herman, Judith. 1997. *Trauma and Recovery: The Aftermath of Violence: From Domestic Abuse to Political Terror.* New York: Basic Books.

Hilberg, Raul. 1993. *Perpetrators, Victims, Bystanders: The Jewish Catastrophe 1933-1945.* New York: Harper Perennial.

Hill, Thomas E. 1973. "Servility and Self Respect." *The Monist* 57 (January): 87–104.

Him, Chanrithy. 2000. *When Broken Glass Floats: Growing Up Under the Khmer Rouge, A Memoir.* New York: Norton.

Hirschman, Albert O. 1970. *Exit, Voice, Loyalty: Responses to Decline in Firms, Organizations and States.* Cambridge, MA: Harvard University Press.

Hodgkinson, Virginia, and Michael Foley, eds. 2003. *The Civil Society Reader.* Lebanon, NH: University Press of New England.

Holmgren, Margaret. 1993. "Forgiveness and the Intrinsic Value of Persons." *American Philosophical Quarterly* 30, no. 4 (October): 341–352.

Honneth, Axel. 1995. *The Fragmented World of the Social: Essays in Social and Political Philosophy.* Albany: State University of New York Press.

———. 1996. *The Struggle for Recognition: The Moral Grammar of Social Conflicts.* Cambridge, MA: Masssachusetts Institute of Technology Press.

Horsbrugh, H. J. N. 1974. "Forgiveness." *Canadian Journal of Philosophy* 4: 269–289.

Human Rights Watch. 1995. "Policy Statement on Accountability for Past Abuses." In *Transitional Justice: How Emerging Democracies Reckon with Former Regimes.* Ed. Neil Kritz. Washington, DC: United States Peace Institute, 3 vols., 1: 217–218.

———. 2006. "Algeria: New Amnesty Law Will Ensure That Atrocities Go Unpunished" (March 1). Available at http://www.hrw.org/english/docs/2006/03/01/algeri12743.htm. Accessed May 23, 2008.

———. 2008. "Zimbabwe: End Crackdown on Peaceful Demonstrators" (October 18). *Human Rights Watch News.* Available at http://www.hrw.org/en/news/2008/10/28/zimbabwe-end-crackdown-peaceful-demonstrators. Accessed December 25, 2008.

Humphrey, Michael. 2002. *The Politics of Atrocity and Reconciliation: From Terror to Trauma.* London: Routledge.

Huntington, Samuel. 1993. *The Third Wave: Democratization in the Late Twentieth Century.* Norman: University of Oklahoma Press.

Huyse, Luc. 2008. "Tradition-Based Approaches in Peacemaking, Transitional Justice and Reconciliation Policies." In *Traditional Justice and Reconciliation after Violent Conflict: Learning from African Experiences.* Ed. Luc Huyse and Mark Salter. Stockholm: Institute for Democracy and Electoral Assistance, 1–21.

Ignatieff, Michael. 1996. "Articles of Faith." *Index on Censorship* 25, no. 5: 110–122.

———. 1998. *The Warrior's Honor: Ethnic War and the Modern Conscience.* New York: Owl Books.

Igreja, Victor, and Beatrice Dias-Lambranca. 2008. "Restorative Justice and the Role of Magamba Spirits in Post-civil War Gorongosa, Central Mozambique." In *Traditional Justice and Reconciliation after Violent Conflict: Learning from African Experiences.* Ed. Luc Huyse and Mark Salter. Stockholm: Institute for Democracy and Electoral Assistance, 61–83.

Ikpeze, Nnaemeka. 2000. "Post-Biafran Marginalization of the Igbo in Nige-
ria." In *The Politics of Memory: Truth, Healing and Social Justice*. Ed. Ifi
Amadiume and Abdullah An-Na'im. London: Zed Books, 90–109.

Ingelaere, Bert. 2008. "The Gacaca Courts in Rwanda." In *Traditional Jus-
tice and Reconciliation after Violent Conflict: Learning from African
Experiences*. Ed. Luc Huyse and Mark Salter. Stockholm: Institute for
Democracy and Electoral Assistance, 51–57.

Iraq. n.d. "Supreme Iraqi Criminal Tribunal Statute." Available at http://www
.ictj.org/static/MENA/Iraq/iraq.statute.engtrans.pdf. Accessed September 12, 2008.

Jaspers, Karl. 1961. *The Question of German Guilt*. New York: Capricorn
Books.

Johnson, Eric A. 1999. *Nazi Terror: The Gestapo, Jews and Ordinary
Germans*. New York: Basic Books.

Johnson, James. 1998. "Arguing for Deliberation: Some Skeptical Considerations." In *Deliberative Democracy*. Ed. Jon Elster. Cambridge: Cambridge University Press, 161–184.

Johnston, Douglas, and Cynthia Sampson, eds. 1994. *Religion: The Missing
Dimension of Statecraft*. New York: Oxford University Press.

Joinet, Louis. 1997. "Set of Principles for the Protection and Promotion of Human Rights through Action to Combat Impunity" (October 2). UN document E/CN.4/Sub.2/1997/20. United Nations. Available at http://www
.unhchr.ch/huridocda/huridoca.nsf/Symbol/E.CN.4.sub.2.1997.20. Accessed
September 23, 2008.

Jones, Adam. 2006a."Why Gendercide? Why Root and Branch? A Comparison of the Vendée Uprising of 1793–94 and the Bosnian War of the
1990s." *Journal of Genocide Research* 8, no. 1 (March): 9–25.

———. 2006b. "Straight as a Rule." *Men and Masculinities* 8, no. 4 (April):
451–469.

Jung, Courtney. 2000. *Then I Was Black: South African Political Identities in
Transition*. New Haven, CT: Yale University Press.

Kant, Immanuel. 1996. *Metaphysics of Morals*. Cambridge: Cambridge University Press.

———. 1998. *Groundwork of the Metaphysics of Morals*. Cambridge: Cambridge University Press.

Keane, John, ed. 1988. *Civil Society and the State*. London: Verso.

Kelsall, Tim. 2005. "Truth, Lies, Ritual: Preliminary Reflections on the Truth
and Reconciliation Commission in Sierra Leone." *Human Rights Quarterly* 27: 361–391.

Kelsen, Hans. 1947. "Will the Judgment in the Nuremberg Trial Constitute
a Precedent in International Law?" *International Law Quarterly* 1: 153–
159.

Kiernan, Ben. 2007. *Blood and Soil: A World History of Genocide and Extermination from Sparta to Darfur*. New Haven, CT: Yale University Press.

Kirchheimer, Otto. 1961. *Political Justice: The Use of Legal Procedure for Political Ends.* Westport, CT: Greenwood Press.

Kirkby, Coel. 2006. "Rwanda's Gacaca Courts: A Preliminary Critique." *Journal of African Law* 50: 94–117.

Kiss, Elizabeth. 2001. "Moral Ambition within and Beyond Political Constraints." In *Truth v. Justice: The Morality of Truth Commissions.* Ed. Robert Rotberg and Dennis Thompson. Princeton, NJ: Princeton University Press, 68–98.

Kleinfeld Belton, Rachel. 2005. "Competing Definitions of the Rule of Law: Implications for Practitioners." Democracy and Rule of Law Project, *Carnegie Papers,* Rule of Law Series. New York: Carnegie Council.

Korsgaard, Christine.1996. *Creating the Kingdom of Ends.* Cambridge: Cambridge University Press.

Kritz, Neil, ed. 1995. *Transitional Justice: How Emerging Democracies Reckon with Former Regimes.* Washington, DC: United States Peace Institute, 3 vols.

Krog, Antjie. 1998. *Country of My Skull: Guilt, Sorrow, and the Limits of Forgiveness in the New South Africa.* New York: Random House.

Kuper, Leo. 1981. *Genocide.* New Haven, CT: Yale University Press.

Laclau, Ernesto. 1990. "Theory, Democracy and Socialism." In *New Reflections on the Revolution of Our Time.* New York: Verso.

———. 1996. *Emancipation(s).* New York: Verso.

Lahav, Pnina. 1992. "The Eichmann Trial, the Jewish Question, and the American-Jewish Intelligentsia." *Boston University Law Review* 72: 559–561.

Langer, Lawrence. 1991. *Holocaust Testimonies: The Ruins of Memory.* New Haven, CT: Yale University Press.

Lawyers Committee for Human Rights. 2002. "Building on Quicksand: The Collapse of the World Bank's Judicial Reform Project in Peru." New York: Lawyers Committee for Human Rights.

Lederach, John Paul. 1999. *Sustainable Reconciliation in Divided Societies.* Washington, DC: United States Institute of Peace Press.

Lefort, Claude. 1986. *The Political Forms of Modern Society.* Cambridge, MA: Massachusetts Institute of Technology Press.

Lehman, Paul. 1986. "Forgiveness." In *The Westminster Dictionary of Christian Ethics.* Ed. James Childress and John Macquerrie. Philadelphia, PA: Westminster Press.

Lehning, Percy B., ed. 1998. *Theories of Secession.* London: Routledge.

Leo, John. 1997. "So Who's Sorry Now?" *U.S. News and World Report* (June 30): 17.

Lester, I. 2000. *Comisiones de la Verdad y Reconciliación Nacional.* Santiago, Chile: Esperanza.

Levine, Robert A., and Donald Campbell. 1972. *Ethnocentrism: Theories of Conflict, Ethnic Attitudes and Group Behavior.* New York: Wiley Press.

Lewis, Clive Staples. 1957. *The Problem of Pain*. London: Fontana Books.

Lewis, Michael. 1980. "On Forgiveness." *Philosophical Quarterly* 30: 236–245.

Lifton, Robert Jay. 1991. *Death In Life: Survivors of Hiroshima*. Chapel Hill: University of North Carolina Press.

Linden, Ian. 1994. "The Right to Truth: Amnesty, Amnesia and Secrecy." *Development in Practice* 4, no. 2: 16–28.

Linz, Juan. 1978. *The Breakdown of Democratic Regimes: Crisis, Breakdown and Reequilibration*. Baltimore: Johns Hopkins University.

Linz, Juan, and Alfred Stepan. 1996. *Problems of Democratic Transition and Consolidation: Southern Europe, South America, and Post-Communist Europe*. Baltimore: Johns Hopkins University.

Lira, Elisabeth. 1997. "Guatemala: Uncovering the Past, Recovering the Future." *Development in Practice* 7, no. 4: 54–64.

Llewellyn, Jennifer. 1999. "Justice for South Africa: Restorative Justice and the South African Truth and Reconciliation Commission." In *Moral Issues in Global Perspective*. Ed. Christine Koggel. Peterborough, Ontario: Broadview, 96–107.

Locke, John. 1983. *A Letter Concerning Toleration*. Indianapolis, IN: Hackett.

Lomasky, Loren. 1991. "Compensation and the Bounds of Rights." In *NOMOS XXXIII: Compensatory Justice*. Ed. John Chapman. New York: New York University Press, 13–44.

Loveman, Brian, and Elizabeth Lira. 2000. *Las Ardientes Cenizas del Olvido: Vía Chilena de la Reconciliación Política 1932–1994*. Santiago, Chile: LOM Ediciones.

Macedo, Stephen, ed. 2006. *Universal Jurisdiction: National Courts and the Prosecution of Serious Crimes under International Law*. Philadelphia: University of Pennsylvania Press.

Mackintosh, L.R. 1927. *The Christian Experience of Forgiveness*. London: n.p.

Mamdani, Mahmood. 1998. "When Does a Settler Become a Native?" *Electronic Mail and Guardian* (May 26). Available at www.mg.co.za/mg/za/links/africa/DRC-all.html. Accessed April 27, 2009.

Mani, Rama. 2002. *Beyond Retribution: Seeking Justice in the Shadows of War*. London: Polity Press.

Manin, Bernard. 1987. "On Legitimacy and Political Deliberation." *Political Theory* 15, no. 3 (August): 338–368.

Manning, Carrie. 2002. *The Politics of Peace in Mozambique: Post Conflict Democratization*. Westport, CT: Praeger.

Martínez, Javier. 1992. "Fear of the State, Fear of Society: On the Opposition Protests in Chile." In *Fear at the Edge: State Terror and Resistance in Latin America*. Ed. Juan Corradi, Patricia Weiss Fagen, and Manuel Antonio Garretón. Berkeley: University of California Press, 142–160.

Marty, Martin. 1998. "The Ethos of Christian Forgiveness." In *Dimensions of Forgiveness: Psychological Research and Theological Forgiveness*.

Ed. Everett L. Worthington, Jr. Philadelphia, PA: Templeton Foundation Press, 9–28.

Mason, T. David, and James D. Meernik, eds. 2006. *Conflict Prevention and Peace Building in Post-War Societies*. London: Routledge.

McAdams, James A., ed. 2001. *Transitional Justice and the Rule of Law in New Democracies*. Notre Dame, IN: University of Notre Dame Press.

Meier, Charles. 1988. *The Unmasterable Past: History, Holocaust and German National Identity*. Cambridge, MA: Harvard University Press.

Méndez, Juan. 1997. "Derecho a la Verdad frente a Graves Violaciones a los Derechos Humanos." In *La Aplicación de los Tratados sobre los Derechos Humanos por los Tribunales Locales*. Ed. Martín Abregú and Cristián Courtis. Buenos Aires: Editorial Del Puerto-CELS, 517–540.

———, ed. 1999. *The (Un)rule of Law and the Underprivileged in Latin America*. Notre Dame, IN: Notre Dame University Press.

Mendus, Susan. 1998. *Justifying Tolerance: Conceptual and Historical Perspectives*. Cambridge: Cambridge University Press.

———, ed. 1999. *The Politics of Toleration*. Edinburgh: Edinburgh University Press.

Menéndez-Carrión, Amparo, and Alfred Joignant, eds. 1999. *La Caja de Pandora: El Retorno de la Transición Chilena*. Santiago, Chile: Planeta/Ariel.

Merwin, William. 1970. "Unchopping a Tree." In *The Miner's Pale Children*. New York: Atheneum Books, 80–88.

Michnik, Adam. 1985. *Letters from Prison and Other Essays*. Berkeley: University of California.

Miller, Donald, and Lorna Touryan Miller. 1999. *Survivors: An Oral History of the Armenian Genocide*. Berkeley: University of California.

Minear, Richard. 2001. *Victors' Justice: The Tokyo War Crimes Trial*. Ann Arbor: University of Michigan.

Minow, Martha. 1998. *Between Vengeance and Forgiveness: Facing History After Genocide and Mass Violence*. Boston: Beacon Press.

Moon, Claire. 2008. *Narrating Political Reconciliation: South Africa's Truth and Reconciliation Commission*. Lanham, MD: Lexington Books.

Moses, A. Dirk. 2007. *German Intellectuals and the Nazi Past*. Cambridge: Cambridge University Press.

Mosse, George. 1991. *Fallen Soldiers: Reshaping the Memory of the World Wars*. Oxford: Oxford University Press.

Mouffe, Chantal. 1997. *The Return of the Political*. New York: Verso.

Moulian, Tomás. 1998. *Chile Actual: Anatomía de un Mito*. Santiago, Chile: LOM ARCIS.

Muller-Fahrenholz, Geiko. 1997. *The Art of Forgiveness: Theological Reflections on Healing and Reconciliation*. Geneva: WCC Publications.

Murphy, Jeffrie. 1995. "Getting Even: The Role of the Victim." In *Punishment and Rehabilitation*. Ed. Jeffrie Murphy. Belmont, CA: Wadsworth, 132–152.

Murphy, Jeffrie, and Jean Hampton. 1988. *Forgiveness and Mercy.* Cambridge: Cambridge University Press.

Narayan, Uma. 1998. "Forgiveness, Moral Reassessment and Reconciliation." In *Explorations of Value.* Ed. Thomas Magnell. Atlanta: Rodopi Press, 169–178.

Nehushtan, Yossi. 2007. "The Limits of Tolerance: A Substantive-Liberal Perspective." *Ratio Juris* 20/2 (June): 230–257.

Neier, Aryeh. 1998. *War Crimes: Brutality, Genocide, Terror, and the Struggle for Justice.* New York: Times Books.

Nersessian David L. 2002. "The Contours of Genocidal Intent: Troubling Jurisprudence from the International Criminal Tribunals." *Texas International Law Journal,* 35–60.

Nesiah, Vasuki. 2006. "Truth v. Justice?: Commissions and Courts." In *Human Rights and Conflict: Exploring the Links between Rights, Law and Peacebuilding.* Ed. Julie Mertus and Jeffrey W. Helsing. Washington, DC: United States Institute of Peace, 375–397.

Newey, Glen. 1999. *Virtue, Reason and Tolerance.* Edinburgh: Edinburgh University Press.

Nietzsche, Friedrich. 1989. *On the Genealogy of Morals.* New York: Vintage Books.

———. 1997. "On the Uses and Disadvantages of History for Life." *Untimely Meditations.* Cambridge: Cambridge University Press, 57–124.

Nino, Carlos Santiago. 1996. *The Constitution of Deliberative Democracy.* New Haven, CT: Yale University Press.

Nobles, Melissa. 2008. *The Politics of Official Apologies.* Cambridge: Cambridge University Press.

Nora, Pierre, ed. 1996. *Realms of Memory: Rethinking the French Past.* New York: Columbia University Press.

Nordstrom, Carolyn. 1997. *A Different Kind of War Story: Ethnography of Political Violence.* Philadelphia: University of Pennsylvania Press.

North, Joanna. 1998. "The 'Ideal' of Forgiveness: A Philosopher's Exploration." In *Exploring Forgiveness.* Ed. Robert D. Enright and Joanna North. Madison: University of Wisconsin Press, 15–34.

Norval, Aletta. 1998. "Memory, Identity and the (Im)possibility of Reconciliation: The Work of the Truth and Reconciliation Commission in South Africa." *Constellations* 5, no. 2: 250–265.

Nossack, Hans Erich. 2004. *The End: Hamburg 1943.* Chicago: University of Chicago Press.

Nozick, Robert. 1974. *Anarchy, State and Utopia.* New York: Basic Books.

———. 1981. *Philosophical Explanations.* Cambridge, MA: Harvard University Press.

Nyatagodien, Ridwan Laher, and Arthur Neal. 2004. "Collective Trauma, Apologies and the Politics of Memory." *Journal of Human Rights* 3, no. 4 (December): 465–475.

O'Donnell, Guillermo, Phillipe C. Schmitter, and Laurence Whitehead, eds. 1986. *Transitions from Authoritarian Rule*. Baltimore: Johns Hopkins University, 4 vols.

Ojera Latigo, James. 2008. "Northern Uganda: Tradition-Based Practices in the Acholi Region." In *Traditional Justice and Reconciliation after Violent Conflict: Learning from African Experiences*. Ed. Luc Huyse and Mark Salter. Stockholm: Institute for Democracy and Electoral Assistance, 85–122.

Okin, Susan. 1999. *Is Multiculturalism Bad for Women?* Princeton, NJ: Princeton University Press.

Orentlicher, Diane. 1990. "Settling Accounts: The Duty to Prosecute Human Rights Violations of a Prior Regime." *Yale Law Journal* 100: 2537–2614.

Orr, Wendy. 2000. "Reparation Delayed Is Healing Retarded." In *Looking Back, Reaching Forward: Reflections on the Truth and Reconciliation Commission of South Africa*. Ed. Charles Villa-Vicencio and Wilhelm Verwoerd. London: Zed Books, 34–60.

Osiel, Mark. 1997. *Mass Atrocity, Collective Memory, and the Law*. New Brunswick, NJ: Transaction.

Paris, Erna. 2001. *Long Shadows: Truth, Lies and History*. New York: Bloomsbury.

Parliament of Australia, Senate Legal and Constitutional References Committee. 2000. *Healing: A Legacy of Generations: The Report into the Federal Government's Implementation of the Recommendations Made by the Human Rights and Equal Commission in Bringing Them Home* (November). Sydney: Government of Australia.

Perelli, Carina. 1992. "Youth, Politics and Dictatorship in Uruguay." In *Fear at the Edge: State Terror and Resistance in Latin America*. Ed. Juan Corradi, Patricia Weiss Fagen, and Manuel Antonio Garretón. Berkeley: University of California Press, 212–235.

Perkumpulan Hak. 2008. "The Hak Association Timor-Leste." Available at http://www.yayasanhak.minihub.org/eng. Accessed September 12, 2008.

Peru. 1995. "Ley N°26479(7)." *El Peruano* (June 14). Lima, Peru.

———. 2003. "Truth and Reconciliation Commission of Peru. Final Report." Available at www.cverdad.org.pe. Accessed January 12, 2009.

Petersen, Rodney L. 2001. "A Theology of Forgiveness: Terminology, Rhetoric, and the Dialectic of Interfaith Relationships." In *Forgiveness and Reconciliation: Religion, Public Policy and Conflict Transformation*. Ed. Raymond C. Helmick and Rodney Petersen. Philadelphia, PA: Templeton Foundation Press, 175–196.

Philip, Mark. 2008. "Peacebuilding and Corruption." *International Peacekeeping* 15, no. 3 (June): 310–327.

Plunkett, Mark. 1998. "Reestablishing Law and Order in Peace-Maintenance." *Global Governance* 4, no. 1: 63–82.

Polonsky, Antony, and Joanna Michlic, eds. 2004. *The Neighbors Respond: The Controversy over the Jedwabne Massacre in Poland.* Princeton, NJ: Princeton University Press.

Post, Robert. 1993. "Managing Deliberation: The Quandary of Democratic Dialogue." *Ethics* 103, no. 4 (July): 654–678.

Prosecutor v. Blaškić. 2004. Judgment, Appeals Chamber, Case No. IT-95-14-A. (July 29). *International Criminal Tribunal for the Former Yugoslavia.*

Prosecutor v. Krstić. 2004. Judgment, Appeals Chamber, Case No. IT-98-33-A (April 19). *International Criminal Tribunal for the Former Yugoslavia.*

Prunier, Gerard. 1997. *The Rwanda Crisis.* New York: Columbia University Press.

Putnam, Robert. 1995. "Bowling Alone: America's Declining Capital." *Journal of Democracy* (January): 65–78.

Ramji, Jaya. 2000. "Reclaiming Cambodian History: The Case for a Truth Commission." *The Fletcher Forum of World Affairs Journal* 24: 137–156.

Rassi, Christopher. 2007. "Lessons Learned from Saddam Trial: Lessons Learned from the Iraqi High Tribunal: The Need for an International Independent Investigation." *Case Western Reserve Journal of International Law* 215: 219–235.

Rawls, John. 2005. *Political Liberalism.* Expanded Edition. New York: Columbia University Press.

Reno, William. 2008. "Anti-Corruption Efforts in Liberia: Are They Aimed at the Right Targets?" *International Peacekeeping* 15, no. 3 (June): 387–404.

Richards, Norvin. 1988. "Forgiveness." *Ethics* 99: 77–97.

Ristchl, Albrecht. 1900. *The Christian Doctrine of Justification and Reconciliation.* London: n.p.: 3 vols.

Robertson, Geoffrey. 2000. *Crimes against Humanity: The Struggle for Global Justice.* London: New Press.

Roht-Arriaza, Namomi. 2002. "Civil Society in Processes of Accountability." In *Post-Conflict Justice.* Ed. M. Cherif Bassiouni. Ardsley, NY: Transnational, 97–114.

———. 2004. "Reparations Decisions and Dilemmas." *Hastings International and Comparative Law Review* 27 (Winter): 157–219.

Roth, Kenneth. 1999. "Human Rights in the Haitian Transition to Democracy." In *Human Rights in Political Transition: Gettysburg to Bosnia.* Ed. Carla Hesse and Robert Post. New York: Zone Books, 93–134.

Roth, Kenneth, and Alison Des Forges. 2002. "Justice or Therapy?" Available at http://bostonreview.net/BR27.3/roth_desforges.php. Accessed April 30, 2009.

Rummel, Rudolph J. 1997. *Statistics of Democide, Genocide, and Mass Murder Since 1900*. Charlottesville: Center for National Security Law, University of Virginia.

Rwanda. 2008. "National Service of the Gacaca Courts." Available at www.inkiko-gacaca.gov.rw. Accessed May 10, 2008.

Samuels, Kirsti. 2006. *Rule of Law Reform in Post-Conflict Countries: Operational Initiatives and Lessons Learnt*. Washington, DC: World Bank (October).

Sandel, Michael. 1998. *Liberalism and the Limits of Justice*. Cambridge: Cambridge University Press.

Savage, Kirk. 1994. "The Savage Politics of Memory: Black Emancipation and the Civil War Monument." In *Commemorations: The Politics of National Identity*. Ed. John Gillis. Princeton, NJ: Princeton University Press, 127–149.

Scanlon, Thomas. 2003. *The Difficulty of Tolerance*. Cambridge: Cambridge University Press.

Scarry, Elaine. 1987. *The Body in Pain: The Making and Unmaking of the World*. Oxford: Oxford University Press.

Schaap, Andrew. 2005. *Political Reconciliation*. London: Routledge.

Schabas, William. 2004. "A Synergistic Relationship: The Sierra Leone Truth and Reconciliation Commission and the Special Court for Sierra Leone." In *Truth Commissions and Courts: The Tension Between Criminal Justice and the Search for Truth*. Ed. William Schabas and Shane Darcy. Berlin: Springer, 3–54.

Scheler, Max. 1973. *Ressentiment*. New York: Noonday Books.

Scher, Steven, and John Darley. 1997. "How Effective Are the Things That People Say to Apologize? Effects of the Realization of the Apology Speech Act." *Journal of Psycholinguistic Research* 26: 127–140.

Scheuerman, William. 1994. *Between the Norm and the Exception: The Frankfurt School and the Rule of Law*. Cambridge, MA: Massachusetts Institute of Technology Press.

Schreiter, Robert J. 1997. *Reconciliation*. Maryknoll, NY: BTI/Orbis Books.

Schwan, Gesine. 1998. "Political Consequences of Silenced Guilt." *Constellations* 5, no. 3: 472–491.

Searle, John. 1969. *Speech Acts: An Essay in the Philosophy of Language*. Cambridge: Cambridge University Press.

Sen, Amartya. 1999. *Development as Freedom*. New York: Anchor Books.

Seré Association for Promoting Memory and Life. 2008. Available at http://www.sere.org.ar. Accessed May 24, 2008.

Shklar, Judith. 1964. *Legalism: Law, Morals, and Political Trials*. Cambridge, MA: Harvard University Press.

Short, Damien. 2008. *Reconciliation and Colonial Power: Indigenous Rights in Australia*. Aldershot, England: Ashgate.

Shriver, Donald, Jr. 1997. *An Ethic for Enemies: Forgiveness in Politics*. Oxford: Oxford University Press.

Sierra Leone. 2008. "Campaign for Good Governance." Available at http://www.slcgg.org/. Accessed September 9, 2008.

———. 2004. "Truth and Reconciliation Commission. Final Report." 2 vols. Available at http://trcsierraleone.org/drwebsite/publish/index.shtml. Accessed September 24, 2008.

Smith, Nick. 2008. *I Was Wrong: The Meaning of Apologies*. Cambridge: Cambridge University Press.

Smith, R. H., J. M. Webster, W. G. Parrott, and H. L. Eyre. 2002. "The Role of Public Exposure in Moral and Nonmoral Shame and Guilt." *Journal of Personality and Social Psychology* 83: 138–159.

Snyder, Jack, and Leslie Vinjamuri. 2004. "Trials and Errors: Principle and Pragmatism in Strategies of International Justice." *International Security* 28/3 (Winter): 5–44.

Solomon, Robert C. 1990. *A Passion for Justice: Emotions and the Origins of the Social Contract*. New York: Addison-Wesley Books.

South Africa. 1995. "Promotion of National Unity and Reconciliation Act." Available at http://www.doj.gov.za/trc/legal/act9534.htm. Accessed April 20, 2009.

South African Truth and Reconciliation Commission. 1995. *South African Truth and Reconciliation Commission Final Report*. New York: Grove's Dictionaries, 5 vols.

Soyinka, Wole. 1999. *The Burden of Memory, the Muse of Forgiveness*. Oxford: Oxford University Press.

Special Court for Sierra Leone. 2003. Available at http://www.sc-sl.org/. Accessed September 12, 2008.

Sriram, Chandra Lekha. 2005. *Globalizing Justice for Mass Atrocities: A Revolution in Accountability*. London: Routledge.

Staub, Ervin. 1989. *The Roots of Evil: The Origins of Genocide and Other Group Violence*. Cambridge: Cambridge University Press.

Steel, Ronald. 1998. "Sorry About That." *The New Republic* (April 20): 9.

Stover, Eric. 2005. *The Witnesses: War Crimes and the Promise of Justice in The Hague*. Philadelphia: University of Pennsylvania Press.

Streich, Gregory. 2002. "Constructing Multicultural Democracy: To Deliberate or Not to Deliberate." *Constellations* 9, no. 1: 127–153.

Suchocki, Marjorie. 1994. *The Fall to Violence: Original Sin in Relational Theology*. New York: Continuum.

Summerfield, Derek. 1995. "Addressing Human Response to War and Atrocity: Major Challenges in Research and Practices and the Limitations of Western Psychiatric Models." In *Beyond Trauma: Cultural and Societal Dynamics*. Ed. Rolf J. Kleber, Charles R. Figley, and Bertolhold P. R. Gersons. New York: Plenum Press, 18–40.

Szymusiak, Moldya (formerly Buth Keo). 1999. *The Stones Cry Out: A Cambodian Childhood, 1975–1980*. Bloomington: Indiana University Press.

Taft, Lee. 2000. "Apology Subverted: The Commodification of Apology." *Yale Law Journal* 109: 1135–1160.

Tajfel, Henri, and John Turner. 1986. "The Social Identity Theory of Intergroup Behavior. In *Psychology of Intergroup Relations*. Ed. Stephen Worchel and William Austin. Chicago: Nelson Hall.

Tavuchis, Nicholas. 1991. *Mea Culpa: A Sociology of Apology and Reconciliation*. Stanford, CA: Stanford University Press.

Taylor, Charles. 1989. *Sources of the Self: The Making of Modern Identity*. Cambridge, MA: Harvard University Press.

———. 1994. "The Politics of Recognition." In *Multiculturalism*. Ed. Amy Gutmann and Charles Taylor. Princeton, NJ: Princeton University Press.

Taylor, John G. 1999. *East Timor: The Price of Freedom*. London: Zed Books.

Teitel, Ruti. 2002. *Transitional Justice*. Oxford: Oxford University Press.

Timerman, Jacobo. 2002. *Prisoner without a Name, Cell without a Number*. Madison: University of Wisconsin.

Torpey, John C. 2006. *Making Whole What Has Been Smashed: On Reparations Politics*. Cambridge, MA: Harvard University Press.

Tuol Sleng Genocide Museum. 2009. Available at www.tuolsleng.com/. Accessed April 23, 2009.

Turner, Victor. 2001. *From Ritual to Theatre: The Human Seriousness of Play*. New York: PAJ.

Tutu, Desmond. 1998. "Without Forgiveness There Is No Future." In *Exploring Forgiveness*. Ed. Robert D. Enright and Joanna North. Madison: University of Wisconsin Press.

———. 1999. No Future without Forgiveness. New York: Doubleday.

Ung, Loung. 2000. *First They Killed My Father: A Daughter of Cambodia Remembers*. New York: Harper Collins.

Unger, Roberto. 1998. *Democracy Realized: The Progressive Alternative*. New York: Verso.

United Nations. 1948. Convention on the Prevention and Punishment of the Crime of Genocide. United Nations: General Assembly of the United Nations, Resolution 2670 (December 9).

———. 1968. Convention on the Non-Applicability of Statutory Limitations to War Crimes and Crimes against Humanity. United Nations: General Assembly of the United Nations, Resolution 2391 XXIII (November).

———. 1999. Rome Statute of the International Criminal Court, U.N. Doc. C.N.604.1999 Treaties-18 (July 12). Available at http://www.icc-cpi.int/. Accessed August 12, 2008.

United Nations Commission on Human Rights. 2005. Resolution 2005/66 "Right to Truth" (April 20).

United Nations Human Rights Council. 2008. Resolution A/HRC/9/L.23 "On the Right to Truth" (September 28).

United Nations Interim Administration Mission in Kosovo. 2001. Appointment and Removal from Office of International Judges and International Prosecutors, UN Doc. UNMIK/REG/2000/6. (January 12).

United Nations Transitional Administration in East Timor. 2000. Organization of Courts in East Timor, UN Doc. UNTAET/REG/2000/11 (March 6).

United States. 1992. Torture Victim Protection Act. United States Code. Section 1350.

Van Boven, Theo. 1993. United Nations Commission on Human Rights: Study Concerning the Right to Restitution, Compensation, and Rehabilitation for Victims of Gross Human Rights Violations and Fundamental Freedoms: Final Report. UN doc. E/CN.4/1990/10, 1990. United Nations: July 8, 1993 (final report).

Van Roermund, Bert. 2001. "Rubbing Off and Rubbing On: The Grammar of Reconciliation." In *Lethe's Law: Justice, Law and Ethics in Reconciliation*. Ed. Emilios Christodoulidis and Scott Veitch. Oxford: Hart.

Verdeja, Ernesto. 2000. Interviews (July–August). Santiago, Chile.

———. 2004. "Derrida and the Impossibility of Forgiveness." *Contemporary Political Theory* 3, no. 1 (April): 23–47.

———. 2006. "A Normative Theory of Reparations in Transitional Democracies." *Metaphilosophy* 37, no. 3/4: 449–468.

———. 2007. Interviews (July). Sarajevo, Bosnia-Herzegovina.

———. 2008. "A Critical Theory of Reparative Justice." *Constellations* 15, no. 2: 208–222.

———. 2009a. "Repair and Justice in Latin America." In *State Violence and Genocide in Latin America*. Ed. Marcia Esparza. New York: Routledge.

———. 2009b. "Official Apologies in the Aftermath of Political Violence." *Metaphilosophy,* forthcoming.

Vergara, Ana Cecilia. 1994. "Justice, Impunity and the Transition to Democracy: A Challenge for Human Rights Education." *Journal of Moral Education* 23, no. 3: 273–284.

Villa-Vicencio, Charles, and Wilhelm Verwoerd. 2001. "Constructing a Report: Writing Up the Truth." In *Truth v. Justice: The Morality of Truth Commissions*. Ed. Robert Rotberg and Dennis Thompson. Princeton: Princeton University Press, 279–294.

Volf, Miroslav. 2001. "Forgiveness, Reconciliation, and Justice: A Christian Contribution to a More Peaceful World." In *Forgiveness and Reconciliation: Religion, Public Policy and Conflict Transformation*. Ed. Raymond

C. Helmick and Rodney Petersen. Philadelphia, PA: Templeton Foundation Press, 27–50.

Volkhart, Heinrich. 2001. "The Role of NGOs in Strengthening the Foundations of South African Democracy." *Voluntas: International Journal of Voluntary and Non-profit Organizations* 12/1 (March): 1–15.

Waldorf, Lars. 2006. "Mass Justice for Mass Atrocity: Rethinking Local Justice as Transitional Justice." *Temple Law Review* 79: 1–87.

Waldron, Jeremy. 1992. "Superseding Historic Injustice." *Ethics* 103 (October): 4–28.

Walker, Margaret Urban. 2006. *Moral Repair: Reconstructing Moral Relations After Wrongdoing.* Cambridge: Cambridge University Press.

Walzer, Michael. 1992. *Regicide and Revolution.* New York: Columbia University Press.

———. 1995. "The Idea of Civil Society." In *Toward a Global Civil Society.* Ed. Michael Walzer. Providence, RI: Bergham Books.

———. 1997. *On Toleration.* New Haven, CT: Yale University Press.

Warnke, Georgia. 2000. "Feminism and Democratic Deliberation." *Philosophy and Social Criticism* 26, no. 3: 61–74.

Warren, Kay. 1998. *Indigenous Movements and Their Critics: Pan-Maya Activism in Guatemala.* Princeton, NJ: Princeton University Press.

Weber, Max. 1958. "Politics as a Vocation." In *From Max Weber: Essays in Sociology.* Ed. Hans H. Gerth and C. Wright Mills. Oxford: Oxford University Press, 77–128.

Weschler, Lawrence. 1997. *A Miracle, A Universe: Settling Accounts with Torturers.* Chicago: Chicago University Press.

Whitmann, Rebecca. 2006. *Beyond Justice: The Auschwitz Trials.* Cambridge, MA: Harvard University Press.

Wilke, Christiane. 2007. "The Shield, the Sword, the Party: Vetting the East German Public Sector." In *Justice as Prevention: Vetting Public Employees in Transitional Societies.* Ed. Alexander Mayer-Rieckh and Pablo de Greiff. New York: Social Science Research Council, 348–401.

Wilson, Richard A. 2001. *The Politics of Truth and Reconciliation in South Africa: Legitimizing the Post-Apartheid State.* Cambridge: Cambridge University Press.

Winter, Jay. 1995. *Sites of Memory, Sites of Mourning.* Cambridge: Cambridge University Press.

World Bank. 2005. *Engaging Civil Society Organizations in Conflict-Affected and Fragile States: Three African Case Studies.* Report No. 32538-GLB. Washington, DC: World Bank.

Young, Iris. 1996. "Communication and the Other: Beyond Deliberative Democracy." In *Democracy and Difference: Contesting the Boundaries of the Political.* Ed. Seyla Benhabib. Princeton, NJ: Princeton University Press.

Zimbabwe Human Rights Forum. 2008. "Political Violence Reports." Available at http://www.hrforumzim.com. Accessed November 26, 2008.

Zimbardo, Philip G. 2004. "A Situationist Perspective on the Psychology of Good and Evil." In *The Social Psychology of Good and Evil*. Ed. Arthur G. Miller. New York: Guilford Press, 21–50.

Index

Ball, Howard, 92
Bangladesh, 5
Barahona de Brito, Alexandra, 4, 70,
    77, 137
Barkan, Elazar, 7, 191n6
Bartoli, Andrea, 10
Barton, Charles K., 194n4
Bashingantahe, 131
Bass, Gary, 97
Bassin, Ari S., 192n5
Beah, Ishmael, 63
Beccaria, Cesare, 44
Belgium, 96
Ben Gurion, David, 106
Benhabib, Seyla, 50, 60–61
Benjamin, Jessica, 49
Bentham, Jeremy, 44
Bhargava, Rajeev, 12, 22–23
Biafra, 5
Bird, Colin, 189n1
Boraine, Alex, 112
Borneman, John, 41
Bosnia and Herzegovina, 95, 157, 165,
    167, 171–172, 175, 192n1, 194n1
Botman, Russell H., 166
Bourdieu, Pierre, 88
Bowman, James, 79
Brazil, 8, 109, 111, 153
Brazil: Never Again, 153–154,
Brilmayer, Lea, 5
Brooks, Roy, 191n6
Brudholm, Thomas, 162–163, 164
Burg, Steven, 6
Burnet, Jennie, 132
Buruma, Ian, 191n10
Burundi, 131–132
Bystanders, 47, 149–152, 189n6

Cambodia, 9, 36–37, 58, 95, 125, 155,
    192n1
Campaign for Good Governance (CGG),
    155–156, 194n6
Canada, 6
Casarjian, Robin, 83
Cassesse, Antonio, 103
Catholic Church, 137, 142, 146, 154
Center for Legal and Social Studies
    (CELS), 155

Chad, 116
Chakravarti, Sonali, 49
Chechnya, 5
Chile, 58, 70, 75, 83–90, 108, 109, 111,
    114, 116, 118, 123, 137, 141, 154,
    158, 163, 167, 173
Civil society, 22, 78, 136–159; 183; and
    accountability, 145; 146, 155; 156;
    159; and challenges, 156–159;
    contributions, 148–156; and critical
    history, 152–153; defined, 138; and
    definition of actor categories, 149–152;
    and deliberation, 144–149; discourse
    theory of, 143–147; and interpersonal
    reconciliation, 168; and policy
    recommendations, 155–156; and
    recognition, 137, 146, 147, 149,
    150–151, 153, 156, 158; and respect,
    145, 147, 148–150, 157, 158, 159; and
    rule of law, 137, 142–143, 145, 146,
    148, 149, 155, 158, 159; "self-limiting"
    theory of, 141–143; and truth, 153,
    154, 158
Cohen, Jean, 68, 77, 144, 146, 148
Cohen, Stanley, 80
Colonialism, 6–7
Comisión para el Esclarecimiento
    Histórico (CEH), 116, 154
Commission on Human Rights
    (Chile), 155
Concannon, Jr., Brian, 105
Couper, David, 83
Crocker, David, 9, 16, 34, 60, 78,
    113, 116, 148, 156, 189n3,
    193n1
Cristina H., 163–165, 168, 178,
    194n1
Curandeiros, 10, 130

Dahl, Robert, 139
Damaska, Mirjan, 98
Danner, Allison Marston, 99
Darley, John, 81
Darwall, Stephen, 189n1
Das, Veena, 177
Dawson, John, 188n8
De Greiff, Pablo, 56, 193n10
De Vito, Daniela, 54

Locke, John, 32
Lomasky, Loren, 56
Lord's Resistance Army, 110, 111
Loveman, Brian, 90

Macedo, Stephen, 193n12
Mackintosh, L. R., 191n7
Mahir P., 165, 194n1
Mamdani, Mahmood, 135
Mani, Rama, 10, 57–58
Manin, Bernard, 190n16
Manning, Carrie, 9
Maria Helena C., 167, 172, 194n1
Marisela P., 173–174, 194n1
Martínez, Javier, 141
Martinez, Jenny S., 99
Marty, Martin, 80, 88, 166
Mason, T. David, 70
Mato oput, 130
McAdams, James A., 4, 70
Meernik, James D., 70
Memory, 67, 73–76; and Berlin
   Holocaust memorial, 191n5; and civil
   society, 154–155; and interpersonal
   reconciliation, 176; memory sites, 67,
   74–76, 85; and respect, 176. *Also see*
   Truth
Méndez, Juan, 34
Mendus, Susan, 32
Menéndez-Carrión, Ampáro, 77,
   190n13
Merwin, William, 184–185
Michlic, Joanna, 11
Michnik, Adam, 139, 141–142, 146
Miller, Donald, 177
Miller, Lourna Touryan, 177
Milošević, Slobodan, 99
Minear, Richard, 106
Minow, Martha, 2, 86, 97
Moon, Claire, 16–17, 36, 38, 187n1
Moses, A. Dirk, 191n5
Mouffe, Chantal, 31, 59–61
Moulian, Tomás, 158
Movement for Democratic Change
   (MDC), 142
Mozambique, 9–11, 77, 109, 130,
   132

Muller-Fahrenholz, Geiko, 83, 188n6
Murphy, Jeffrie, 9, 42, 162, 194n3

Narayan, Uma, 169
National Coordinator for Human Rights
   (CNDDHH), 153, 194n4
Neal, Arthur, 82–83
Nehushtan, Yossi, 32
Neier, Aryeh, 97
Nersessian, David L., 4
Nesiah, Vasuki, 120
New Zealand, 6
Newey, Glen, 32
Nicaragua, 71, 111
Nietzsche, Friedrich, 40, 75, 152, 162,
   188n4
Nino, Carlos, 57, 190n16
Nobles, Melissa, 85
Nora, Pierre, 67
Nordstrom, Carolyn, 10
North, Joanna, 87
Norval, Aletta, 187n1
Nozick, Robert, 97, 140, 162
Nuremberg Tribunal, 92, 94, 102, 103,
   105, 126
Nyatagodien, Ridwan, 82–83

O'Donnell, Guillermo, 69, 136
Ojera Latigo, James, 132
Okin, Susan Moller, 51
Orentlicher, Diane, 98
Orr, Wendy, 190n10
Osiel, Mark, 36, 73, 101, 183

Pardon, 19; partial, 169–175
Paris, Erna, 191n4
Partition, Political, 5–6
Perkumpulan Hak, 153
Perrelli, Carina, 141
Peru, 55, 108, 109, 111, 113–117, 151,
   153, 155
Peruvian Association of History and
   Reconciliation, 152
Petar L., 171–172, 194n1
Petersen, Robin, 166
Petersen, Rodney, 16
Philip, Mark, 73

Ernesto Verdeja is an Assistant Professor of Political Science and Peace Studies at the University of Notre Dame.